Bill Bryson is

'An adopted national treasure after the publication of *Notes from a Small Island* in which he pottered around Britain, observing the country and its characteristics with far more fondness and hilarity than the way we Brits view ourselves'
Daily Telegraph

'Laugh-out-loud'
Observer

'Not to be read in public, for fear of emitting loud snorts'
The Times

'Seriously funny'
Sue Townsend, *Sunday Times*

'Hilarious'
Independent on Sunday

'Hugely funny (not snigger-snigger funny, but great-big-belly-laugh-till-you-cry funny)'
Daily Telegraph

Bill Bryson's opening lines were:

'I come from Des Moines. Someone had to'.

This is what followed:

The Lost Continent

A road trip around the puzzle that is small-town America introduces the world to the adjective 'Brysonesque'.

> *'A very funny performance, littered with wonderful lines and memorable images'* LITERARY REVIEW

Neither Here Nor There

Europe never seemed funny until Bill Bryson looked at it.

> *'Hugely funny (not snigger-snigger funny but great-big-belly-laugh-till-you-cry funny)'* DAILY TELEGRAPH

Made in America

A compelling ride along the Route 66 of American language and popular culture gets beneath the skin of the country.

> *'A tremendous sassy work, full of zip, pizzazz and all those other great American qualities'* INDEPENDENT ON SUNDAY

Notes from a Small Island

A eulogy to Bryson's beloved Britain captures the very essence of the original 'green and pleasant land'.

> *'Not a book that should be read in public, for fear of emitting loud snorts'* THE TIMES

A Walk in the Woods

Bryson's punishing (by his standards) hike across the celebrated Appalachian Trail, the longest footpath in the world.

> *'This is a seriously funny book'* SUNDAY TIMES

Notes from a Big Country

Bryson brings his inimitable wit to bear on that strangest of phenomena – the American way of life.

> *'Not only hilarious but also insightful and informative'* INDEPENDENT ON SUNDAY

Down Under
An extraordinary journey to the heart of another big country – Australia.

> 'Bryson is the perfect travelling companion . . . When it comes to travel's peculiars the man still has no peers' THE TIMES

A Short History of Nearly Everything
Travels through time and space to explain the world, the universe and everything.

> 'Truly impressive . . . It's hard to imagine a better rough guide to science' GUARDIAN

The Life and Times of the Thunderbolt Kid
Quintessential Bryson – a funny, moving and perceptive journey through his childhood.

> 'He can capture the flavour of the past with the lightest of touches' SUNDAY TELEGRAPH

At Home
On a tour of his own house, Bill Bryson gives us an instructive and entertaining history of the way we live.

> 'A work of constant delight and discovery . . . don't leave home without it" SUNDAY TELEGRAPH

One Summer
Bryson travels back in time to a forgotten summer, when America came of age, took centre stage and changed the world for ever.

> 'Has history ever been so enjoyable?' MAIL ON SUNDAY

The Road to Little Dribbling
Two decades after Notes from a Small Island, Bill Bryson takes a new amble round Britain, to rediscover the beautiful, eccentric and endearing country he calls home.

> 'Is it the funniest travel book I've read all year? Of course it is' DAILY TELEGRAPH

By

Bill Bryson

The Lost Continent

Mother Tongue

Troublesome Words

Neither Here Nor There

Made in America

Notes from a Small Island (published in the
USA as *I'm a Stranger Here Myself*)

A Walk in the Woods

Notes from a Big Country

Down Under (published in the USA as *In a
Sunburned Country*)

African Diary

A Short History of Nearly Everything

The Life and Times of the Thunderbolt Kid

Shakespeare (Eminent Lives Series)

Bryson's Dictionary for Writers and Editors

Icons of England

At Home

One Summer

The Road to Little Dribbling

BILL BRYSON

The LOST CONTINENT

TRAVELS IN SMALL-TOWN AMERICA

BLACK SWAN

TRANSWORLD PUBLISHERS
61–63 Uxbridge Road, London W5 5SA
www.transworldbooks.co.uk

Transworld is part of the Penguin Random House group of companies
whose addresses can be found at global.penguinrandomhouse.com

First published in Great Britain in 1989 by Secker & Warburg Ltd
Abacus edition published 1990
Black Swan edition published 1999
Black Swan edition reissued 2015

A CIP catalogue record for this book
is available from the British Library.

ISBN
9781784161804

Typeset in Great Britain by Hewer Text UK Ltd
Printed and bound in Great Britain by Clays Ltd, Elcograf S.p.A.

Penguin Random House is committed to a sustainable
future for our business, our readers and our planet. This book
is made from Forest Stewardship Council® certified paper.

7 9 10 8

To my father

Acknowledgements

I WOULD LIKE TO thank the following people for their kind and various assistance in helping me during the preparation of this book: Hal and Lucia Horning, Robert and Rita Schmidt, Stan and Nancy Kluender, Mike and Sherry Bryson, Peter Dunn, Cynthia Mitchell, Nick Tosches, Paul Kingsbury and, above all, my mother, Mary Bryson, who still has the best legs in Des Moines.

PART ONE

Chapter one

I COME FROM Des Moines. Somebody had to.

When you come from Des Moines you either accept the fact without question and settle down with a local girl named Bobbi and get a job at the Firestone factory and live there for ever and ever, or you spend your adolescence moaning at length about what a dump it is and how you can't wait to get out, and then you settle down with a local girl named Bobbi and get a job at the Firestone factory and live there for ever and ever.

Hardly anyone ever leaves. This is because Des Moines is the most powerful hypnotic known to man. Outside town there is a big sign that says WELCOME TO DES MOINES. THIS IS WHAT DEATH IS LIKE. There isn't really. I just made that up. But the place does get a grip on you. People who have nothing to do with Des Moines drive in off the interstate, looking for gas or hamburgers, and stay for ever. There's a New Jersey couple up the street from my parents' house whom you see wandering around from time to time looking faintly puzzled but strangely serene. Everybody in Des Moines is strangely serene.

The only person I ever knew in Des Moines who wasn't serene was Mr Piper. Mr Piper was my parents' neighbour, a leering cherry-faced idiot who was forever getting drunk and crashing his car into telephone poles. Everywhere you went you encountered telephone poles and road signs

13

leaning dangerously in testimony to Mr Piper's driving habits. He distributed them all over the west side of town, rather in the way dogs mark trees. Mr Piper was the nearest possible human equivalent to Fred Flintstone, but less charming. He was a Shriner and a Republican – a Nixon Republican – and he appeared to feel he had a mission in life to spread offence. His favourite pastime, apart from getting drunk and crashing his car, was to get drunk and insult the neighbours, particularly us because we were Democrats, though he was prepared to insult Republicans when we weren't available.

Eventually, I grew up and moved to England. This irritated Mr Piper almost beyond measure. It was worse than being a Democrat. Whenever I was in town, Mr Piper would come over and chide me. 'I don't know what you're doing over there with all those Limeys,' he would say provocatively. 'They're not clean people.'

'Mr Piper, you don't know what you're talking about,' I would reply in my affected English accent. 'You are a cretin.' You could talk like that to Mr Piper because (1) he *was* a cretin and (2) he never listened to anything that was said to him.

'Bobbi and I went over to London two years ago and our hotel room didn't even have a *bathroom* in it,' Mr Piper would go on. 'If you wanted to take a leak in the middle of the night you had to walk about a mile down the hallway. That isn't a clean way to live.'

'Mr Piper, the English are paragons of cleanliness. It is a well-known fact that they use more soap per capita than anyone else in Europe.'

Mr Piper would snort derisively at this. 'That doesn't mean diddly-squat, boy, just because they're cleaner than a bunch of Krauts and Eyeties. My God, a *dog's* cleaner than a bunch of Krauts and Eyeties. And I'll tell you something else: if his Daddy hadn't bought Illinois for him, John F. Kennedy would never have been elected President.'

I had lived around Mr Piper long enough not to be thrown by this abrupt change of tack. The theft of the 1960 presidential election was a long-standing plaint of his, one that he brought into the conversation every ten or twelve minutes regardless of the prevailing drift of the discussion. In 1963, during Kennedy's funeral, someone in the Waveland Tap punched Mr Piper in the nose for making that remark. Mr Piper was so furious that he went straight out and crashed his car into a telephone pole. Mr Piper is dead now, which is of course one thing that Des Moines prepares you for.

When I was growing up I used to think that the best thing about coming from Des Moines was that it meant you didn't come from anywhere else in Iowa. By Iowa standards, Des Moines is a Mecca of cosmopolitanism, a dynamic hub of wealth and education, where people wear three-piece suits and dark socks, often simultaneously. During the annual state high school basketball tournament, when the hayseeds from out in the state would flood into the city for a week, we used to accost them downtown and snidely offer to show them how to ride an escalator or negotiate a revolving door. This wasn't always so far from reality. My friend Stan, when he was about sixteen, had to go and stay with his cousin in some remote, dusty hamlet called Dog Water or Dunceville or some such improbable spot – the kind of place where if a dog gets run over by a truck everybody goes out to have a look at it. By the second week, delirious with boredom, Stan insisted that he and his cousin drive the fifty miles into the county town, Hooterville, and find something to do. They went bowling at an alley with warped lanes and chipped balls and afterwards had a chocolate soda and looked at a *Playboy* in a drugstore, and on the way home the cousin sighed with immense satisfaction and said, 'Gee thanks, Stan. That was the best time I ever had in my whole life!' It's true.

I had to drive to Minneapolis once, and I went on a back road just to see the country. But there was nothing to see. It's just flat and hot, and full of corn and soya beans and hogs. Every once in a while you come across a farm or some dead little town where the liveliest thing is the flies. I remember one long, shimmering stretch where I could see a couple of miles down the highway and there was a brown dot beside the road. As I got closer I saw it was a man sitting on a box by his front yard, in some six-house town with a name like Spigot or Urinal, watching my approach with inordinate interest. He watched me zip past and in the rear-view mirror I could see him still watching me going on down the road until at last I disappeared into a heat haze. The whole thing must have taken about five minutes. I wouldn't be surprised if even now he thinks of me from time to time.

He was wearing a baseball cap. You can always spot an Iowa man because he is wearing a baseball cap advertising John Deere or a feed company, and because the back of his neck has been lasered into deep crevasses by years of driving a John Deere tractor back and forth in a blazing sun. (This does not do his mind a whole lot of good either.) His other distinguishing feature is that he looks ridiculous when he takes off his shirt because his neck and arms are chocolate brown and his torso is as white as a sow's belly. In Iowa it is called a farmer's tan and it is, I believe, a badge of distinction.

Iowa women are almost always sensationally overweight – you see them at Merle Hay Mall in Des Moines on Saturdays, clammy and meaty in their shorts and halter tops, looking a little like elephants dressed in children's clothes, yelling at their kids, calling out names like Dwayne and Shauna. Jack Kerouac, of all people, thought that Iowa women were the prettiest in the country, but I don't think he ever went to Merle Hay Mall on a Saturday. I will say this, however – and it's a strange, strange thing – the teenaged daughters of these fat women are always utterly delectable, as soft and gloriously rounded and naturally fresh-smelling as a basket of fruit. I don't know what it is that happens to them, but it must be awful to marry one of those nubile cuties knowing that there is a time bomb ticking away in her that will at some unknown date make her bloat out into something huge and grotesque, presumably all of a sudden and without much notice, like a self-inflating raft from which the stopper has been yanked.

Even without this inducement, I don't think I would have stayed in Iowa. I never felt altogether at home there, even when I was small. In about 1957, my grandparents gave me a Viewmaster for my birthday and a packet of discs with the title 'Iowa – Our Glorious State'. I can remember thinking even then that the selection of glories was a trifle on the thin side. With no natural features of note, no national parks, no battlefields or famous birthplaces, the Viewmaster people had to stretch their creative 3-D talents to the full. Putting the Viewmaster to your eyes

17

and clicking the white handle gave you, as I recall, a shot of Herbert Hoover's birthplace, impressively three-dimensional, followed by Iowa's other great treasure, the Little Brown Church in the Vale (which inspired the song whose tune nobody ever quite knows), the highway bridge over the Mississippi River at Davenport (all the cars seemed to be hurrying towards Illinois), a field of waving corn, the bridge over the Missouri River at Council Bluffs and the Little Brown Church in the Vale again, taken from another angle. I can remember thinking even then that there must be more to life than that.

Then one grey Sunday afternoon when I was about ten I was watching TV and there was a documentary on about movie-making in Europe. One clip showed Anthony Perkins walking along some sloping city street at dusk. I don't remember now if it was Rome or Paris, but the street was cobbled and shiny with rain and Perkins was hunched deep in a trench coat and I thought, 'Hey, *c'est moi!*' I began to read – no, I began to *consume* – *National Geographics*, with their pictures of glowing Lapps and mist-shrouded castles and ancient cities of infinite charm. From that moment, I wanted to be a European boy. I wanted to live in an apartment across from a park in the heart of a city, and from my bedroom window look out on a crowded vista of hills and roof-tops. I wanted to ride trams and understand strange languages. I wanted friends named Werner and Marco who wore short pants and played soccer in the street and owned toys made of wood. I cannot for the life of me think why. I wanted my mother to send me out to buy long loaves of bread from a shop with a wooden pretzel hanging above the entrance, I wanted to step outside my front door and *be* somewhere.

As soon as I was old enough I left. I left Des Moines and Iowa and the United States and the war in Vietnam and Watergate, and settled across the world. And now when I came home it was to a foreign country, full of serial murderers and sports teams in the wrong towns (the Indianapolis Colts? the Toronto Blue Jays?) and a personable old fart who was President. My mother knew that personable old fart when he was a sports caster called Dutch Reagan at WHO Radio in Des Moines. 'He was just a nice, friendly, kind of dopey guy,' my mother says.

Which, come to that, is a pretty fair description of most Iowans. Don't get me wrong. I am not for a moment suggesting that Iowans are mentally deficient. They are a decidedly intelligent and sensible people who, despite their natural conservatism, have always been prepared to elect a conscientious, clear-thinking liberal in preference to some cretinous conservative. (This used to drive Mr Piper practically insane.) And Iowans, I am proud to tell you, have the highest literacy rate in the nation: 99.5 per cent of grown-ups there can read. When I say they are kind of dopey I mean they are trusting and amiable and open. They are a tad slow, certainly – when you tell an Iowan a joke, you can see a kind of race going on between his brain and his expression – but it's not because they're incapable of high-speed mental activity, it's only that there's not much call for it. Their wits are dulled by simple, wholesome faith in God and the soil and their fellow man.

Above all, Iowans are friendly. You go into a strange diner in the South and everything goes quiet, and you realize all the other customers are looking at you as if they are sizing up the risk involved in murdering you for your wallet and leaving your body in a shallow grave some-

19

where out in the swamps. In Iowa you are the centre of attention, the most interesting thing to hit town since a tornado carried off old Frank Sprinkel and his tractor last May. Everybody you meet acts like he would gladly give you his last beer and let you sleep with his sister. Everyone is happy and friendly and strangely serene.

The last time I was home, I went to Kresge's downtown and bought a bunch of postcards to send back to England. I bought the most ridiculous ones I could find – a sunset over a feed lot, a picture of farmers bravely grasping a moving staircase beside the caption 'We rode the escalator at Merle Hay Mall!', that sort of thing. They were so uniformly absurd that when I took them up to the check-out, I felt embarrassed by them, as if I were buying dirty magazines, and hoped somehow to convey the impression that they weren't really for me. But the check-out lady regarded each of them with interest and deliberation – just as they always do with dirty magazines, come to that.

When she looked up at me she was almost misty-eyed. She wore butterfly glasses and a beehive hairdo. 'Those are real nice,' she said. 'You know, honey, I've bin in a lot of states and seen a lot of places, but I can tell you that this is just about the purtiest one I ever saw.' She really said purtiest. She really meant it. The poor woman was in a state of terminal hypnosis. I glanced at the cards and to my surprise I suddenly saw what she meant. I couldn't help but agree with her. They *were* purty. Together, we made a little pool of silent admiration. For one giddy, careless moment, I was almost serene myself. It was a strange sensation, and it soon passed.

*　　*　　*

My father liked Iowa. He lived his whole life in the state, and is even now working his way through eternity there, in Glendale Cemetery in Des Moines. But every year he became seized with a quietly maniacal urge to get out of the state and go on vacation. Every summer, without a whole lot of notice, he would load the car to groaning, hurry us into it, take off for some distant point, return to get his wallet after having driven almost to the next state, and take off again for some distant point. Every year it was the same. Every year it was awful.

The big killer was the tedium. Iowa is in the middle of the biggest plain this side of Jupiter. Climb onto a roof-top almost anywhere in the state and you are confronted with a featureless sweep of corn for as far as the eye can see. It is 1,000 miles from the sea in any direction, 400 miles from the nearest mountain, 300 miles from skyscrapers and muggers and things of interest, 200 miles from people who do not habitually stick a finger in their ear and swivel it around as a preliminary to answering any question addressed to them by a stranger. To reach anywhere of even passing interest from Des Moines by car requires a journey that in other countries would be considered epic. It means days and days of unrelenting tedium, in a baking steel capsule on a ribbon of highway.

In my memory, our vacations were always taken in a big blue Rambler station-wagon. It was a cruddy car – my dad always bought cruddy cars, until he got to the male menopause and started buying zippy red convertibles – but it had the great virtue of space. My brother, sister and I in the back were miles away from my parents up front, in effect in another room. We quickly discovered during illicit forays into the picnic hamper that if you stuck a

21

bunch of Ohio Blue Tip matches into an apple or hard-boiled egg, so that it resembled a porcupine, and casually dropped it out the tailgate window, it was like a bomb. It would explode with a small bang and a surprisingly big flash of blue flame, causing cars following behind to veer in an amusing fashion.

My dad, miles away up front, never knew what was going on and could not understand why all day long cars would zoom up alongside him with the driver gesticulating furiously, before tearing off into the distance. 'What was that all about?' he would say to my mother in a wounded tone.

'I don't know, dear,' my mother would answer mildly. My mother only ever said two things. She said, 'I don't know, dear.' And she said, 'Can I get you a sandwich, honey?' Occasionally on our trips she would volunteer other pieces of intelligence like, 'Should that dashboard light be glowing like that, dear?' or, 'I think you hit that dog/man/blind person back there, honey,' but mostly she wisely kept quiet. This was because on vacations my father was a man obsessed. His principal obsession was with trying to economize. He always took us to the crummiest hotels and motor lodges, and to the kind of roadside eating-houses where they only washed the dishes weekly. You always knew, with a sense of doom, that at some point before finishing you were going to discover someone else's congealed egg-yolk lurking somewhere on your plate or plugged between the tines of your fork. This, of course, meant cooties and a long, painful death.

But even that was a relative treat. Usually we were forced to picnic by the side of the road. My father had an instinct for picking bad picnic sites – on the apron of a busy truck

22

stop or in a little park that turned out to be in the heart of some seriously deprived ghetto, so that groups of children would come and stand silently by our table and watch us eating Hostess Cupcakes and crinkle-cut potato chips – and it always became incredibly windy the moment we stopped, so that my mother spent the whole of lunch-time chasing paper plates over an area of about an acre.

In 1957 my father invested $19.98 in a portable gas stove that took an hour to assemble before each use and was so wildly temperamental that we children were always ordered to stand well back when it was being lit. This always proved unnecessary, however, because the stove would flicker to life only for a few seconds before puttering out, and my father would spend many hours turning it this way and that to keep it out of the wind, simultaneously addressing it in a low, agitated tone normally associated with the chronically insane. All the while my brother, sister and I would implore him to take us some place with airconditioning, linen table-cloths and ice-cubes clinking in glasses of clear water. 'Dad,' we would beg, 'you're a successful man. You make a good living. Take us to a Howard Johnson's.' But he wouldn't have it. He was a child of the Depression and where capital outlays were involved he always wore the haunted look of a fugitive who had just heard bloodhounds in the distance.

Eventually, with the sun low in the sky, he would hand us hamburgers that were cold and raw and smelled of butane. We would take one bite and refuse to eat any more. So my father would lose his temper and throw everything into the car and drive us at high speed to some roadside diner where a sweaty man with a floppy hat would sling hash while grease-fires danced on his grill.

And afterwards, in a silent car filled with bitterness and unquenched basic needs, we would mistakenly turn off the main highway and get lost and end up in some no-hope hamlet with a name like Draino, Indiana, or Tapwater, Missouri, and get a room in the only hotel in town, the sort of rundown place where if you wanted to watch TV it meant you had to sit in the lobby and share a cracked leatherette sofa with an old man with big sweat circles under his arms. The old man would almost certainly have only one leg and probably one other truly arresting deficiency, like no nose or a caved-in forehead, which meant that although you were sincerely intent on watching *Laramie* or *Our Miss Brooks*, you found your gaze being drawn, ineluctably and sneakily, to the amazing eaten-away body sitting beside you. You couldn't help yourself. Occasionally the man would turn out to have no tongue, in which case he would try to engage you in lively conversation. It was all most unsatisfying.

After a week or so of this kind of searing torment, we would fetch up at some blue and glinting sweep of lake or sea in a bowl of pine-clad mountains, a place full of swings and amusements and the gay shrieks of children splashing in water, and it would all almost be worth it. Dad would become funny and warm and even once or twice might take us out to the sort of restaurant where you didn't have to watch your food being cooked and where the glass of water they served you wasn't autographed with lipstick. This was living. This was heady opulence.

It was against this disturbed and erratic background that I became gripped with a curious urge to go back to the land of my youth and make what the blurb writers like to call a journey of discovery. On another continent, 4,000 miles away, I became quietly seized with that nostalgia that overcomes you when you have reached the middle of your life and your father has recently died and it dawns on you that when he went he took some of you with him. I wanted to go back to the magic places of my youth – to Mackinac Island, the Rocky Mountains, Gettysburg – and see if they were as good as I remembered them. I wanted to hear the long, low sound of a Rock Island locomotive calling across a still night and the clack of it receding into the distance. I wanted to see lightning bugs, and hear cicadas shrill, and be inescapably immersed in that hot, crazy-making August weather that makes your underwear scoot up every crack and fissure and cling to you like latex, and drives mild-mannered men to pull out hand-guns in bars and light up the night with gunfire. I wanted to look for Ne-Hi Pop and Burma Shave signs and go to a ball game and sit at a marble-topped soda-fountain and drive through the kind of small towns that Deanna Durbin and Mickey Rooney used to inhabit in the movies. I wanted to travel around. I wanted to see America. I wanted to come home.

So I flew to Des Moines and acquired a sheaf of road-maps, which I studied and puzzled over on the living-room floor, drawing an immense circular itinerary that would take me all over this strange and giant semi-foreign land. My mother, meantime, made me sandwiches and said, 'Oh, I don't know, dear,' when I asked her questions about the vacations of my childhood. And one September dawn in my thirty-sixth year I crept out of my childhood home, slid behind the wheel of an ageing Chevrolet Chevette lent by my sainted and trusting mother and guided it out through the flat, sleeping streets of the city. I cruised down an empty freeway, the only person with a mission in a city of 250,000 sleeping souls. The sun was already high in the sky and promised a blisteringly hot day. Ahead of me lay about a million square miles of quietly rustling corn. At the edge of town I joined Iowa Highway 163 and with a light heart headed towards Missouri. And it isn't often you hear anyone say that.

Chapter two

I N BRITAIN IT had been a year without summer. Wet spring had merged imperceptibly into bleak autumn. For months the sky had remained a depthless grey. Sometimes it rained, but mostly it was just dull, a land without shadows. It was like living inside Tupperware. And here suddenly the sun was dazzling in its intensity. Iowa was hysterical with colour and light. Roadside barns were a glossy red, the sky a deep, hypnotic blue; fields of mustard and green stretched out before me. Flecks of mica glittered in the rolling road. And here and there in the distance mighty grain elevators, the cathedrals of the Middle West, the ships of the prairie seas, drew the sun's light and bounced it back as pure white. Squinting in the unaccustomed brilliance, I followed the highway to Otley.

My intention was to retrace the route my father always took to my grandparents' house in Winfield – through Prairie City, Pella, Oskaloosa, Hedrick, Brighton, Coppock, Wayland and Olds. The sequence was tattooed on my memory. Always having been a passenger before, I had never paid much attention to the road, so I was surprised to find I kept coming up against odd turns and abrupt T-junctions, requiring me to go left here for a couple of miles, then right for a few miles, then left again, and so on. It would have been much more straightforward to take

Highway 92 to Ainsworth and then head south to Mount Pleasant. I couldn't imagine by what method of reasoning my father had ever settled on this route, and now of course I never would know. This seemed a pity, particularly as there was almost nothing he would have liked better than to cover the dining-room table with maps and consider at length possible routings. In this he was like most Midwesterners. Directions are very important to them. They have an innate need to be oriented, even in their anecdotes. Any story related by a Midwesterner will wander off at some point into a thicket of interior monologue along the lines of 'We were staying at a hotel that was eight blocks north-east of the state capitol building. Come to think of it, it was north-west. And I think it was probably more like nine blocks. And this woman without any clothes on, naked as the day she was born except for a coonskin cap, came running at us from the south-west . . . or was it the south-east?' If there are two Midwesterners present and they both witnessed the incident, you can just about write off the anecdote because they will spend the rest of the afternoon arguing points of the compass and will never get back to the original story. You can always tell a Midwestern couple in Europe because they will be standing on a traffic island in the middle of a busy intersection looking at a windblown map and arguing over which way is west. European cities, with their wandering streets and undisciplined alleys, drive Midwesterners practically insane.

This geographical obsession probably has something to do with the absence of landmarks throughout middle America. I had forgotten just how flat and empty it is. Stand on two phone books almost anywhere in Iowa and you get a view. From where I was now I could look out on a sweep of landscape about the size of Belgium, but there was nothing on it except for a few widely-separated farms, some scattered stands of trees and two water-towers, brilliant silver glints signifying distant, unseen towns. Far off in the middle distance a cloud of dust chased a car up a gravel road. The only things that stood out from the landscape were the grain elevators, but even they looked all the same, and there was nothing much to distinguish one view from another.

And it's so quiet. Apart from the ceaseless fidgeting of the corn, there is not a sound. Somebody could sneeze in a house three miles away and you would hear it ('Bless you!' 'Thank you!'). It must nearly drive you crazy to live a life so devoid of stimulus, where no passing aeroplane ever draws your gaze and no car horns honk, where time shuffles forward so slowly that you half expect to find the people still watching *Ozzie and Harriet* on TV and voting for Eisenhower. ('I don't know how far you folks in Des Moines have got, but we're only up to 1958 here in Fudd County.')

Small towns are equally unhelpful in offering distinguishing features. About all that separates them are their names. They always have a gas station, a grocery store, a grain elevator, a place selling farm equipment and fertilizers, and something improbable like a microwave oven dealer or a dry cleaner's, so you can say to yourself as you glide through town, 'Now what would they be doing with a dry cleaner's in Fungus City?' Every fourth or fifth community will be a county town, built around a square. A handsome brick courthouse with a Civil War cannon and a monument to the dead of at least two wars will stand on one side of the square and on the other sides will be businesses: a five and dime, a luncheonette, two banks, a hardware store, a Christian bookstore, a barber's, a couple of hairdressers, a place selling the sort of men's clothing that only someone from a very small town would wear. At least two of the businesses will be called Vern's. The central area of the square will be a park, with fat trees and a bandstand and a pole with an American flag and scattered benches full of old men in John Deere caps sitting around talking about the days when they had something else to do other than sit around and talk about the days when they had something else to do. Time in these places creaks along.

The best county town in Iowa is Pella, forty miles south-east of Des Moines. Pella was founded by Dutch immigrants and every May it still holds a big tulip festival for which they get somebody important like the mayor of The Hague to fly in and praise their bulbs. I used to like Pella when I was little because many of the residents put little windmills in their front yards, which made it kind of interesting. I wouldn't say it made it *outstandingly* interesting, but you learned from an early age to take what pleasures you could find on any trip across Iowa. Besides, Pella had a Dairy Queen on the edge of town where my father would sometimes stop and buy us ice-cream cones dipped in chocolate, and for this alone I have always felt a special fondness for the place. So I was pleased to note, as I rolled into the town on this fine September morn, that there were still windmills whirling in many a front yard. I stopped at the square and got out to stretch my legs. Being a Sunday, the old men from the square had the day off – they would be on sleeping-in-front-of-the-TV duty all day – but in every other respect Pella was as perfect as I remembered it. The square was thick with trees and flower-beds of blazing salvias and glowing marigolds. It had its own windmill, a handsome green one with white blades, nearly full-sized, standing on one corner. The stores around the square were of the cereal box architecture favoured by small-town stores throughout the Midwest, but with gingerbread cornices and other cheery embellishments. Every business had a solid, trustworthy Dutch name: Pardekooper's Drug Store, Jaarsma Bakery, Van Gorp Insurers, Gosselink's Christian Book Store, Vander Ploeg Bakery. All were shut, of course. Sundays are still closely observed in places like Pella. Indeed, the whole town was eerily quiet. It was steeped in that kind of dead silence that makes you begin to wonder, if you are of a suitably hysterical nature, if perhaps everybody has been poisoned in the night by a leak of odourless gas – which even now could be taking insidious control of your own central nervous system – turning Pella into a kind of Pompeii of the plains. I briefly imagined people from all over coming to look at the victims and being especially enthralled at the worried-looking young man in spectacles on the town square, forever clutching his throat and trying to get his car door open. But then I saw a man walking a dog at the far end of the square and realized that any danger was safely past.

I hadn't intended to linger, but it was such a splendid morning that I wandered off down a nearby street, past neat wooden-framed houses with cupolas and gables and front porches with two-seater swings that creaked in the breeze. There was no other sound, apart from the scuffling of my feet through dried leaves. At the bottom of the street, I came across the campus of Central College, a small institution run by the Dutch Reformed Church, with a campus of redbrick buildings overlooking a serpentine with an arching wooden footbridge. The whole place was as tranquil as a double dose of Valium. It looked like the sort of tidy, friendly, clean-thinking college that Clark Kent would have attended. I crossed the bridge and at the far side of the campus found further evidence that I was not the only living person in Pella. From an open window high up in a dormitory building came the sound of a stereo turned up far too loud. It blared for a moment – something by Frankie Goes to Hollywood, I believe – and then from someplace indiscernible there came a booming voice that said, 'IF YOU DON'T TURN THAT THING THE FUCK OFF RIGHT NOW I'M GONNA COME OVER THERE AND POUND YOUR HEAD IN!' It was the voice of a large person – someone, I fancied, with the nickname Moose. Immediately the music stopped and Pella slept again.

I continued on east, through Oskaloosa, Fremont, Hedrick, Martinsburg. The names were familiar, but the towns themselves awoke few memories. By this stage on most trips I was on the floor in a boredom-induced stupor, calling out at fifteen-second intervals, 'How much longer? When are we going to be there? I'm bored. I feel sick. How much longer? When are we going to be there?' I vaguely recognized a bend in the road near Coppock, where we once spent four hours caught in a blizzard waiting for a snow-plough to come through, and several spots where we had paused to let my sister throw up, including a gas station at Martinsburg where she tumbled out of the car and was lavishly sick in the direction of a pump attendant's ankles (boy did that guy dance!), and another at Wayland where my father nearly left me at the side of the road after discovering that I had passed the time by working loose all the rivets on one of the back door panels, exposing an interesting view of the interior mechanism, but unfortunately rendering both the window and door forever inoperable. However, it wasn't until I reached the turning off for Winfield, just past Olds, a place where my father would announce with a sort of delirious joy that we were practically there, that I felt a pang of recognition. I had not been down this road for at least a dozen years, but its gentle slopes and isolated farms were as familiar to me as my own left leg. My heart soared. This was like going back in time. I was about to be a boy again.

Arriving in Winfield was always thrilling. Dad would turn off Highway 78 and bounce us down a rough gravel road at far too high a speed, throwing up clouds of white dust, and then to my mother's unfailing alarm would drive with evident insanity towards some railroad tracks on a blind bend in the road, remarking gravely, 'I hope there's not a train coming.' My mother didn't discover until years later that there were only two trains a day along those tracks, both in the dead of night. Beyond the tracks, standing alone in a neglected field, was a Victorian mansion like the one in the Charles Addams cartoons in the *New Yorker*. No-one had lived in it for decades, but it was still full of furniture, under dank sheets. My sister and brother and I used to climb in through a broken window and look through trunks of musty clothes and old *Collier's* magazines and photographs of strangely worried-looking people. Upstairs was a bedroom in which, according to my brother, lay the shrivelled body of the last occupant, a woman who had died of heartbreak after being abandoned at the altar. We never went in there, though once, when I was about four, my brother peered through the keyhole, let out a howl, cried 'She's coming!' and ran headlong down the stairs. Whimpering, I followed, squirting urine at every step. Beyond the mansion was a wide field, full of black and white cows, and beyond that was my grandparents' house, pretty and white beneath a canopy of trees, with a big red barn and acres of lawn. My grandparents were always waiting at the gate. I don't know whether they could see us coming and raced to their positions or whether they just waited there hour after hour. Quite possibly the latter because, let's face it, they didn't have a whole lot else to do. And then it would be four or five days of fun. My grandfather had a Model T Ford, which he let us kids drive around the yard, to the distress of his chickens and the older women. In the winter he would attach a sleigh to the back and take us for long cold rides down snowy roads. In the evenings we would all play cards around the kitchen table and stay up late. It was always Christmas at my grandparents' house, or Thanksgiving, or the Fourth of July, or somebody's birthday. There was always happiness there.

When we arrived, my grandmother would scuttle off to pull something fresh-baked out of the oven. This was always something unusual. My grandmother was the only person I ever knew – possibly the only person who ever lived – who actually made things from the recipes on the backs of food packets. These dishes always had names like 'Rice Krispies 'n' Banana Chunks Upside-Down Cake' or

'Del Monte Lima Bean 'n' Pretzels Party Snacks'. Generally they consisted of suspiciously large amounts of the man-ufacturer's own products, usually in combinations you wouldn't think of except perhaps in an especially severe famine. The one thing to be said for these dishes was that they were novel. When my grandmother offered you a steaming slab of cake or wedge of pie it might contain almost anything – Niblets sweet corn, chocolate chips, Spam, diced carrots, peanut butter. Generally it would have some Rice Krispies in it somewhere. My grandmother was particularly partial to Rice Krispies and would add a couple of shovelfuls to whatever she made, even if the recipe didn't call for it. She was about as bad a cook as you can be without actually being hazardous.

It all seems so long ago now. And it was. It was so long ago, in fact, that my grandparents had a crank telephone, the kind that hung on the wall and had a handle you turned and said, 'Mabel, get me Gladys Scribbage. I want to ask her how she makes her Frosted Flakes 'n' Cheez Whiz Party Nuggets.' And it would turn out that Gladys Scribbage was already listening in, or somebody else listening in would know how to make Frosted Flakes 'n' Cheez Whiz Party Nuggets. Everybody listened in. My grandmother often listened in when things were slow around the house, covering the mouthpiece with a hand and relaying to the rest of the room vivid accounts of colonic irrigations, prolapsed wombs, husbands who ran off to Burlington with the barmaid from Vern's Uptown Tavern and Supper Club, and other crises of small-town life. We always had to maintain the strictest silence during these sessions. I could never entirely understand why, because if things got really juicy my grandmother would often butt in. 'Well, I think Merle's a real skunk,' she would say. 'Yes, that's right, it's Maude Bryson here, and I just want to say that I think he's an absolute stinker to do that to poor Pearl. And I'll tell you something else, Mabel, you know you could get those support bras a dollar cheaper in Columbus Junction.' In about 1962 the telephone company came and put a normal phone without a party line in my grandmother's house, possibly at the request of the rest of the town. It drove a hole right through her life from which she never entirely recovered.

I didn't really expect my grandparents to be waiting for me at the gate, on account of them both having been dead for many years. But I suppose I had vaguely hoped that another nice old couple might be living there now and would invite me in to look around and share my reminiscences. Perhaps they would let me be their grandson. At the very least, I had assumed that my grandparents' house would be just as I had last seen it.

It was not to be. The road leading to the house was still gravelled with gleaming gypsum pebbles and still threw up satisfying clouds of dust, but the railroad tracks were gone. There was no sign that they had ever been there. The Victorian mansion was gone too, replaced by a ranch-house-style home with cars and propane gas cylinders scattered around the yard like a toddler's playthings. Worse still, the field of cows was now an estate of box houses. My grandparents' home had stood well outside the town, a cool island of trees in an ocean of fields. Now cheap little houses crowded in on it from all sides. With shock, I realized that the barn was gone. Some jerk had torn down my barn! And the house itself – well, it was a shack. Paint had abandoned it in chunks.

Bushes had been pointlessly uprooted, trees chopped down. The grass was high and littered with overspill from the house. I stopped the car on the road out front and just gaped. I cannot describe the sense of loss. Half my memories were inside that house. After a moment a hugely overweight woman in pink shorts, talking on a phone with an apparently endless cord, came and stood in the open doorway and stared at me, wondering what I was doing staring at her.

I drove on into the town. When I was growing up, Main Street in Winfield had two grocery stores, a variety store, a tavern, a pool hall, a newspaper, a bank, a barbershop, a post office, two gas stations – all the things you would expect of any thriving little town. Everyone shopped locally; everyone knew everyone else. Now all that was left was a tavern and a place selling farm equipment. There were half a dozen vacant lots, full of patchy grass, where buildings had been torn down and never replaced. Most of the remaining buildings were dark and boarded up. It was like an abandoned film set which had long since been left to decay.

I couldn't understand what had happened. People now must have to drive thirty miles to buy a loaf of bread. Outside the tavern a group of young thuggy-looking motorcyclists were hanging out. I was going to stop to ask them what had happened to their town, but one of them, seeing me slow down, gave me the finger. For no reason. He was about fourteen. Abruptly, I drove on, back out towards Highway 78, past the scattered farms and gentle slopes that I knew like my own left leg. It was the first time in my life that I had turned my back on a place knowing that I would never see it again. It was all very sad, but I should have known better. As I always used to tell Thomas Wolfe, there are three things you just can't do in life. You can't beat the phone company, you can't make a waiter see you until he's ready to see you, and you can't go home again.

Chapter three

I DROVE ON, without the radio or much in the way of thoughts, to Mount Pleasant, where I stopped for coffee. I had the Sunday *New York Times* with me – one of the greatest improvements in life since I had been away was that you could now buy the *New York Times* out of machines on the day of publication in a place like Iowa, an extraordinary feat of distribution – and I spread out with it in a booth. Boy, do I love the Sunday *New York Times*. Apart from its many virtues as a newspaper, there is just something wonderfully reassuring about its very bulk. The issue in front of me must have weighed ten or twelve pounds. It could've stopped a bullet at twenty yards. I read once that it takes 75,000 trees to produce one issue of the Sunday *New York Times* – and it's well worth every trembling leaf. So what if our grandchildren have no oxygen to breathe? Fuck 'em.

My favourite parts of the *Times* are the peripheral bits – the parts that are so dull and obscure that they exert a kind of hypnotic fascination, like the home improvements column ('All You Need to Know About Fixings and Fastenings') and the stamps column ('Post Office Marks 25 Years of Aeronautic Issues'). Above all, I love the advertising supplements. If a Bulgarian asked me what life was like in America, I would without hesitation tell him to get hold of a stack of *New York Times* advertising supplements. They show a life of richness and variety beyond the wildest dreams of most foreigners. As if to illustrate my point, the issue before me contained a gift catalogue from the Zwingle Company of New York offering scores of products of the things-you-never-knew-you-needed variety – musical shoe-trees, an umbrella with a transistor radio in the handle, an electric nail buffer. What a great country! My favourite was a small electric hotplate you could put on your desk to keep your coffee from going cold. This must be a real boon to people with brain damage, the sort of injuries that lead them to wander off and neglect their beverages. And epileptics all over America must be feeling equally grateful. ('Dear Zwingle Company: I can't tell you how many times I have come around from a *grand mal* seizure to find myself lying on the floor thinking, "Oh God, I bet my coffee's gone cold again."') Really, who buys these things – silver toothpicks and monogrammed underpants and mirrors that say Man of the Year on them? I have often thought that if I ran one of these companies I would produce a polished mahogany plaque with a brass plate on it saying 'Hey, how about me? I paid $22.95 for this completely useless piece of crap.' I'm certain they would sell like hot cakes.

Once in a deranged moment I bought something myself from one of these catalogues, knowing deep in my mind that it would end in heartbreak. It was a little reading light that you clipped on to your book so as not to disturb your bedmate as she slumbered beside you. In this respect it was outstanding because it barely worked. The light it cast was absurdly feeble (in the catalogue it looked like the sort of thing you could signal ships with if you got lost at sea) and left all but the first two lines of a page in darkness. I have seen more luminous insects. After about four minutes its little beam fluttered and failed altogether, and it has never been used again. And the thing is that I knew all along that this was how it was going to end, that it would all be a bitter disappointment. On second thought, if I ever ran one of those companies I would just send people an empty box with a note in it saying 'We have decided not to send you the item you've ordered because, as you well know, it would never properly work and you would only be disappointed. So let this be a lesson to you for the future.'

From the Zwingle catalogue I moved on to the food and household products advertisements. There is usually a wodge of these bright and glossy inducements to try out exciting new products – things with names like Hunk o' Meat Beef Stew 'n' Gravy ('with rich 'n' meaty chunks of beef-textured fibre') and Sniffa-Snax ('An Exciting New Snack Treat You Take Through the Nose!') and Country Sunshine Honey-Toasted Wheat Nut 'n' Sugar Bits Breakfast Cereal ('Now with Vitamin-Enriched Chocolate-Covered Raisin Substitute!'). I am endlessly fascinated by these new products. Clearly, some time ago makers and consumers of American junk food passed jointly through some kind of sensibility barrier in the endless quest for new taste sensations. Now they are a little like those desperate junkies who have tried every known drug and are finally reduced to mainlining toilet bowl cleanser in an effort to get still higher. All over America you can see countless flabby-butted couples quietly searching supermarket shelves for new combinations of flavours, hoping to find some untried product that will tingle in their mouths and excite, however briefly, their leaden tastebuds.

The competition for this market is intense. The food

41

inserts not only offered 50¢ discounts and the like, but also if you sent off two or three labels the manufacturers would dispatch to you a Hunk o' Meat Beach Towel, or Country Sunshine Matching Apron and Oven Mitt, or a Sniffa-Snax hotplate for keeping your coffee warm while you slipped in and out of consciousness from a surfeit of blood sugar. Interestingly, the advertisements for dog food were much the same, except that they weren't usually chocolate-flavoured. In fact, every single product – from the lemon-scented toilet bowl cleansers to the scent-o-pine trash bags – promised to give you a brief buzz. It's no wonder that so many Americans have a glazed look. They are completely junked out.

I drove on south on Highway 218 to Keokuk. This stretch of the road was marked on my map as a scenic route, though these things are decidedly relative. Talking about a scenic route in south-east Iowa is like talking about a good Barry Manilow album. You have to make certain allowances. Compared with an afternoon in a darkened room, it wasn't bad. But compared with, say, the coast road along the Sorrentine peninsula, it was perhaps a little tame. Certainly it didn't strike me as being any more or less scenic than any of the other roads I had been on today. Keokuk is a Mississippi river town where Iowa, Illinois and Missouri face each other across a broad bend in the river. I was heading towards Hannibal in Missouri and was hoping to see a bit of the town *en route* to the bridge south. But before I knew it. I found myself on a bridge going east to Illinois. I was so disconcerted by this that I only caught a glimpse of the river, a glistening smear of brown stretching off in two directions, and then, chagrined, I was in Illinois.

I had really looked forward to seeing the Mississippi. Crossing it as a child had always been an adventure. Dad would call, 'Here's the Mississippi, kids!' and we would scramble to the window to find ourselves on a bridge practically in the clouds, so high it made our breath catch, and the silvery river far, far below, wide, majestic, serene, going about its timeless business of just rolling on. You could see for miles – a novel experience in Iowa. You could see barges and islands and riverside towns. It looked wonderful. And then, abruptly, you were in Illinois and it was flat and full of corn and you realized with a sinking heart that that was it. That was your visual stimulation for the day. Now you had hundreds more miles of arid cornland to cross before you would experience even the most fractional sense of pleasure.

And now here I was in Illinois, and it was flat and full of corn and boring. A childlike voice in my head cried, 'When are we going to be there? I'm bored. Let's go home. When are we going to be there?' Having confidently expected at this stage to be in Missouri, I had my book of maps opened to the Missouri page, so I pulled over to the side of the road, in a state of some petulance, to make a cartographical adjustment. A sign just ahead of me said BUCKLE UP. ITS THE LAW IN ILLINOIS. Clearly, however, it was not an offence to be unable to punctuate. Frowning, I studied my maps. If I turned off at Hamilton just down the road, I could drive along the east bank of the river and cross into Missouri at Quincy. It was even marked on the map as a scenic route; perhaps my blundering would turn out to be no bad thing.

I followed the road through Warsaw, a run-down little river town. A steep hill plunged down towards the river, but then turned inland and again I caught no more than a glimpse of the river. Almost immediately, the landscape spread out into a broad alluvial plain. The sun was sinking in the sky. To the left hills rose up, flecked with trees that were just beginning to show a blush of autumn colour. To the right the land was as flat as a table-top. Teams of combine harvesters laboured in the fields, kicking up dust, working late to bring in the harvest. In the far distance, grain elevators caught the fading sun and glowed an opalescent white, as if lit from within. Somewhere out there, unseen, was the river.

I drove on. The road was completely unsignposted. They do this to you a lot in America, particularly on country roads that go from nowhere to nowhere. You are left to rely on your own sense of direction to find your way – which in my case, let us not forget, had only recently delivered me to the wrong state. I calculated that if I were going south the sun should be to my right (a conclusion I reached by imaging myself in a tiny car driving across a big map of America), but the road twisted and wandered, causing the sun to drift teasingly in front of me, first to this side of the road, then to that. For the first time all day, I had a sense of being in the heart of a vast continent, in the middle of nowhere.

Abruptly the highway turned to gravel. Gypsum nuggets, jagged as arrowheads, flew up against the underside of the car and made a fearful din. I had visions of hosepipes rupturing, hot oil spraying everywhere, me rolling to a steamy, hissing halt out here on this desolate road. The wandering sun was just settling on to the horizon, splashing the sky with faint pinks. Uneasily I drove on, and steeled myself for the prospect of a night spent beneath the stars, with dog-like animals sniffing at my feet and snakes finding warmth up a trouser leg. Ahead of me on the road an advancing storm of dust became after a moment a pickup truck, which passed in a hell-bent fashion, spraying the car with rocky projectiles, which thumped against the sides and bounced off the windows with a cracking sound, and then left me adrift in a cloud of dust. I trundled on, peering helplessly through the murk. It cleared just in time to show me that I was twenty feet from a T-Junction with a stop sign. I was going fifty miles an hour, which on gravel leaves you with a stopping distance of about three miles. I jumped on the brakes with all my feet and made a noise like Tarzan missing a vine as the car went into a skid. It slid sideways past the stop sign and out onto a paved highway, where it came to a halt, rocking gently from side to side. At that instant an enormous semi-trailer truck – all silver horns and flashing lights – blared mightily at me as it swept past, setting the car rocking again. Had I slid out on to the highway three seconds earlier it would have crushed the car into something about the size of a stock cube. I pulled on to the shoulder and got out to examine the damage. It looked as if the car had been dive-bombed with bags of flour. Bits of raw metal showed through where the paint had been pinged away. I thanked God that my mother was so much smaller than me. I sighed, suddenly feeling lost and far from home, and noticed ahead a road sign pointing the way to Quincy. I had come to a halt facing in the right direction, so at least something had come of it.

It was time to stop. Just down the road stood a little town, which I shall call Dullard lest the people recognize themselves and take me to court or come to my house and batter me with baseball bats. On the edge of town was an old motel which looked pretty seedy, though judging by the absence of charred furniture in the front yard it was clearly a step up from the sort of place my dad would have chosen. I pulled on to the gravel drive and went inside. A woman of about seventy-five was sitting behind the desk. She wore butterfly glasses and a beehive hairdo. She was doing one of those books that require you to find words in a mass of letters and circle them. I think it was called 'Word Puzzles for Morons'.

'Help yew?' she drawled without looking up.

'I'd like a room for the night, please.'

'That'll be thirty-eight dollars and fifty cents,' she replied as her pen fell greedily on the word YUP.

I was nonplussed. In my day a motel room cost about $12. 'I don't want to *buy* the room,' I explained. 'I just want to sleep in it for one night.'

She looked at me gravely over the tops of her glasses. 'The room is thirty-eight dollars and fifty cents. Per night. Plus tax. You want it or not?' She had one of those disagreeable accents that add a syllable to every word. 'Tax' came out as 'tayax'.

We both knew that I was miles from anywhere. 'Yes, please,' I said contritely. I signed in and crunched across the gravel to my *suite du nuit*. There appeared to be no other customers. I went into my room with my bag and had a look around, as you do in a new place. There was a black and white TV which appeared to get only one channel and three bent coat-hangers. The bathroom mirror was cracked, and the shower curtains didn't match. The toilet seat had a strip of paper across it saying 'Santitized For Your Protection', but floating beneath it was a cigarette butt, adrift in a little circle of nicotine. Dad would have liked it here, I thought.

I had a shower – that is to say, water dribbled onto my head from a nozzle in the wall – and afterwards went out to check out the town. I had a meal of gristle and baked wiffle ball at a place called – aptly – Chuck's. I didn't think it was possible to get a truly bad meal anywhere in the Midwest, but Chuck managed to provide it. It was the worst food I had ever had – and remember, I've lived in Britain. It had all the attributes of chewing-gum, except flavour. Even now when I burp I can taste it.

Afterwards I had a look around the town. There wasn't much. It was mostly just one street, with a grain silo and railroad tracks at one end and my motel at the other, with a couple of gas stations and grocery stores in between. Everyone regarded me with interest. Years ago, in the midst of a vivid and impressionable youth, I read a chilling story by Richard Matheson about a remote hamlet whose inhabitants waited every year for a lone stranger to come to town so that they could roast him for their annual barbecue. The people here watched me with barbecue eyes.

Feeling self-conscious I went into a dark place called Vern's Tap and took a seat at the bar. I was the only customer, apart from an old man in the corner with only one leg. The barmaid was friendly. She wore butterfly glasses and a beehive hairdo. You could see in an instant that she had been the local good-time girl since about 1931. She had 'Ready for Sex' written all over her face, but 'Better Bring a Paper Bag' written all over her body. Somehow she had managed to pour her capacious backside into some tight red toreador pants and to stretch a clinging blouse over her bosom. She looked as if she had dressed in

47

her granddaughter's clothes by mistake. She was about sixty. It was pretty awful. I could see why the guy with one leg had chosen to sit in the farthest corner.

I asked her what people in Dullard did for fun. 'What exactly did you have in mind, honey?' she said, and rolled her eyes suggestively. The 'Ready for Sex' signs flickered, an occurrence I found unsettling. I wasn't used to being hustled by women, though somehow I had always known that when the moment came it would be in some place like downstate Illinois with a sixty-year-old grandmother. 'Well, perhaps something in the way of legitimate theatre or maybe an international chess congress,' I croaked weakly. However, once we established that I was only prepared to love her for her mind, she became quite sensible and even rather charming. She told me in great and frank detail about her life, which seemed to have involved a dizzying succession of marriages to guys who were now in prison or dead as a result of shoot-outs, and dropped in breathtakingly candid disclosures like: 'Now Jimmy kilt his mother, I never did know why, but Curtis never kilt nobody except once by accident when he was robbing a gas station and his gun went off. And Floyd – he was my fourth husband – he never kilt nobody either, but he used to break people's arms if they got him riled.'

'You must have some interesting family reunions,' I ventured politely.

'I don't know what ever became of Floyd,' she went on. 'He had a little cleft in his chin rot year' – after a moment I realized that this was downstate Illinois for 'right here, on this very spot indicated' – 'that made him look kind of like Kirk Douglas. He was real cute, but he had a temper on him. I got a two-foot scar right across my back where he cut me with an ice-pick. You wanna see it?' She started to hoist up her blouse, but I stopped her. She went on and on like that for ages. Every once in a while the guy in the corner, who was clearly eavesdropping would grin, showing large yellow teeth. I expect Floyd had torn his leg off in a moment of high spirits. At the end of our conversation, the barmaid gave me a sideways look, as if I had been slyly trying to fool her, and said, 'Say, where do you come from anyway, honey?'

I didn't feel like giving her my whole life story, so I just said, 'Great Britain.'

'Well, I'll tell you one thing, honey,' she said, 'for a foreigner you speak English real good.'

Afterwards I retired with a six-pack to my motel, where I discovered that the bed, judging by its fragrance and shape, had only recently been vacated by a horse. It had a sag in it so severe that I could only see the TV at its foot by splaying my legs to their widest extremity. It was like lying in a wheel-barrow. The night was hot and the air conditioner, an aged Philco window unit, expended so much energy making a noise like a steelworks that it could only manage to emit the feeblest and most occasional puffs of cool air. I lay with the six-pack on my chest, effectively immobilized, and drank the beers one by one. On the TV was a talk show presided over by some smooth asshole in a blazer whose name I didn't catch. He was the kind for whom personal hair care was clearly a high priority. He exchanged some witless banter with the band-leader, who of course had a silvery goatee, and then turned to the camera and said in a solemn voice, 'But seriously, folks. If you've ever had a personal problem or trouble at work or you just can't seem to get a grip on life, I know you're gonna be real interested in what our first guest has to tell you tonight. Ladies and gentlemen: Dr Joyce Brothers.'

As the band launched into a perky tune and Joyce Brothers strode onstage, I sat up as far as the bed would allow me and cried, 'Joyce! Joyce Brothers!' as if to an old friend. I couldn't believe it. I hadn't seen Joyce Brothers for years and she hadn't changed a bit. Not one hair on her head had altered a fraction since the last time I saw her, droning on about menstrual flow, in 1962. It was as if they had kept her in a box for twenty-five years. This was as close as I would ever come to time travel. I watched agog as she and Mr Smoothie chattered away about penis envy and Fallopian tubes. I kept expecting him to say to her, 'Now seriously, Joyce, here's a question all America has been wanting me to ask you: what sort of preparations do you take to keep yourself looking like that? Also, when are you going to do something about that hairstyle? And finally, why is it, do you think, that talk show bozos like me all over America keep inviting you back again and again?' Because, let's be frank, Joyce Brothers is pretty dull. I mean, if you turn on the *Johnny Carson Show* and she is one of the guests you know that absolutely everybody in town must be at some really big party or première. She is like downstate Illinois made flesh.

Still, like most immensely boring things, there is something wonderfully comforting about her. Her cheery visage on the glowing box at the foot of my bed made me feel strangely warm and whole and at peace with the world. Out here in this crudbucket motel in the middle of a great empty plain I began for the first time to feel at home. I somehow knew that when I awoke I would see this alien land in a new but oddly familiar light. With a happy heart, I fell asleep and dreamt gentle dreams of southern Illinois and the rolling Mississippi River and Dr Joyce Brothers. And it's not often you hear anyone say that either.

Chapter four

I N THE MORNING I crossed the Mississippi at Quincy; somehow it didn't look as big or majestic as I had remembered it. It was stately. It was imposing. It took whole minutes to cross. But it was also somehow flat and dull. This may have had something to do with the weather, which was likewise flat and dull. Missouri looked precisely the same as Illinois, which had looked precisely the same as Iowa. The only difference was that the car licence plates were a different colour.

Near Palmyra, I stopped at a roadside café for breakfast and took a seat at the counter. At this hour, just after eight in the morning, it was full of farmers. If there is one thing farmers sure do love it is to drive into town and spend half a day (a whole day in winter) sitting at a counter with a bunch of other farmers drinking coffee and teasing the waitress in a half-assed sort of way. I had thought that this was the busiest time of their year, but they didn't seem to be in any rush. Every once in a while one of them would put a quarter on the counter, get up with the air of a man who has just loaded six gallons of coffee into his belly, tell Tammy not to do anything he wouldn't do, and depart. A moment later we would hear the grip of his pickup truck's wheels on the gravel drive, someone would say something candid about him, provoking appreciative laughter, and the conversation would drift lazily back to hogs, state politics, Big Eight football and – when Tammy was out of earshot – sexual predilections, not least Tammy's.

The farmer next to me had only three fingers on his right hand. It is a little-noticed fact that most farmers have parts missing off them. This used to trouble me when I was small. For a long time I assumed that it was because of the hazards of farming life. After all, farmers deal with lots of dangerous machinery. But when you think about it, a lot of people deal with dangerous machinery, and only a tiny proportion of them ever suffer permanent injury. Yet there is scarcely a farmer in the Midwest over the age of twenty who has not at some time or other had a limb or digit yanked off and thrown into the next field by some noisy farmyard implement. To tell you the absolute truth, I think farmers do it on purpose. I think working day after day beside these massive threshers and balers with their grinding gears and flapping fan belts and complex mechanisms they get a little hypnotized by all the noise and motion. They stand there staring at the whirring machinery and they think, 'I wonder what would happen if I just stuck my finger in there a little bit.' I know that sounds crazy. But you have to realize that farmers don't have a whole lot of sense in these matters because they feel no pain.

It's true. Every day in the *Des Moines Register* you can find a story about a farmer who has inadvertently torn off an arm and then calmly walked six miles into the nearest town to have it sewn back on. The stories always say, 'Jones, clutching his severed limb, told his physician, "I seem to have cut my durn arm off, Doc." ' It's never 'Jones, spurting blood, jumped around hysterically for twenty minutes, fell into a swoon and then tried to run in four directions at once,' which is how it would be with you or me. Farmers simply don't feel pain – that little voice in your head that tells you not to do something because it's foolish and will hurt like hell and for the rest of your life somebody will have to cut up your food for you doesn't speak to them. My grandfather was just the same. He would often be repairing the car when the jack would slip and he would call out to you to come and crank it up again as he was having difficulty breathing, or he would run over his foot with the lawn-mower, or touch a live wire, shorting out the whole of Winfield but leaving himself unscathed apart from a ringing in the ears and a certain lingering smell of burnt flesh. Like most people from the rural Midwest, he was practically indestructible. There are only three things that can kill a farmer: lightning, rolling over in a tractor, and old age. It was old age that got my grandfather.

I drove on forty miles south to Hannibal, and went to see Mark Twain's boyhood home, a trim and tidy white-washed house with green shutters set incongruously in the middle of the downtown. It cost $2 to get in and was a disappointment. It purported to be a faithful reproduction of the original interiors, but there were wires and water sprinklers clumsily evident in every room. I also very much doubt that young Samuel Clemens's bedroom had Arm-strong vinyl on the floor (the same pattern as in my mother's kitchen, I was interested to note) or that his sister's bedroom had a plywood partition in it. You don't actually go in the house; you look at it through the windows. At each window there is a recorded message telling you about that room as if you were a moron: 'This is the kitchen. This is where Mrs Clemens would prepare the family's meals . . .'. The whole thing is pretty shabby, which wouldn't be so awful if it were owned by some underfunded local literary society and they were doing the best they could with it. In fact, it is owned by the city of Hannibal and it draws 135,000 visitors a year. It's a little gold mine for the town.

I proceeded from window to window behind a bald fat guy, whose abundant rolls of flesh made him look as if he were wearing an assortment of inner tubes beneath his shirt. 'What do you think of it?' I asked him. He fixed me with that instant friendliness Americans freely adopt with strangers. It is their most becoming trait. 'Oh, I think it's great. I come here whenever I'm in Hannibal – two, three times a year. Sometimes I go out of my way to come here.'

'Really?' I tried not to sound dumbfounded.

'Yeah. I must have been here twenty, thirty times by now. This is a real shrine, you know.'

'You think it's well done?'

'Oh, for sure.'

'Would you say the house is just like Twain described it in his books?'

'I don't know,' the man said thoughtfully, 'I've never read one of his books.'

Next door, attached to the house, was a small museum, which was better. There were cases of Twain memorabilia – first editions, one of his typewriters, photographs, some letters. There was precious little to link him to the house or the town. It is worth remembering that Twain got the hell out of both Hannibal and Missouri as soon as he could, and was always disinclined to come back. I went outside and looked around. Beside the house was a white fence with a sign saying TOM SAWYER'S FENCE. HERE STOOD THE BOARD

FENCE WHICH TOM SAWYER PERSUADED HIS GANG TO PAY HIM FOR THE PLEASURE OF WHITE-WASHING. TOM SAT BY AND SAW THAT IT WAS WELL DONE. Really wakes up your interest in literature, doesn't it? Next door to the Twain house and museum – and I mean absolutely right next to it – was the Mark Twain Drive-In Restaurant and Dinette, with cars parked in little bays and people grazing off trays attached to their windows. It really lent the scene a touch of class. I began to understand why Clemens didn't just leave town but also changed his name.

I strolled around the business district. The whole area was a dispiriting combination of auto parts stores, empty buildings and vacant lots. I had always thought that all river towns, even the poor ones, had something about them – a kind of faded elegance, a raffish air – that made them more interesting than other towns, that the river served as a conduit to the larger world and washed up a more interesting and sophisticated brand of detritus. But not Hannibal. It had obviously had better days, but even they couldn't have been all that great. The Hotel Mark Twain was boarded up. That's a sad sight – a tall building with every window plugged with plywood. Every business in town appeared to trade on Twain and his books – the Mark Twain Roofing Company, the Mark Twain Savings and Loan, the Tom 'n' Huck Motel, the Injun Joe Campground and Go-Kart Track, the Huck Finn Shopping Center. You could even go and be insane at the Mark Twain Mental Health Center – a possibility that would, I imagine, grow increasingly likely with every day spent in Hannibal. The whole place was sad and awful. I had been planning to stay for lunch, but the thought of having to face a Tom Sawyer

Burger or Injun Joe Cola left me without any appetite for either food or Hannibal.

I walked back to the car. Every parked car along the street had a licence plate that said 'Missouri – the Show Me State'. I wondered idly if this could be short for 'Show Me the Way to Any Other State'. In any case, I crossed the Mississippi – still muddy, still strangely unimpressive – on a long, high bridge and turned my back on Missouri without regret. On the other side a sign said BUCKLE UP. ITS THE LAW IN ILLINOIS. Just beyond it another said AND WE STILL CAN'T PUNCTUATE.

I plunged east into Illinois. I was heading for Springfield, the state capital, and New Salem, a restored village where Abraham Lincoln lived as a young man. My dad had taken us there when I was about five and I thought it was wonderful. I wondered if it still was. I also wanted to see if Springfield was in any way an ideal town. One of the things I was looking for on this trip was the perfect town. I've always felt certain that somewhere out there in America it must exist. When I was small, WHO TV in Des Moines used to show old movies every afternoon after school, and when other children were out playing kick the can or catching bullfrogs or encouraging little Bobby Birnbaum to eat worms (something he did with surprising amenability), I was alone in a curtained room in front of the TV, lost in a private world, with a plate of Oreo cookies on my lap and Hollywood magic flickering on my glasses. I didn't realize it at the time, but the films WHO showed were mostly classic – *The Best Years of Our Lives, Mr Smith Goes to Washington, Never Give a Sucker an Even Break, It Happened One Night*. The one constant in these pictures was the background. It was always the same place, a trim and sunny little city with a tree-lined Main Street full of friendly merchants ('Good morning, Mrs Smith!') and a courthouse square, and wooded neighbourhoods where fine houses slumbered beneath graceful elms. There was always a paper-boy on a bike slinging papers onto front porches, and a genial old fart in a white apron sweeping the sidewalk in front of his drugstore and two men striding briskly past. These two background men always wore suits, and they always strode smartly, never strolled or ambled, but strode in perfect harmony. They were really good at it. No matter what was going on in the foreground – Humphrey Bogart blowing away a bad guy with a .45, Jimmy Stewart earnestly explaining his ambitions to Donna Read, W.C. Fields lighting a cigar with the cellophane still on it – the background was always this timeless, tranquil place. Even in the midst of the most dreadful crises, when monster ants were at large in the streets or buildings were collapsing from some careless scientific experiment out at State University, you could still generally spot the paper-boy slinging newspapers somewhere in the background and those two guys in suits striding along like Siamese twins. They were absolutely imperturbable.

And it wasn't just in the movies. Everybody on TV – Ozzie and Harriet, Wally and Beaver Cleaver, George Burns and Gracie Allen – lived in this middle-class Elysium. So did the people in the advertisements in magazines and on the commercials on television and in the Norman Rockwell paintings on the covers of the *Saturday Evening Post*. In books it was the same. I used to read Hardy Boys mysteries one after the other, not for the plots, which even at the age of eight I could see were ridiculously improbable ('Say,

Frank, do you suppose those fellows with the funny accents that we saw at Moose Lake yesterday weren't really fishermen, but German spies, and that the girl in the bottom of their canoe with the bandage around her mouth wasn't really suffering from pyorrhoea but was actually Dr Rorschack's daughter? I've got a funny feeling those fellows might even be able to tell us a thing or two about the missing rocket fuel!'). No, I read them for Franklin W. Dixon's evocative, albeit incidental, descriptions of Bayport, the Hardy Boys' home town, a place inexpressibly picturesque, where houses with porch swings and picket fences peeked out on a blue sweep of bay full of sail-boats and skimming launches. It was a place of constant adventures and summers without end.

It began to bother me that I had never seen this town. Every year on vacation we would drive hundreds and hundreds of miles across the country, in an insane pursuit of holiday happiness, toiling over blue hills and brown prairies, through towns and cities without number, but without ever going through anywhere even remotely like that dreamy town in the movies. The places we passed through were hot and dusty and full of scrawny dogs, closed-down movie theatres, grubby diners and gas stations that looked as if they would be grateful to get two customers a week. But I felt sure that it must exist somewhere. It was inconceivable that a nation so firmly attached to small-town ideals, so dedicated in its fantasies to small-town notions, could not have somewhere built one perfect place – a place of harmony and industry, a place without shopping malls and oceanic parking lots, without factories and drive-in churches, without Kwik-Kraps and Jiffi-Shits and commercial squalor from one end to the other. In this timeless place Bing Crosby would be the priest, Jimmy Stewart the mayor, Fred Macmurray the high school principal, Henry Fonda a Quaker farmer. Walter Brennan would run the gas station, a boyish Mickey Rooney would deliver groceries, and somewhere at an open window Deanna Durbin would sing. And in the background, always, would be the kid on a bike and those two smartly striding men. The place I was looking for would be an amalgam of all those towns I had encountered in fiction. Indeed, that might well be its name – Amalgam, Ohio, or Amalgam, North Dakota. It could exist almost anywhere, but it had to exist. And on this trip, I intended to find it.

I drove and drove, through flat farming country and little towns devoid of life: Hull, Pittsfield, Barry, Oxville. On my map, Springfield was about two inches to the right of Hannibal, but it seemed to take hours to get there. In fact it does take hours to get there. I was only slowly adjusting to the continental scale of America, where states are the size of countries. Illinois is nearly twice as big as Austria, four times the size of Switzerland. There is so much emptiness, so much space between towns. You go through a little place and the dinette looks crowded, so you think, 'Oh, I'll wait till I get to Fuddville before I stop for coffee,' because it's only just down the road, and then you get out on the highway and a sign says FUDDVILLE 102 MILES. And you realize that you are dealing with another scale of geography altogether. There is a corresponding lack of detail on the maps. On British maps every church and public house is dutifully recorded. Rivers of laughable minuteness – rivers you can step across – are landmarks of importance, known for miles around. In America whole towns go missing – places with schools, businesses, hundreds of quiet little lives, just vanish, as effectively as if they had been vaporized.

And the system of roads is only cruelly hinted at. You look at the map and think you spy a short cut between, say, Weinerville and Bewilderment, a straight grey line of county road that promises to shave thirty minutes from your driving time. But when you leave the main highway, you find yourself in a network of unrecorded back roads, radiating out across the countryside like cracks in a pane of broken glass.

The whole business of finding your way around becomes laden with frustration, especially away from the main roads. Near Jacksonville I missed a left turn for Springfield and had to go miles out of my way to get back to where I wanted to be. This happens a lot in America. The highway authorities are curiously reluctant to impart much in the way of useful information, like where you are or what road you are on. This is all the more strange when you consider that they are only too happy to provide all kinds of peripheral facts – NOW ENTERING BUBB COUNTY SOIL CONSERVATION DISTRICT, NATIONAL SPRAT HATCHERY 5 MILES, NO PARKING WED 3 A.M. TO 6 A.M., DANGER: LOW-FLYING GEESE, NOW LEAVING BUBB COUNTY SOIL CONSERVATION DISTRICT. Often on country roads you will come to a crossroads without signposts and then have to drive twenty miles or more without having any confidence in where you are. And then abruptly, without warning, you round a bend and find yourself at an eight-lane intersection with fourteen traffic lights and the most bewildering assortment of signs, all with arrows pointing in different directions. Lake

Maggot State Park this way. Curtis Dribble Memorial Expressway over there. US Highway 41 South. US Highway 53 North. Interstate 11/78. Business District this way. Dextrose County Teachers' College that way. Junction 17 West. Junction 17 Not West. No U-Turn. Left Lane Must Turn Left. Buckle Your Seat Belt. Sit Up Straight. Did You Brush Your Teeth This Morning?

Just as you realize that you should be three lanes to the left, the lights change and you are swept off with the traffic, like a cork on a fast river. This sort of thing used to happen to my father all the time. I don't think Dad ever went through a really big and important intersection without getting siphoned off to somewhere he didn't want to be – a black hole of one-way streets, an expressway into the desert, a long and expensive toll bridge to some offshore island, necessitating an embarrassing and costly return trip. ('Hey, mister, didn't you come through here a minute ago from the other direction?') My father's particular speciality was the ability to get hopelessly lost without ever actually losing sight of the target. He never arrived at an amusement park or tourist attraction without first approaching it from several directions, like a pilot making passes over an unfamiliar airport. My sister and brother and I, bouncing on the back seat, could always see it on the other side of the freeway and cry, 'There it is! There it is!' Then after a minute we would spy it from another angle on the far side of a cement works. And then across a broad river. And then on the other side of the freeway again. Sometimes all that would separate us from our goal would be a high chain-link fence. On the other side you could see happy, carefree families parking their cars and getting ready for a wonderful day. 'How did they get in there?'

my dad would cry, the veins of his forehead lively. 'Why can't the city put up some signs, for Christ's sake? It's no wonder you can't find your way into the place,' he would add, conveniently overlooking the fact that 18,000 other people, some of them of decidedly limited mental acuity, had managed to get on to the right side of the barbed wire without too much difficulty.

Springfield was a disappointment. I wasn't really surprised. If it were a nice place, someone would have said to me, 'Say, you should go to Springfield. It's a nice place.' I had high hopes for it only because I had always thought it sounded promising. In a part of the world where so many places have harsh, foreign-sounding names full of hard consonants – De Kalb, Du Quoin, Keokuk, Kankakee – Springfield is a little piece of poetry, a name suggesting grassy meadows and cool waters. In fact, it was nothing of the sort. Like all small American cities, it had a downtown of parking lots and tallish buildings surrounded by a sprawl of shopping centres, gas stations and fast food joints. It was neither offensive nor charming. I drove around a little bit, but finding nothing worth stopping for, I drove on to New Salem, twelve miles to the north.

New Salem had a short and not very successful life. The original settlers intended to cash in on the river trade that passed by, but in fact the river trade did just that – passed by – and the town never prospered. In 1837 it was abandoned and would no doubt have been lost to history altogether except that one of its residents from 1831 to 1837 was a young Abraham Lincoln. So now, on a 620-acre site, New Salem has been rebuilt just as it was when Lincoln lived there, and you can go and see why everybody

was pretty pleased to clear off. Actually it was very nice. There were about thirty or forty log cabins distributed around a series of leafy clearings. It was a gorgeous autumn afternoon, with a warm breeze and soft sunlight adrift in the trees. It all looked impossibly quaint and appealing. You are not allowed to go in the houses. Instead you walk up to each one and peer through the windows or front door and you get an idea of what life was like for the people who lived there. Mostly it must have been pretty uncomfortable. Every house had a sign telling you about its residents. The historical research was impressively diligent. The only problem was that it all became a little repetitive after a while. Once you have looked through the windows of fourteen log cabins, you find yourself approaching number fifteen with a certain diminution of enthusiasm, and by the time you reach number twenty it is really only politeness that impels you onward. Since they've taken the trouble to build all these cabins and scour the country digging out old rocking-chairs and chamber-pots, you feel that the least you can do is walk around and feign interest at each one. But in your heart you are really thinking that if you never saw a log cabin again you'd be pretty damn pleased. I'm sure that was what Lincoln was thinking when he packed his cases and decided not to be a backwoods merchant any more, but to take up a more rewarding career emancipating Negroes and being President.

Down at the far end of the site, I met an older couple plodding towards me, looking tired. The man gave me a sympathetic look as he passed and said, 'Only two more to go.' Down the path from where they had come I could see one of the two remaining cabins, looking distant and small. I waited until the older couple were safely out of sight around a bend, and then sat down beneath a tree, a handsome oak into whose leaves a first trace of autumn gold was delicately bleeding. I felt a weight lifting from my shoulders and wondered why it was that I had been so enchanted by this place when I was five years old. Were childhoods so boring back then? I knew my own little boy, if driven to this place, would drop to the ground and start hyperventilating at the discovery that he had spent a day and a half sealed in a car only to come and see a bunch of boring log cabins. And looking at it now, I couldn't have blamed him. I mused for a few moments on the question of which was worse, to lead a life so boring that you are easily enchanted or a life so full of stimulus that you are easily bored.

But then it occured to me that musing is a pointless waste of anyone's time, and instead I went off to see if I could find a Baby Ruth candy bar, a far more profitable exercise.

After New Salem, I took Interstate 55 south, and drove for an hour and a half towards St Louis. It was boring, too. On a road as straight and as wide as an American interstate, fifty-five miles an hour is just too slow. It feels like walking speed. Cars and trucks coming towards you on the opposite carriageway seem to be travelling on one of those pedestrian conveyor belts you find in airports. You can see the people inside, get a long, lingering glimpse into their lives, as they slide past. And there's no sense of driving. You need to put a hand to the wheel occasionally just to confirm your course, but you can take time out to do the most intricate things – count your money, brush your hair, tidy up the car, use the rear-view mirror to search-and-destroy blackheads, read maps and guidebooks, put on or discard articles of clothing. If your car possessed cruise control you could just about climb in the back and take a nap. It is certainly quite easy to forget that you are in charge of two tons of speeding metal, and it is only when you start to scatter emergency cones at roadworks sites or a truck honks at you as you drift into its path that you are jolted back to reality and you realize that henceforth you probably shouldn't leave your seat to search for snack food.

The one thing that can be said is that it leaves you time to think, and to consider questions like why is it that the trees along highways never grow? Some of them must have been there for forty years by now, and yet they are still no more than six feet tall and with only fourteen leaves on them. Is it a particular low-maintenance strain, do you suppose? And here's another one. Why can't they make cereal boxes with pouring spouts? Is some guy at General Foods splitting his sides at the thought that every time people pour out a bowl of cornflakes they spill some of it on the floor? And why is that when you clean a sink, no matter how long you let the water run or how much you wipe it with a cloth there's always a strand of hair and some bits of wet fluff left behind? And just what *do* the Spanish see in flamenco music?

In a forlorn effort to keep from losing my mind, I switched on the radio, but then I remembered that American radio is designed for people who have already lost their minds. The first thing I came across was a commercial for Folger's Coffee. An announcer said in a confidential whisper, 'We went to the world famous Napa Valley Restaurant in California and – without telling the customers – served them Folger's instant coffee instead of the restaurant's usual brand. Then we listened in on hidden microphones.' There followed an assortment of praise for the coffee along the lines of 'Hey, this coffee is fantastic!', 'I've never tasted such rich, full-bodied coffee before!', 'This coffee is so good I can hardly stand it!' and that sort of thing. Then the announcer leapt out and told the diners that it was Folger's coffee, and they all shared a good laugh – and an important lesson about the benefits of drinking quality instant coffee. I twirled the dial. A voice said, 'We'll return to our discussion of maleness in sixty seconds.' I twirled the dial. The warbling voice of a female country singer intoned:

> His hands are tiny
> His arms are short
> But I lean upon him
> For my child support.

I twirled the dial. A voice said, 'This portion of the news is brought to you by the Airport Barber Shop, Biloxi.' There was then a commercial for the said barber shop, followed by thirty seconds of news, all of it related to deaths by cars, fires and gunfire in Biloxi in the last twenty-four hours. There was no hint that there might be a wider, yet more violent world beyond the city limits. Then there was another commercial for the Airport Barber Shop, in case you were so monumentally cretinous that you had forgotten about it during the preceding thirty seconds of news. I switched the radio off.

At Litchfield, I left the interstate vowing not to get on again if I could possibly help it, and joined a state highway, Illinois 127, heading south towards Murphysboro and Carbondale. Almost immediately life became more interesting. There were farms and houses and little towns to look at. I was still going fifty-five miles an hour, but now I seemed to be fairly skimming along. The landscape flashed past, more absorbing than before, more hilly and varied, and the foliage was a darker blur of green. Signs came and went: TEE PEE MINI MART, B-RITE FOOD STORE, BETTY'S BEAUTY BOX, SAV-A-LOT FOOD CENTER, PINCKNEYVILLE COON CLUB, BALD KNOB TRAILER COURT, DAIRY DELITE, ALL U CAN EAT. In between these shrines to dyslexia and free enterprise there were clearings on the hillsides where farmhouses stood. Almost everyone had a satellite dish in the yard, pointed to the sky as if tapping into some life-giving celestial force. I suppose in a sense they were. Here in the hills, the light failed more quickly. I noticed with surprise that it was past six o'clock and I decided that I had better find a room. As if on cue, Carbondale hove into view.

It used to be that when you came to the outskirts of a town you would find a gas station and a Dairy Queen, maybe a motel or two if it was a busy road or the town had a college. Now every town, even a quite modest one, has a mile or more of fast food places, motor inns, discount cities, shopping malls – all with thirty-foot-high revolving signs and parking lots the size of Shropshire. Carbondale appeared to have nothing else. I drove in on a road that became a two-mile strip of shopping centres and gas stations, K-Marts, J.C. Penneys, Hardees and McDonald's. And then, abruptly, I was in the country again. I turned around and drove back through town on a parallel street that offered precisely the same sorts of things but in slightly different configurations and then I was in the country again. The town had no centre. It had been eaten by shopping malls.

I got a room in the Heritage Motor Inn, then went out for a walk to try once more to find Carbondale. But there was nothing there. I was perplexed and disillusioned. Before I had left on the trip I had lain awake at night in my bed in England and pictured myself stopping each evening at a motel in a little city, strolling into town along sidewalks, dining on the blue plate special at Betty's Family Restaurant on the town square, then plugging a scented toothpick in my mouth and going for a stroll around the town, very probably stopping off at Vern's Midnite Tavern for a couple of draws and a game of eight-ball with the boys or taking in a movie at the Regal or looking in at the Val-Hi Bowling Alley to kibitz the Mid-Week Hairdressers' League matches before rounding off the night with a couple of games of pinball and a grilled cheese sandwich. But here there was no square to stroll to, no Betty's, no blue plate specials, no Vern's Midnite Tavern, no movie theatre, no bowling alley. There was no town, just six-lane highways and shopping malls. There weren't even any sidewalks. Going for a walk, as I discovered, was a ridiculous and impossible undertaking. I had to cross parking lots and gas station forecourts, and I kept coming up against little white-painted walls marking the boundaries between, say, Long John Silver's Seafood Shoppe and Kentucky Fried Chicken. To get from one to the other, it was necessary to clamber over the wall, scramble up a grassy embankment and pick your way through a thicket of parked cars. That is if you were on foot. But clearly from the looks people gave me as I lumbered breathlessly over the embankment, no-one had ever tried to go from one of these places to another under his own motive power. What you were supposed to do was get in your car, drive twelve feet down the street to another parking lot, park the car and get out. Glumly I clambered my way to a Pizza Hut and went inside, where a waitress seated me at a table with a view of the parking lot.

All around me people were eating pizzas the size of bus wheels. Directly opposite, inescapably in my line of vision, an overweight man of about thirty was lowering wedges into his mouth whole, like a sword swallower. The menu was dazzling in its variety. It went on for pages. There were so many types and sizes of pizza, so many possible permutations, that I felt quite at a loss. The waitress appeared. 'Are you ready to order?'

'I'm sorry,' I replied, 'I need a little more time.'

'Sure,' she said. 'You take your time.' She went off to somewhere out of my line of vision, counted to four and came back. 'Are you ready to order now?' she asked.

'I'm sorry,' I said, 'I really need just a little more time.'

'OK,' she said, and left. This time she may have counted as high as twenty, but when she returned I was still nowhere near understanding the many hundreds of options open to me as a Pizza Hut patron.

'You're kinda slow arentcha?' she observed brightly.

I was embarrassed. 'I'm sorry. I'm out of touch. I've . . . just got out of prison.'

Her eyes widened. 'Really?'

'Yes. I murdered a waitress who rushed me.'

With an uncertain smile she backed off and gave me lots and lots of time to make up my mind. In the end I had a medium-sized deep dish pepperoni pizza with extra onions and mushrooms, and I can recommend it without hesitation.

Afterwards, to round off a perfect evening, I clambered over to a nearby K-Mart and had a look around. K-Marts are a chain of discount stores and they are really depressing places. You could take Mother Theresa to a K-Mart and she would get depressed. It's not that there's anything wrong with the K-Marts themselves, it's the customers. K-Marts are always full of the sort of people who give their children names that rhyme: Lonnie, Donnie, Ronnie, Connie, Bonnie. The sort of people who would stay in to watch *The Munsters*. Every woman there has at least four children and they all look as if they have been fathered by a different man. The woman always weighs 250 pounds. She is always walloping a child and bawling, 'If you don't behave, Ronnie, I'm not gonna bring you back here no more!' As if Ronnie could give a toss about never going to a K-Mart again. It's the place you would go if you wanted to buy a stereo system for under $35 and didn't care if it sounded like the band was playing in a mailbox under water in a distant lake. If you go shopping at K-Mart you know that you've touched bottom. My dad liked K-Marts.

I went in and looked around. I picked up some disposable razors and a pocket notebook, and then, just to make an occasion of it, a bag of Reese's Peanut Butter Cups, which were attractively priced at $1.20. I paid for these and went outside. It was 7.30 in the evening. The stars were rising above the parking lot. I was alone with a small bag of pathetic treats in the most boring town in America and frankly I felt sorry for myself. I clambered over a wall and dodged across the highway to a Kwik-Krap mini supermarket, purchased a cold six-pack of Pabst Blue

Ribbon beer, and returned with it to my room where I watched cable TV, drank beer, messily ate Reese's Peanut Butter Cups (wiping my hands on the sheets) and drew meagre comfort from the thought that in Carbondale, Illinois, that was about as good a time as you were ever likely to get.

Chapter five

IN THE MORNING I rejoined Highway 127 south. This was marked on my map as a scenic route and for once this proved to be so. It really was attractive countryside, better than anything I knew Illinois possessed, with rolling hills of winebottle green, prosperous-looking farms and deep woods of oak and beech. Surprisingly, considering I was heading south, the foliage here was more autumnal than elsewhere – the hillsides were a mixture of mustard, dull orange and pale green, quite fetching – and the clear, sunny air had an agreeable crispness to it. I could live here, in these hills, I thought.

It took me a while to figure out what was missing. It was billboards. When I was small, billboards thirty feet wide and fifteen feet high stood in fields along every roadside. In places like Iowa and Kansas they were about the only stimulation you got. In the 1960s Lady Bird Johnson, in one of those misguided campaigns in which Presidents' wives are always engaging themselves, had most of the roadside billboards removed as part of a highway beautification programme. In the middle of the Rocky Mountains this was doubtless a good thing, but out here in the lonesome heartland billboards were practically a public service. Seeing one standing a mile off you would become interested to see what it said, and would watch with mild absorption as it advanced towards you and passed. As roadside excitements went, it was on about a par with the little windmills in Pella, but it was better than nothing.

The superior billboards would have a three-dimensional element to them – the head of a cow jutting out if it was for a dairy, or a cut-out of a bowling ball scattering pins if it was for a bowling alley. Sometimes the billboard would be for some coming attraction. There might be a figure of a ghost and the words: VISIT SPOOK CAVERNS! OKLAHOMA'S GREAT FAMILY ATTRACTION! JUST 69 MILES! A couple of miles later there would be another sign saying PLENTY OF FREE PARKING AT SPOOK CAVERNS, JUST 67 MILES! And so it would go, with sign after sign promising the most thrilling and instructive afternoon any family could ever hope to have, at least in Oklahoma. These promises would be supported by illustrations showing eerily-lit underground chambers, the size of cathedrals, in which the stalactites and stalagmites had magically fused into the shapes of witches' houses, bubbling cauldrons, flying bats and Casper the Friendly Ghost. It all looked extremely promising. So we children in the back would begin suggesting that we stop and have a look, taking it in turns to say, in a sincere and moving way, 'Oh, *please* Dad, oh, pleeeeease.'

Over the next sixty miles my father's position on the matter would proceed through a series of well-worn phases, beginning with a flat refusal on the grounds that it was bound to be expensive and anyway our behaviour since breakfast had been so disgraceful that it didn't warrant any special treats, to studiously ignoring our pleas (this phase would last for up to eleven minutes), to asking my mother privately in a low voice what she thought about the idea and receiving an equivocal answer, to ignoring us again in the evident hope that we would forget about it and stop nagging (one minute, twelve seconds), to saying that we *might* go if we started to behave and kept on behaving more or less forever, to saying that we definitely would *not* go because, just look at us, we were already squabbling again and we hadn't even gotten there, to finally announcing – sometimes in an exasperated bellow, sometimes in a death-bed whisper – that all right, we would go. You could always tell when Dad was on the brink of acceptance because his neck would turn red. It was always the same. He always said yes in the end. I never understood why he didn't just accede to our demands at the outset and save himself thirty minutes of anguish. Then he would always quickly add, 'But we're only going for half an hour – and you're not going to buy anything. Is that clear?' This seemed to restore to him a sense that he was in charge of things.

By the last two or three miles, the signs for Spook Caverns would be every couple of hundred yards, bringing us to a fever pitch of excitement. Finally there would be a billboard the size of a battleship with a huge arrow telling us to turn right here and drive eighteen miles. 'Eighteen miles!' Dad would cry shrilly, his forehead veins stirring to life in preparation for the inevitable discovery that after eighteen miles of bouncing down a dirt road with knee-deep ruts there would be no sign of Spook Caverns, that, indeed, after nineteen miles the road would end in a desolate junction without any clue to which way to turn, and that Dad would turn the wrong way. When eventually found, Spook Caverns would prove to be rather less than advertised – in fact, would give every appearance of being in the last stages of solvency. The caverns, damp and ill-lit and smelling like a long-dead horse, would be about the size of a garage and the stalactites and stalagmites wouldn't look the least bit like witches' houses and Casper the Ghost. They would look like – well, like stalactites and stalagmites. It would all be a huge let-down. The only possible way of assuaging our disappointment, we would discover, would be if Dad bought us each a rubber Bowie knife and bag of plastic dinosaurs in the adjoining gift shop. My sister and I would drop to the ground and emit mournful noises to remind him what a fearful thing unassuaged grief can be in a child.

So, as the sun sank over the brown flatness of Oklahoma and Dad, hours behind schedule, embarked on the difficult business of not being able to find a room for the night (ably assisted by my mother, who would misread the maps and mistakenly identify almost every approaching building as a possible motel), we children would pass the time in the back by having noisy and vicious knife fights, breaking off at intervals to weep, report wounds and complain of hunger, boredom and the need for toilet facilities. It was a kind of living hell. And now there appeared to be almost no billboards along the highways. What a sad loss.

I headed for Cairo, which is pronounced Kay-ro. I don't know why. They do this a lot in the South and Midwest. In Kentucky, Athens is pronounced AY-thens and Versailles is pronounced Vur-SAYLES. Bolivar, Missouri, is BAW-liv-er. Madrid, Iowa, is MAD-rid. I don't know whether the people in these towns pronounce them that way because they are backward undereducated shitkickers who don't know any better or whether they know better but don't care that everybody thinks they are backward undereducated shitkickers. It's not really the sort of question you can

ask them, is it? At Cairo I stopped for gas and in fact I did
ask the old guy who doddered out to fill my tank why they
pronounced Cairo as they did.

'Because that's its *name*,' he explained as if I were kind of
stupid.

'But the one in Egypt is pronounced Ki-ro.'

'So I've heard,' agreed the man.

'And most people, when they see the name, think Ki-ro,
don't they?'

'Not in Kay-ro they don't,' he said, a little hotly.

There didn't seem to be much to be gained by pursuing
the point, so I let it rest there, and I still don't know why
the people call it Kay-ro. Nor do I know why any citizen of
a free country would choose to live in such a dump,
however you pronounce it. Cairo is at the point where
the Ohio River, itself a great artery, joins the Mississippi,
doubling its grandeur. You would think that at the con-
fluence of two such mighty rivers there would be a great
city, but in fact Cairo is a poor little town of 6,000 people.
The road in was lined with battered houses and unpainted
tenements. Aged black men sat on the porches and stoops
on old sofas and rocking-chairs, waiting for death or
dinner, whichever came first. This surprised me. You don't
expect to see tenements and porches full of black people in
the Midwest – at least not outside big cities like Chicago
and Detroit. But then I realized that I was no longer really
in the Midwest. The speech patterns of southern Illinois
are more Southern than Midwestern. I was nearly as far
south as Nashville. Mississippi was only 160 miles away.
And Kentucky was just across the river. I crossed it now, on
a long, high bridge. From here on down to Louisiana the
Mississippi is immensely broad. It looks safe and lazy, but

in fact it is full of danger. Scores of people die in it every year. Farmers out fishing stare at the water and think, 'I wonder what would happen if I just stuck my toe in there a little bit,' and the next thing you know their bodies bob in the Gulf of Mexico, bloated but looking strangely serene. The river is deceptively fierce. In 1927, when the Mississippi overflowed, it flooded an area the size of Scotland. That is a serious river.

On the Kentucky side of the river I was greeted by huge signs everywhere saying FIREWORKS! In Illinois fireworks are illegal; in Kentucky they are not. So if you live in Illinois and want to blow your hand off, you drive across the river to Kentucky. You used to see a lot more of this sort of thing. If one state had a lower sales tax on cigarettes than a neighbouring state, all the state-line gas stations and cafés would put big signs on their roofs saying TAX-FREE CIGARETTES! 40 CENTS A PACK! NO TAX! and all the people from the next state would come and load their cars up with cut-price cigarettes. Wisconsin used to ban margarine to protect its dairy farmers, so everybody in Wisconsin, including all the dairy farmers, would drive to Iowa where there were big signs everywhere saying MARGARINE FOR SALE! All the Iowans, in the meantime, were driving off to Illinois, where there was no sales tax on anything, or Missouri where the sales tax on gasoline was fifty per cent lower. The other thing you used to get a lot of was states going their own way in terms of daylight saving time, so in the summer Illinois might be two hours adrift from Iowa and one hour behind Indiana. It was all kind of crazy, but it made you realize to what an extent the United States is really fifty independent countries (forty-eight countries in those days). Most of that seems to have gone now, yet another sad loss.

I drove through Kentucky thinking of sad losses and was abruptly struck by the saddest loss of all – the Burma Shave sign. Burma Shave was a shaving cream that came in a tube. I don't know if it's still produced. In fact, I never knew anyone who ever used it. But the Burma Shave company used to put clever signs along the highway. They came in clusters of five, expertly spaced so that you read them as a little poem as you passed: IF HARMONY/IS WHAT YOU CRAVE/THEN GET/A TUBA/BURMA SHAVE. Or: BEN MET/ANNA/MADE A HIT/NEGLECTED BEARD/BEN-ANNA SPLIT. Great, eh? Even in the 1950s the Burma Shave signs were pretty much a thing of the past. I can only remember seeing half a dozen in all the thousands of miles of highway we covered. But as roadside diversions went they were outstanding, ten times better than billboards and Pella's little twirling windmills. The only things that surpassed them for diversion value were multiple car pile-ups with bodies strewn about the highway.

Kentucky was much like southern Illinois – hilly, sunny, attractive – but the scattered houses were less tidy and prosperous-looking than in the north. There were lots of wooded valleys and iron bridges over twisting creeks, and an abundance of dead animals pasted to the road. In every valley stood a little white Baptist church and all along the road were signs to remind me that I was now in the Bible Belt: JESUS SAVES. PRAISE THE LORD. CHRIST IS KING.

I was out of Kentucky almost before I knew it. The state tapers to a point at its western edge, and I was cutting across a chunk of it only forty miles wide. In a veritable eyeblink in terms of American travelling time I was in Tennessee. It isn't often you can dispense with a state in less than an hour, and Tennessee would not detain me much longer. It is an odd-looking state, shaped like a Dutch brick, stretching more than 500 miles from east to west, but only 100 miles from top to bottom. Its landscape was much the same as that of Kentucky and Illinois – indeterminate farming country laced with rivers, hills and religious zealots – but I was surprised, when I stopped for lunch at a Burger King in Jackson, at how warm it was. It was eighty-three degrees, according to a sign on the drive-in bank across the street, a good twenty degrees higher than it had been in Carbondale that morning. I was still obviously deep in the Bible Belt. A sign in the yard of a church next door said CHRIST IS THE ANSWER. (The question, of course, is: What do you say when you strike your thumb with a hammer?) I went into the Burger King. A girl at the counter said, 'Kin I hep yew?' I had entered another country.

Chapter six

J UST SOUTH OF Grand Junction, Tennessee, I passed over
the state line into Mississippi. A sign beside the highway said WELCOME TO MISSISSIPPI. WE SHOOT TO KILL. It didn't
really. I just made that up. This was only the second time I
had ever been to the Deep South and I entered it with a
sense of foreboding. It is surely no coincidence that all
those films you have ever seen about the South – *Easy
Rider, In the Heat of the Night, Cool Hand Luke, Brubaker,
Deliverance* – depict Southerners as murderous, incestuous,
shitty-shoed rednecks. It really is another country. Years
ago, in the days of Vietnam, two friends and I drove to
Florida during college spring break. We all had long hair.
En route we took a short cut across the back roads of
Georgia and stopped late one afternoon for a burger at a
dinette in some dreary little crudville, and when we took
our seats at the counter the place fell silent. Fourteen people
just stopped eating, their food resting in their mouths, and
stared at us. It was so quiet in there you could have heard a
fly fart. A whole roomful of good ole boys with cherry-
coloured cheeks and bib overalls watched us in silence and
wondered whether their shotguns were loaded. It was
disconcerting. To them, out here in the middle of nowhere,
we were at once a curiosity – some of them had clearly
never seen no long-haired, nigger-loving, Northern, college-
edjicated, commie hippies in the flesh before – and yet

81

unspeakably loathsome. It was an odd sensation to feel so deeply hated by people who hadn't really had a proper chance to acquaint themselves with one's shortcomings. I remember thinking that our parents didn't have the first idea where we were, other than that we were somewhere in the continental vastness between Des Moines and the Florida Keys, and that if we disappeared we would never be found. I had visions of my family sitting around the living room in years to come and my mother saying, 'Well, I wonder whatever happened to Billy and his friends. You'd think we'd have had a postcard by now. Can I get anybody a sandwich?'

That sort of thing did really happen down there, you know. This was only five years after three freedom riders were murdered in Mississippi. They were a twenty-one-year-old black from Mississippi named James Chaney and two white guys from New York, Andrew Goodman, twenty, and Michael Schwerner, twenty. I give their names because they deserve to be remembered. They were arrested for speeding, taken to the Neshoba County Jail in Philadelphia, Mississippi, and never seen again – at least not until weeks later when their bodies were hauled out of a swamp. These were kids, remember. The police had released them to a waiting mob, which had taken them away and done things to them that a child wouldn't do to an insect. The sheriff in the case, a smirking, tobacco-chewing fat boy named Lawrence Rainey, was acquitted of negligent behaviour. No-one was ever charged with murder. To me this was and always would be the South.

I followed Highway 7 south towards Oxford. It took me along the western edge of the Holly Springs National Forest, which seemed to be mostly swamp and scrubland.

I was disappointed. I had half expected that as soon as I crossed into Mississippi there would be Spanish mosses hanging from the trees and women in billowy dresses twirling parasols and white-haired colonels with handle-bar moustaches drinking mint juleps on the lawn while darkies gathered the cotton and sang sweet hymns. But this landscape was just scrubby and hot and nondescript. Occasionally there would be a shack set up on bricks, with an old black man in a rocking-chair on the porch, but precious little sign of life or movement elsewhere.

At the town of Holly Springs stood a sign for Senatobia, and I got briefly excited. Senatobia! What a great name for a Mississippi town! All the stupidity and pomposity of the Old South seemed to be encapsulated in those five golden syllables. Maybe things were picking up. Maybe now I would see chain-gangs toiling in the sun and a prisoner in heavy irons legging it across fields and sloshing through creeks while pursued by bloodhounds, and lynch mobs roaming the streets and crosses burning on lawns. The prospect enlivened me, but I had to calm down because a state trooper pulled up alongside me at a traffic light and began looking me over with that sort of casual disdain you often get when you give a dangerously stupid person a gun and a squad car. He was sweaty and overweight and sat low in his seat. I assume he was descended from the apes like all the rest of us, but clearly in his case it had been a fairly gentle slope. I stared straight ahead with a look that I hoped conveyed seriousness of purpose mingled with a warm heart and innocent demeanour. I could *feel* him looking at me. At the very least I expected him to gob a wad of tobacco juice down the side of my head. Instead, he said, 'How yew doin'?'

This so surprised me that I answered, in a cracking voice, 'Pardon?'

'I said how yew doin'?'

'I'm fine,' I said. And then added, having lived some years in Britain, 'Thank you.'

'Y'on vacation?'

'Yup.'

'Hah doo lack Miss Hippy?'

'Pardon?'

'I say, Hah doo lack Miss Hippy?'

I was quietly distressed. The man was armed and Southern and I couldn't understand a word he was saying to me. 'I'm sorry,' I said, 'I'm kind of slow, and I don't understand what you're saying.'

'I say' – and he repeated it more carefully – 'how doo yew *lack* Mississippi?'

It dawned on me. 'Oh! I like it fine! I like it heaps! I think it's wonderful. The people are so friendly and helpful.' I wanted to add that I had been there for an hour and hadn't been shot at once, but the light changed and he was gone, and I sighed and thought, 'Thank you, Jesus.'

I drove on to Oxford, home of the University of Mississippi, or 'Ole Miss', as it's known. The people named the town after Oxford in England in the hope that this would persuade the state to build the university there, and the state did. This tells you most of what you need to know about the workings of the Southern mind. Oxford appeared to be an agreeable town. It was built around a square, in the middle of which stood the Lafayette County Courthouse, with a tall clock-tower and Doric columns, basking grandly in the Indian summer sunshine. Around the perimeter of the square were attractive stores and a tourist information office. I went into the tourist information office to get directions to Rowan Oak, William Faulkner's home. Faulkner lived in Oxford for the whole of his life, and his home is now a museum, preserved as it was on the day he died in 1962. It must be unnerving to be so famous that you know they are going to come in the moment you croak and hang velvet cords across all the doorways and treat everything with reverence. Think of the embarrassment if you left a copy of *Reader's Digest Condensed Books* on the bedside table.

Behind the desk sat a large, exceptionally well-dressed black woman. This surprised me a little, this being Mississippi. She wore a dark two-piece suit, which must have been awfully warm in the Mississippi heat. I asked her the way to Rowan Oak.

'You parked on the square?' she said. Actually she said, 'You pocked on the skwaya?'

'Yes.'

'Okay, honey, you git in yo' car and you makes the skwaya. You goes out the other end, towards the university, goes three blocks, turns rat at the traffic lats, goes down the hill and you there, un'stan?'

'No.'

She sighed and started again. 'You git in yo' car and you makes the skwaya—'

'What, I drive around the square?'

'That's rat, honey. You *makes* the skwaya.' She was talking to me the way I would talk to a French person. She gave me the rest of the instructions and I pretended to understand, though they meant almost nothing to me. All I kept thinking was what funny sounds they were to be emerging from such an elegant-looking woman. As I went out the door she called out, 'Hit doan really matter any-how cuz hit be's closed now.' She really said hit; she really said be's.

I said, 'Pardon?'

'Hit be's closed now. You kin back arond the grounz if you woan, but you caint go insod.'

I wint outsod think that Miss Hippy was goan be hard work. I walked around the square looking at the stores, most of them selling materials for a country club life-style. Handsome, well-dressed women bounded in and out. They were all tanned and rich-looking. On one of the corners was a bookstore with a magazine stand. I went in and looked around. At the magazine stand I picked up a *Playboy* and browsed through it. As one does. I was dis-tressed to see that *Playboy* is now printed on that awful glossy paper that makes the pages stick together like wet paper towels. You can't flick through it any more. You have to prise each page apart, like peeling paper off a stick of butter. Eventually I peeled my way to the main photo spread. It was of a naked paraplegic. I swear to God. She was sprawled – perhaps not the best choice of words in the context – in various poses on beds and divans, looking pert and indisputably attractive, but with satiny material draped artfully over her presumably withered legs. Now is it me, or does that seem just a little bit strange?

Clearly *Playboy* had lost its way, and this made me feel old and sad and foreign, because *Playboy* had been a cornerstone of American life for as long as I could re-member. Every man and boy I knew read *Playboy*. Some men, like my dad, pretended not to. He used to get embarrassed if you caught him looking at it at the super-market, and would pretend that he was really looking for

Better Homes and Gardens or something. But he read it. He even had a little stash of men's magazines in an old hatbox at the back of his clothes closet. Every kid I knew had a father with a little stash of men's magazines which the father thought was secret and which the kids knew all about. Once in a while we would swap our dads' magazine among ourselves and then imagine their perplexity when they went to the closet and found that instead of last month's issue of *Gent* they now possessed a two-year-old copy of *Nugget* and, as a bonus, a paperback book called *Ranchhouse Lust.* You could do this knowing that your dad would never say a word to you about it. All that would happen would be that the next time you went back the stash would be in a different place. I don't know whether women in the 1950s didn't sleep with their husbands or what, but this dedication to girlie magazines was pretty well universal. I think it may have had something to do with the war.

The magazines our fathers read had names like *Dude* and *Swell* and the women in them were unappealing, with breasts like deflated footballs and hips of abundant fleshiness. The women in *Playboy* were young and pretty. They didn't look like somebody you'd meet on shore leave. Beyond the incalculable public service *Playboy* performed by printing pictures of attractive naked women was the way it offered a whole attendant life-style. It was like a monthly manual telling you how to live, how to play the stock market and buy a hi-fi and mix sophisticated cocktails and intoxicate women with your wit and sense of style. Growing up in Iowa, you could use help with such matters. I used to read every issue from cover to cover, even the postal regulations at the bottom of the contents page.

We all did. Hugh Hefner was a hero to all of us. Looking back now. I can hardly believe it because really – let's be frank – Hugh Hefner has always struck me as a kind of an asshole. I mean honestly, if you had all that money, would you want a huge circular bed and to spend your life in a silk dressing-gown and carpet slippers? Would you want to fill a wing of your house with the sort of girls who would be happy to engage in pillow-fights in the nude and wouldn't mind you taking pictures of them while so occupied for publication in a national magazine? Would you want to come downstairs of an evening and find Buddy Hackett, Sammy Davis Jr and Joey Bishop standing around the piano in your living room? Do I hear a chorus of 'Shit, no's' out there? Yet I bought it whole. We all did.

Playboy was like an older brother to my generation. And over the years, just like an older brother, it had changed. It had had a couple of financial reversals, a little problem with gambling, and had eventually moved out to the coast. Just like real brothers do. We had lost touch. I hadn't really thought about it for years. And then here suddenly, in Oxford, Mississippi, of all places, who should I run into but *Playboy*. It was exactly like seeing an old high school hero and discovering he was bald and boring and still wearing those lurid V-neck sweaters and shiny black shoes with gold braid that you thought were so neat in about 1961. It was a shock to realize that both *Playboy* and I were a lot older than I had thought and that we had nothing in common any more. Sadly I returned the *Playboy* to the rack and realized it would be a long time – well, thirty days anyway – before I picked up another one.

I looked at the other magazines. There were at least 200 of them, but they all had titles like *Machine-Gun Collectors*,

Obese Bride, Christian Woodworker, Home Surgery Digest.
There was nothing for a normal person, so I left.

I drove out on South Lamar Street towards Rowan Oak,
having first made the square, following the tourist lady's
instructions as best I could, but I couldn't for the life of me
find it. To tell you the truth, this didn't disturb me a whole
lot because I knew it was closed and in any case I have
never managed to read a William Faulkner novel beyond
about page three (roughly half-way through the first
sentence), so I wasn't terribly interested in what his house
looked like. At any rate, in driving around I came across
the campus of the University of Mississippi and that was
much more interesting. It was a handsome campus, full of
fine buildings that looked like banks and courthouses.
Long shadows fell across the lawns. Young people, all
looking as healthy and as wholesome as a bottle of milk,
walked along with books tucked under their arms or sat at
tables doing homework. At one table, a black student sat
with white people. Things had clearly changed. It so
happened that twenty-five years ago to the very week there
had been a riot on this campus when a young black named
James Meredith, escorted by 500 federal marshals, enrolled as a student at Ole Miss. The people of Oxford
were so inflamed at the thought of having to share their
campus with a 'Niggra boy' that they wounded thirty of the
marshals and killed two journalists. Many of the parents of
these serene-looking students must have been among the
rioters, hurling bricks and setting cars alight. Was it really
possible that that kind of hate could have been extin-
guished in just one generation? It seemed unlikely. But
then it was impossible to imagine these tranquil students
ever rioting over a matter of race. Come to that, it was

89

impossible to imagine such a well-scrubbed straight-arrow group of young people rioting over anything – except perhaps the number of chocolate chips in the dining-hall cookies.

I decided on an impulse to drive on to Tupelo, Elvis Presley's hometown, thirty-five miles to the east. It was a pleasant drive, with the sun low and the air warm. Black woods pressed in on the road from both sides. Here and there in clearings there were shacks, usually with large numbers of black youngsters in the yard, passing footballs or riding bikes. Occasionally there were also nicer houses – white people's houses – with big station wagons standing in the driveways and a basketball hoop over the garage and large, well-mown lawns. Often these houses were remarkably close – sometimes right next door – to a shack. You would never see that in the North. It struck me as notably ironic that Southerners could despise blacks so bitterly and yet live comfortably alongside them, while in the North people by and large did not mind blacks, even respected them as humans and wished them every success, just so long as they didn't have to mingle with them too freely.

By the time I reached Tupelo it was dark. Tupelo was a bigger place than I had expected, but by now I was coming to expect things to be not like I expected them to be, if you see what I mean. It had a long, bright strip of shopping malls, motels and gas stations. Hungry and weary, I saw for the first time the virtue of these strips. Here it all was, laid out for you – a glittering array of establishments offering every possible human convenience, clean, comfortable, reliable, reasonably-priced places where you could rest, eat, relax and re-equip with the minimum of physical and mental exertion. On top of all this they give you glasses of iced water and free second cups of coffee, not to mention free matchbooks and scented toothpicks wrapped in paper to cheer you on your way. What a wonderful country, I thought, as I sank gratefully into Tupelo's welcoming bosom.

Chapter seven

I N THE MORNING I went to Elvis Presley's birthplace. It was early, and I expected it to be closed, but it was open and there were already people there, taking photographs beside the house or waiting to file in at the front door. The house, tidy and white, stood in a patch of shade in a city park. It was amazingly compact, shaped like a shoe-box, with just two rooms: a front room with a bed and dresser, and a plain kitchen behind. But it looked comfortable and had a nice homey feel. It was certainly superior to most of the shacks I had seen along the highway. A pleasant lady with meaty arms sat in a chair and answered questions. She must get asked the same questions about a thousand times a day, but she didn't seem to mind. Of the dozen or so people there, I was the only one under the age of sixty. I'm not sure if this was because Elvis was so clapped-out by the end of his career that his fans were all old people, or whether it is just that old people are the only ones with the time and inclination to visit the homes of dead celebrities.

A path behind the house led to a gift shop where you could buy Elvis memorabilia – albums, badges, plates, posters. Everywhere you looked his handsome, boyish face was beaming down at you. I bought two postcards and six books of matches, which I later discovered, with a strange sense of relief, I had lost somewhere. There was a visitors' book by the door. All the visitors came from towns with nowhere names like Coleslaw, Indiana, Dead Squaw, Oklahoma, Frigid, Minnesota, Dry Heaves, New Mexico, Colostomy, Montana. The book had a column for remarks. Reading down the list they said, 'Nice', 'Real nice', 'Very nice', 'Nice'. Such eloquence. I turned back to an earlier page. One visitor had misunderstood the intention of the remarks column and had written 'Visit'. Every other visitor on that page and the facing page had written 'Visit', 'Visit', 'Re-visit', 'Visit', until someone had turned the page and they got back on the right track.

The Elvis Presley house is in Elvis Presley Park on Elvis Presley Drive, just off the Elvis Presley Memorial Highway. You may gather from this that Tupelo is proud of its most famous native son. But it hadn't done anything tacky to exploit his fame, and you had to admire it for that. There weren't scores of gift shops and wax museums and souvenir emporia all trying to make a quick killing from Presley's fading fame, just a nice little house in a shady park. I was glad I had stopped.

From Tupelo I drove due south towards Columbus, into a hot and rising sun. I saw my first cotton fields, dark and scrubby but with fluffs of real cotton poking out from every plant. The fields were surprisingly small. In the Midwest you get used to seeing farms that sweep away to the horizon; here they were the size of a couple of vegetable patches. There were more shacks as well, a more or less continuous line of them along the highway. It was like driving through the world's roomiest slum. And these were real shacks. Some of them looked dangerously uninhabitable, with sagging roofs and walls that looked as if they had been cannon-balled. Yet as you passed you would see someone lurking in the doorway, watching you. There

93

were many roadside stores as well, more than you would have thought such a poor and scattered populace could support, and they all had big signs announcing a motley of commodities; GAS, FIREWORKS, FRIED CHICKEN, LIVE BAIT. I wondered just how hungry I would have to be to eat fried chicken prepared by a man who also dealt in live bait. All the stores had Coke machines and gas pumps out front, and almost all of them had rusting cars and assorted scrap scattered around the yard. It was impossible to tell if they were still solvent or not by their state of dereliction.

Every once in a while I would come to a town, small and dusty, with loads of black people hanging around outside the stores and gas stations, doing nothing. That was the most arresting difference about the South – the number of black people everywhere. I shouldn't really have been surprised by it. Blacks make up thirty-five per cent of the population in Mississippi and not much less in Alabama, Georgia and South Carolina. In some counties in the South, blacks outnumber whites by four to one. Yet until as recently as twenty-five years ago, in many of those counties not a single black person was registered to vote.

With so much poverty everywhere, Columbus came as a welcome surprise. It was a splendid little city, hometown of Tennessee Williams, with a population of 30,000. During the Civil War it was briefly the state capital, and it still had some large *ante bellum* homes lining the well-shaded road in from the highway. But the real jewel was its downtown, which seemed hardly to have changed since about 1955. Crenshaw's Barber Shop had a rotating pole out front and across the street was a genuine five and dime called McCrory's and on the corner was the Bank of Mississippi in an imposing building with a big clock hanging over the sidewalk. The country courthouse, city hall and post office were all handsome and imposing edifices but built to a small-town scale. The people looked prosperous. The first person I saw was an obviously well-educated black man in a three-piece suit carrying a *Wall Street Journal*. It was all deeply pleasing and encouraging. This was a first-rate town. Combine it with Pella's handsome square and you would almost have my long-sought Amalgam. I was beginning to realize that I was never going to find it in one place. I would have to collect it piecemeal – a courthouse here, a fire station there – and here I had found several pieces.

I went for a cup of coffee in a hotel on Main Street and bought a copy of the local daily paper, the *Commercial Dispatch* ('Mississippi's Most Progressive Newspaper'). It was an old-fashioned paper with a banner headline across eight columns on page one that said 'Taiwanese Business Group to Visit Golden Triangle Area', and beneath that a crop of related single-column subheadings all in different sizes, typefaces and degrees of coherence.

Visitors Are Looking
At Opportunities
For Investment

AS PART
OF TRADE
MISSION

Group To Arrive In
Golden Triangle
Thursday

STATE OFFICIALS
COORDINATE VISIT

All the stories inside suggested a city ruled by calmness and compassion: 'Trinity Place Home-makers Give Elderly A Helping Hand', 'Lamar Landfill Is Discussed', 'Pickens School Budget Adopted'. I read the police blotter. 'During the past twenty-four hours,' it said, 'the Colombus Police Department had a total of thirty-four activities.' What a wonderful place – the police here didn't deal with crimes, they had activities. According to the blotter the most exciting of these activities had been arresting a man for driving on a suspended licence. Elsewhere in the paper I discovered that in the past twenty-four hours six people had died – or had death activities, as the police blotter might have put it – and three births had been recorded. I developed an instant affection for the *Commercial Dispatch* (which I rechristened in my mind the *Amalgam Commercial Dispatch*) and with the town it served.

I could live here, I thought. But then the waitress came over and said, 'Yew honestly a breast menu, honey?' and I realized that it was out of the question. I couldn't understand a word these people said to me. She might as well have addressed me in Dutch. It took many moments and much gesturing with a knife and fork to establish that what she had said to me was, 'Do you want to see a breakfast menu, honey?'

In fact I had been hoping to see a lunch menu, but rather than spend the afternoon trying to convey this notion, I asked for a Coca-Cola, and was enormously relieved to find that this did not elicit any subsidiary questions.

It isn't just the indistinctness with which Southerners speak that makes it so difficult to follow, it's also the slowness. This begins to get to you after a while. The average Southerner has the speech patterns of someone slipping in and out of consciousness. I can change my shoes and socks faster than most people in Mississippi can speak a sentence. Living there would drive me crazy. Slowly.

Columbus is just inside the state boundary line and I found myself, twenty minutes after leaving town, in Alabama, heading for Tuscaloosa by way of Ethelsville, Coal Fire and Reform. A sign by the highway said DON'T LITTER, KEEP ALABAMA THE BEAUTIFUL. 'OK, I the will,' I replied cheerfully.

I put the radio on. I had been listening to it a lot in the last couple of days, hoping to be entertained by backward and twangy radio stations playing songs by artists with names like Hank Wanker and Brenda Buns. This is the way it always used to be. My brother, who was something of a scientific wizard, once built a short-wave radio from old baked bean cans and that sort of thing, and late at night when we were supposed to be asleep he would lie in bed in the dark twiddling his knob (so to speak), searching for distant stations. Often he would pick up stations from the South. They would always be manned by professional hillbillies playing twangy music. The stations were always crackly and remote, as if the broadcasts were being beamed to us from another planet. But now there were hardly any backward-sounding people. In fact, there were hardly any Southern accents at all. All the disc jockeys sounded as if they came from Ohio.

Outside Tuscaloosa I stopped for gas and was surprised that the young man who served me also sounded as if he came from Ohio. In point of fact he did. He had a girlfriend at the University of Alabama, but he hated the South because it was so slow and backward. I asked him about the voices on the radio since he seemed to be an on-the-ball sort of guy. He explained that Southerners had become so sensitive about their reputation for being shit-squishing red-necks that all the presenters on TV and radio tried to sound as if they came from the North and had never in their whole lives nibbled a hush puppy or sniffed a grit. Nowadays it was the only way to get a job. Apart from anything else, the zippier Northern cadences meant the radio stations could pack in three or four commercials in the time it would take the average Southerner to clear his throat. That was certainly very true, and I tipped the young man 35¢ for his useful insight.

From Tuscaloosa, I followed Highway 69 south into Selma. All Selma meant to me was vague memories from the civil rights campaigns in the 1960s, when Martin Luther King led hundreds of blacks on forty-mile marches from there to Montgomery, the state capital, to register to vote. It was another surprisingly attractive town – this corner of the South seemed to be awash with them. It was about the same size as Columbus, and just as shady and captivating. Trees had been planted along the streets downtown and the sidewalks had recently been repaved in brick. Benches had been set out, and the waterfront area, where the city ended in a sharp bluff overlooking the Alabama River, had been cleaned up. It all had an agreeable air of prosperity. At a tourist information office I picked up some pamphlets extolling the town, including one boasting of its black heritage. I was heartened by this. I had seen nothing even faintly praiseworthy of blacks in Mississippi. Moreover, blacks and whites here seemed to be on far better terms. I could see them chatting at bus-stops, and I saw a black nurse and white nurse travelling together in a car, looking like old friends. Altogether, it seemed a much more relaxed atmosphere than in Mississippi.

I drove on, through rolling, open countryside. There were some cotton fields still, but mostly this was dairy country, with green fields and bright sunshine. In the late afternoon, almost the early evening, I reached Tuskegee, home of the Tuskegee Institute. Founded by Booker T. Washington and developed by George Washington Carver, it is America's premier college for blacks. It is also the seat of one of the poorest counties in America. Eighty-two per cent of the county population is black. More than half the county residents live below the poverty level. Almost a third of them still don't have indoor plumbing. That is really poor. Where I come from you are poor if you can't afford a refrigerator that makes its own ice-cubes and your car doesn't have automatic windows. Not having running water in the house is something beyond the realms of the imaginable to most Americans.

The most startling thing about Tuskegee was that it was completely black. It was in every respect a typical small American city, except that it was poor, with lots of boarded shopfronts and general dereliction, and that every person in every car, every pedestrian, every storekeeper, every fireman, every postman, every last soul was black. Except me. I had never felt so self-conscious, so visible. I suddenly appreciated what a black person must feel like in North Dakota. I stopped at a Burger King for a cup of coffee. There must have been fifty people in there. I was the only person who wasn't black, but no-one seemed to notice or care. It was an odd sensation – and rather a relief, I must say, to get back out on the highway.

I drove on to Auburn, twenty miles to the north-east. Auburn is also a college town and roughly the same size as Tuskegee, but the contrast could hardly have been more striking. Auburn students were white and rich. One of the first sights I saw was a blonde sweeping past in a replica Dusenberg that must have cost her daddy $25,000. It was obviously a high school graduation present. If I could have run fast enough to keep up, I would happily have urinated all down the side of it. Coming so soon after the poverty of Tuskegee, it made me feel strangely ashamed.

However, I must say that Auburn appeared to be a pleasant town. I've always liked college towns anyway. They are about the only places in America that manage to combine the benefits of a small-town pace of life with a dash of big city sophistication. They usually have nice bars and restaurants, more interesting shops, an altogether more worldly air. And there is a pleasing sense of being around 20,000 young people who are having the best years of their lives.

In my day, the principal concerns of university students were sex, smoking dope, rioting and learning. Learning was something you did only when the first three weren't available, but at least you did it. Nowadays, American students' principal concerns seem to be sex and keeping their clothes looking nice. I don't think learning comes into it very much. Just at this time, there was an outcry in

America over the contagion of ignorance that appeared to be sweeping through the nation's young people. The principal focus of this nationwide hand-wringing was a study by the National Endowment for the Humanities. It had recently tested 8,000 high school seniors and found that they were as stupid as pig dribble. More than two thirds of them did not know when the US Civil War took place, couldn't identify Stalin or Churchill, and didn't know who wrote *The Canterbury Tales*. Almost half thought World War 1 started before 1900. A third thought that Roosevelt was President during the Vietnam war and that Columbus sailed to America after 1750. Forty-two per cent – this is my favourite – couldn't name a single country in Asia. I would scarcely have believed all this myself except that the summer before I had taken two American high school girls for a drive around Dorset – bright girls, both of them now enrolled in colleges of high repute – and neither of them had ever heard of Thomas Hardy. How can you live to be eighteen years old and never have at least *heard* of Thomas Hardy?

I don't know the answer to that, but I suspect you could spend a week in Auburn kissing the ass of every person who had ever heard of Thomas Hardy and not get chapped lips. Perhaps that is a grossly unjustified comment. For all I know, Auburn may be a hotbed of Hardy scholarship. But what I do know, from having spent only a short while there, is that it hasn't got a single decent bookstore. How can a university town not have a decent bookstore? There was a bookstore, but all it sold was textbooks and a decidedly unliterary assortment of sweat-shirts, stuffed animals and other paraphernalia bearing the Auburn University seal. Most American universities like Auburn have 20,000 students or more, and upwards of 800 or 1,000 professors and lecturers. How can any community with that many educated people not support a single decent bookstore? If I were the National Endowment for the Humanities, I would find that at least as compelling a question as why high school seniors do so poorly on general knowledge tests.

Incidentally, I'll tell you why they do so poorly. They answer the questions as fast as they can, at random, and then sleep. We used to do it all the time. Once a year in high school, our principal, Mr Toerag, would file the whole school into the auditorium and make us spend a tedious day answering multiple choice questions on a variety of subjects for some national examination. It didn't take you long to deduce that if you filled in the circles without bothering to look at the questions, you could complete the work in a fraction of the time, and then shut your eyes and lose yourself in erotic eyelid movies until it was time for the next test. As long as your pencil was neatly stowed and you didn't snore, Mr Toerag, whose job it was to wander up and down the rows looking for miscreants, would leave you alone. That was what Mr Toerag did for a living, wander around all day looking for people misbe-having. I always imagined him at home in the evening walking around the dining-room table and poking his wife with a ruler if she slouched. He must have been hell to live with. His name wasn't really Mr Toerag, of course. It was Mr Superdickhead.

Chapter eight

I DROVE THROUGH bright early-morning sunshine. Here and there the road plunged into dense pine forests and led past collections of holiday cabins in the woods. Atlanta was only an hour's drive to the north and the people here-abouts were clearly trying to cash in on that proximity. I passed through a little town called Pine Mountain, which seemed to have everything you could want in an inland resort. It was attractive and had nice shops. The only thing it lacked was a mountain, which was a bit of a disappointment considering its name. I had intentionally chosen this route because Pine Mountain conjured up to my simple mind a vision of clean air, craggy precipices, scented forests and tumbling streams – the sort of place where you might bump into John-Boy Walton. Still, who could blame the locals if they stretched the truth a little in the pursuit of a dollar? You could hardly expect people to drive miles out of their way to visit something called Pine Flat-Place.

The countryside became gradually more hilly, though obstinately uncraggy, before the road made a gentle descent into Warm Springs. For years I had been harbouring an urge to go there. I'm not sure why. I knew nothing about the place except that Franklin Roosevelt had died there. In the Register and Tribune Building in Des Moines the main corridor was lined with historic front pages which I found strangely absorbing when I was small. One of them said 'President Roosevelt Dies at Warm Springs', and I thought even then that it sounded like such a nice place to pass away.

In the event, Warm Springs was a nice place. There was just a main street, with an old hotel on one side and a row of shops on the other, but they had been restored as expensive boutiques and gift shops for visitors from Atlanta. It was all patently artificial – there was even outdoor Muzak, if you can stand it – but I quite liked it.

I drove out to the Little White House, about two miles outside town. The parking lot was almost empty, except for an old bus from which a load of senior citizens were disembarking. The bus was from the Calvary Baptist Church in some place like Firecracker, Georgia, or Bare-assed, Alabama. The old people were noisy and excited, like schoolchildren, and pushed in front of me at the ticket booth, little realizing that I wouldn't hesitate to give an old person a shove, especially a Baptist. But I just smiled benignly and stood back, comforted by the thought that soon they would be dead.

I bought my ticket and quickly overtook the old people on the slope up to the Roosevelt compound. The path led through woods of tall pine trees that seemed to go up and up forever and sealed out the sunlight so effectively that the ground at their bases was bare, as if it had just been swept. The path was lined with large rocks from each state. Every governor had evidently been asked to contribute some hunk of native stone and here they were, lined up like a guard of honour. It's not often you see an idea that stupid brought to fruition. Many had been cut in the shape of the state, then buffed to a glossy finish and engraved.

But others, clearly not catching the spirit of the enterprise, were just featureless hunks with a terse little plaque saying 'Delaware. Granite.' Iowa's contribution was, as expected, carefully middling. The stone had been cut to the shape of the state, but by someone who had clearly never attempted such a thing before. I imagine he had impulsively put in the lowest bid and was surprised to get the contract. At least the state had found a rock to send. I had half feared it might be a clump of dirt.

Beyond this unusual diversion was a white bungalow, which had formerly been a neighbouring home and was now a museum. As always with these things in America, it was well done and interesting. Photographs of Roosevelt at Warm Springs covered the walls and lots of his personal effects were on display in glass cases – his wheelchairs, crutches, leg-braces and other such implements. Some of these were surprisingly elaborate and exerted a morbid interest because F.D.R. was always careful not to let the public see him as the cripple he was. And here we were viewing him with his trousers off, so to speak. I was particularly taken with a room full of all the handmade gifts that had been given to him when he was President and then presumably stuck at the back of a very large cupboard. There were carved walking-sticks by the dozen and maps of America made of inlaid wood and portraits of F.D.R. scratched on walrus tusks and etched with acid into slate. The amazing thing was how well done they all were. Every one of them represented hundreds of hours of delicate carving and tireless polishing, and all to be given away to a stranger for whom it would be just one more item in a veritable cavalcade of personalized keepsakes. I became so absorbed in these items that I scarcely noticed when the old people barged in, a trifle breathless but none the less lively. A lady with a bluish tint to her hair pushed in front of me at one of the display cases. She gave me a brief look that said, 'I am an old person. I can go where I want,' and then she dismissed me from her mind. 'Say, Hazel,' she called in a loud voice, 'did you know you shared a birthday with Eleanor Roosevelt?'

'Is that so?' answered a grating voice from the next room.

'I share a birthday with Eisenhower myself,' the lady with the bluish hair went on, still loudly, consolidating her position in front of me with a twitch of her ample butt. 'And I've got a cousin who shares a birthday with Harry Truman.'

I toyed for a moment with the idea of grabbing the woman by both ears and driving her forehead into my knee, but instead passed into the next room where I found the entrance to a small cinema in which they showed us a crackling black and white film all about Roosevelt's struggle with polio and his long stays at Warm Springs trying to rub life into his spindly legs, as if they had merely gone to sleep. It too was excellent. Written and narrated by a correspondent from UPI, it was moving without being mawkish, and the silent home movies, with their jerky movements that made all the participants look as if someone just out of camera range was barking at them to hurry up, exerted the same sort of voyeuristic fascination as F.D.R.'s legbraces. Afterwards we were at last released to see the Little White House itself. I fairly bounded ahead in order not to have to share the experience with the old people. It was down another path, through more pine trees and beyond a white sentry-box. I was surprised at how small it was. It was just a little white cottage in the woods, all on one floor, with five small rooms, all panelled in dark wood. You would never believe that this could be the property of a President, particularly a rich President like Roosevelt. He did, after all, own most of the surrounding countryside, including the hotel on Main Street, several cottages and the springs themselves. Yet the very compactness of the cottage made it all the more snug and appealing. Even now, it looked comfy and lived-in. You couldn't help but want it for yourself, even if it meant coming to Georgia to enjoy it. In every room there was a short taped commentary, which explained how Roosevelt worked and underwent therapy at the cottage. What it didn't tell you was that what he really came here for was a bit of rustic bonking with his secretary, Lucy Mercer. Her bedroom was on one side of the living-room and his was on the other. The taped recording made nothing of this, but it did point out that Eleanor's bedroom, tucked away at the back and decidedly inferior to the secretary's, was mostly used as a guest-room because Eleanor seldom made the trip south.

From Warm Springs I went some miles out of my way to take the scenic road into Macon, but there didn't seem to be a whole lot scenic about it. It wasn't unscenic particularly, it just wasn't scenic. I was beginning to suspect that the scenic route designations on my maps had been applied somewhat at random. I imagined some guy who had never been south of Jersey City sitting in an office in New York and saying, 'Warm Springs to Macon? Ooh, that sounds nice,' and then carefully drawing in the orange dotted line that signifies a scenic route, his tongue sticking ever so slightly out of the corner of his mouth.

Macon was nice – all the towns in the South seemed to be nice. I stopped at a bank for money and was served by a lady from Great Yarmouth, something that brought a little excitement to both of us, and then continued on my way over the Otis Redding Memorial Bridge. There is a fashion in many parts of America, particularly the South, to name things made out of concrete after some local worthy – the Sylvester C. Grubb Memorial Bridge, the Chester Ovary Levee, that sort of thing. It seems a very odd practice to me. Imagine working all your life, clawing your way to the top, putting in long hours, neglecting your family, stabbing people in the back and generally being thought a shit by everyone you came in contact with, just to have a highway bridge over the Tallapoosa River named after you. Doesn't seem right somehow. Still, at least this one was named after someone I had heard of.

I headed east for Savannah, down Interstate 16. It was a 173-mile drive of unspeakable tedium across the red-clay plain of Georgia. It took me five hot and unrewarding hours to reach Savannah. While you, lucky reader, have only to flit your eyes to the next paragraph.

I stood agog in Lafayette Square in Savannah, amid brick paths, trickling fountains and dark trees hung with Spanish moss. Before me rose up a cathedral of exquisite linen-fresh whiteness with twin Gothic spires, and around it stood 200-year-old houses of weathered brick, with hurricane shutters that were still clearly used. I did not know that such perfection existed in America. There are twenty such squares in Savannah, cool and quiet beneath a canopy of trees, and long straight side-streets equally dark and serene. It is only when you stumble out of this urban rain forest, out into the open streets of the modern city, exposed to the glare of the boiling sun, that you realize just how sweltering the South can be. This was October, a time of flannel shirts and hot toddies in Iowa, but here summer was unrelenting. It was only eight in the morning and already businessmen were loosening their ties and mopping their foreheads. What must it be like in August? Every store and restaurant is air-conditioned. You step inside and the sweat is freeze-dried on your arms. Step back outside and the air meets you as something hot and unpleasant, like a dog's breath. It is only in its squares that the climate achieved a kind of pleasing equilibrium.

Savannah is a seductive city and I found myself wandering almost involuntarily for hours. The city has more than 1,000 historic buildings, many of them still lived in as houses. This was, New York apart, the first American city I had ever been in where people actually lived downtown. What a difference it makes, how much more vibrant and alive it all seems, to see children playing ball in the street or skipping rope on the front stoops. I wandered along the cobbled sidewalk of Oglethorpe Avenue to the Colonial Park Cemetery, full of mouldering monuments and densely packed with the gravestones of people famous to the state's history – Archibald Bulloch, the first president of Georgia, James Habersham, 'a leading merchant', and Button Gwinnett, who is famous in America for being one of the signatories of the Declaration of Independence and for having the silliest first name in Colonial history. The people of Savannah, in a careless moment, appear to have lost old Button. The historical marker said that he might be buried where I was standing now or then again he might be over in the corner or possibly somewhere else altogether. You could walk around all day and never know when you were on the Button, so to speak.

The business district in Savannah was frozen in a perpetual 1959 – the Woolworth's store didn't appear to have changed its stock since about then. There was a handsome old movie-house, Weis's, but it was shut. Downtown movie-houses are pretty much a thing of the past in America, alas, alas. You are always reading how buoyant the movie industry is in America, but all the theatres now are at shopping malls in the suburbs. You go to the movies there and you get a choice of a dozen pictures, but each theatre is about the size of a large fridge-freezer and only marginally more comfortable. There are no balconies. Can you imagine that? Can you imagine movie theatres without balconies? To me, going to the movies means sitting in the front row of the balcony with your feet up, dropping empty candy boxes on to the people below (or, during the more boring love-scenes, dribbling Coke) and throwing Nibs at the screen. Nibs were a liquorice-flavoured candy, thought to be made from rubber left over from the Korean War, which had a strange popularity in the 1950s. They were practically inedible, but if you sucked on one of them for a minute and then threw it at the screen, it would stick with an interesting 'pock' sound. It was a tradition on Saturdays for everybody to take the bus downtown to the Orpheum, buy a box of Nibs and spend the afternoon bombarding the screen.

You had to be careful when you did this because the theatre manager employed vicious usherettes, dropouts from Tech High School whose one regret in life was that they hadn't been born into Hitler's Germany, who patrolled the aisles with high-powered flash-lights looking for children who were misbehaving. Two or three times during the film their darting lights would fix on some hapless youngster, half out of his seat, poised in throwing position with a moistened Nib in his hand, and they would rush to subdue him. He would be carried off squealing. This never happened to my friends or me, thank God, but we always assumed that the victims were taken away and tortured with electrical instruments before being turned over to the police for a long period of mental readjustment in a reform school. Those were the days! You cannot tell me that some suburban multiplex with shoe-box theatres and screens the size of bath towels can offer anything like the enchantment and community spirit of a cavernous downtown movie-house. Nobody seems to have noticed it yet, but ours could well be the last generation for which movie-going has anything like a sense of magic.

On this sobering thought I strolled to Water Street, on the Savannah River, where there was a new riverside walk. The river itself was dark and smelly and on the South Carolina side opposite there was nothing to look at but down-at-heel warehouses and, further downriver, factories dispensing billows of smoke. But the old cotton warehouses overlooking the river on the Savannah side were splendid. They had been restored without being over-gentrified. They contained boutiques and oyster bars on the ground floor, but the upper floors were left a tad shabby, giving them that requisite raffish air I had been looking for since Hannibal. Some of the shops were just a bit twee, I must admit. One of them was called The Cutest Little Shop in Town, which made me want to have the Quickest Little Puke in the County. A sign on the door said 'Absotively, posilutely no food or drink in shop.' I sank to my knees and thanked God that I had never had to meet the proprietor. The shop was closed so I wasn't able to go inside and see what was so cute about it.

Towards the end of the street stood a big new Hyatt Regency hotel, an instantly depressing sight. Massive and made of shaped concrete, it was from the Fuck You school of architecture so favoured by the big American hotel chains. There was nothing about it in scale or appearance even remotely sympathetic to the old buildings around it. It just said, 'Fuck you, Savannah.' The city is particularly ill-favoured in this respect. Every few blocks you come up against some discordant slab – the De Soto Hilton, the Ramada Inn, the Best Western Riverfront, all about as appealing as spittle on a johnny cake, as they say in Georgia. Actually, they don't say anything of the sort in Georgia. I just made it up. But it has a nice Southern ring to it, don't you think? I was just about at the point where I was starting to get personally offended by the hotels, and in serious danger of becoming tiresome here, when my attention was distracted by a workman in front of the city courthouse, a large building with a gold dome. He had a leaf blower, a noisy contraption with miles of flex snaking back into the building behind him. I had never seen such a thing before. It looked something like a vacuum cleaner – actually, it looked like one of the Martians in *It Came From Outer Space* – and it was very noisy. The idea, I gathered, was that you would blow all the leaves into a pile and then gather them up by hand. But every time the man assembled a little pile of leaves, a breeze would come along and unassemble it. Sometimes he would chase one leaf half a block or more with his blower, whereupon all the leaves back at base would seize the opportunity to scuttle off in all directions. It was clearly an appliance that must have looked nifty in the catalogue but would never work in the real world, and I vaguely wondered, as I strolled past, whether the people at the Zwingle Company were behind it in some way.

I left Savannah on the Herman Talmadge Memorial Bridge, a tall, iron-strutted structure that rises up and up and up and flings you, wide-eyed and quietly gasping, over the Savannah River and into South Carolina. I drove along what appeared on my map to be a meandering coast road, but was in fact a meandering inland road. This stretch of coast is littered with islands, inlets, bays, and beaches of rolling sand dunes, but I saw precious little of it. The road was narrow and slow. It must be hell in the summer when millions of vacationers from all over the eastern seaboard head for the beaches and resorts – Tybee Island, Hilton Head, Laurel Bay, Fripp Island.

It wasn't until I reached Beaufort (pronounced Bewfurt) that I got my first proper look at the sea. I rounded a bend to find myself, suddenly and breathtakingly, gazing out on a looking-glass bay full of boats and reed beds, calm and bright and blue, the same colour as the sky. According to my *Mobil Travel Guide*, the three main sources of income in the area are tourism, the military and retired people. Sounds awful, doesn't it? But in fact Beaufort is lovely, with many mansions and an old-fashioned business district. I parked on Bay Street, the main road through town, and was impressed to find that the meter fee was only 5¢. That must be just about the last thing a nickel will buy you in America – thirty minutes of peace of mind in Beaufort, South Carolina. I strolled down to a little park and marina, which had been recently built, from the look of it. This was only the fourth time I had seen the Atlantic from this side. When you come from the Midwest, the ocean is a thing rarely encountered. The park was full of signs instructing you not to enjoy yourself or do anything impertinent. They were every few yards, and said NO SWIMMING OR DIVING FROM SEA-WALL. NO BIKE-RIDING IN PARK. CUTTING OR DAMAGING FLOWERS, PLANTS, TREES OR SHRUBS PROHIBITED. NO CONSUMPTION OR POSSESSION OF BEER, WINE, OR ALCOHOLIC BEVERAGES IN CITY PARKS WITHOUT SPECIAL PERMISSION OF THE CITY. VIOLATORS WILL BE PROSECUTED. I don't know what sort of mini-Stalin they have running the council in Beaufort, but I've never seen a place so officially unwelcoming. It put me off so much that I didn't want to be there any more, and abruptly I left, which was a shame really because I still had twelve minutes of unexpired time on the meter.

As a result of this, I arrived in Charleston twelve minutes earlier than planned, which was good news. I had thought that Savannah was the most becoming American city I had ever seen, but it thumped into second place soon after my arrival in Charleston. At its harbour end, the city tapers to a rounded promontory which is packed solid with beautiful old homes, lined up one after the other along straight, shady streets like oversized books on a crowded shelf. Some are of the most detailed Victorian ornateness, like fine lace, and some are plain white clapboard with black shutters, but all of them are at least three storeys high and imposing – all the more so as they loom up so near the road. Almost no-one has any yard to speak of – though everywhere I looked there were Vietnamese gardeners minutely attending to patches of lawn the size of table-cloths – so children play on the street and women, all of them white, all of them young, all of them rich, gossip on the front steps. This isn't supposed to happen in America. Wealthy children in America don't play on the street; there isn't any need. They lounge beside the pool or sneak reefers in the $3,000 treehouse that daddy had built for them for their ninth birthday. And their mothers, when they wish to gossip with a neighbour, do it on the tele-phone or climb into their air-conditioned station wagons and drive a hundred yards. It made me realize how much cars and suburbs – and indiscriminate wealth – have spoiled American life. Charleston had the climate and ambience of a Naples, but the wealth and style of a big American city. I was enchanted. I walked away the after-noon, up and down the peaceful streets, secretly admiring all these impossibly happy and good-looking people and their wonderful homes and rich, perfect lives.

The promontory ended in a level park, where children wheeled and bounced on BMXs and young couples strolled hand in hand and Frisbees sailed through the long strips of dark and light caused by the lowering sun filtering through the magnolia trees. Every person was youthful, good-looking and well-scrubbed. It was like wandering into a Pepsi commercial. Beyond the park, a broad stone promenade overlooked the harbour, vast and shimmery and green. I went and peered over the edge. The water slapped the stone and smelled of fish. Two miles out you could see the island of Fort Sumter where the Civil War began. The promenade was crowded with cyclists and sweating joggers, who weaved expertly among the pedestrians and shuffling tourists. I turned around and walked back to the car, the sun warm on my back, and had the sneaking feeling that after such perfection things were bound to be downhill from now on.

Chapter nine

FOR THE SAKE of haste I got on Interstate 26, which runs in a 200-mile diagonal across South Carolina, through a landscape of dormant tobacco fields and salmon-coloured soil. According to my *Mobil Travel Guide*, I was no longer in the Deep South but in the Middle Atlantic states. But it had the heat and glare of the South and the people in gas stations and cafés along the way sounded Southern. Even the radio announcers sounded Southern, in attitude as much as accent. According to one news broadcast, the police in Spartanburg were looking for two black men 'who raped a white girl'. You wouldn't hear *that* outside the South.

As I neared Columbia, the fields along the road began to fill with tall signs advertising motels and quick food places. These weren't the squat, rectangular billboards of my youth, with alluring illustrations and three-dimensional cows, but just large unfriendly signs standing atop sixty-foot-high metal poles. Their messages were terse. They didn't invite you to do anything interesting or seductive. The old signs were chatty and would say things like WHILE IN COLUMBIA, WHY NOT STAY IN THE MODERN SKYLINER MOTOR INN, WITH OUR ALL NEW SENSUMATIC VIBRATING BEDS. YOU'LL LOVE 'EM! SPECIAL RATES FOR CHILDREN. FREE TV. AIR-COOLED ROOMS. FREE ICE. PLENTY OF PARKING. PETS WELCOME. ALL-U-CAN-EAT CATFISH BUFFET EVERY TUES 5–7 P.M. DANCE NITELY

TO THE VERNON STURGES GUITAR ORCHESTRA IN THE STARLITE
ROOM. (PLEASE – NO NEGROES). The old signs were like oversized postcards, with helpful chunks of information. They
provided something to read, a little food for thought, a
snippet of insight into the local culture. Attention spans
had obviously contracted since then. The signs now simply
announced the name of the business and how to get there.
You could read them from miles away: HOLIDAY INN, EXIT
26E, 4 MI. Sometimes these instructions were more complex and would say things like: BURGER KING – 31 MILES. TAKE
EXIT 17B 5 MI TO US49 SOUTH, TURN RIGHT AT LIGHTS, THEN WEST
PAST AIRPORT FOR 2½ MI. Who could want a Whopper that
much? But the signs are effective, no doubt about it.
Driving along in a state of idle mindlessness, suffering
from hunger and a grease deficiency, you see a sign that
says MCDONALD'S – EXIT HERE, and it's almost instinctive to
swerve onto the exit ramp and follow it. Over and over
through the weeks I found myself sitting at plastic tables
with little boxes of food in front of me which I didn't want
or have time to eat, all because a sign had instructed me to
be there.

At the North Carolina border, the dull landscape ended
abruptly, as if by decree. Suddenly the countryside rose
and fell in majestic undulations, full of creeping thickets of
laurel, rhododendron and palmetto. At each hilltop the
landscape opened out to reveal hazy views of the Blue
Ridge Mountains, part of the Appalachian chain. The
Appalachians stretch for 2,100 miles from Alabama to
Canada and were once higher than the Himalayas (I read
that on a book of matches once and have been waiting
years for an opportunity to use it), though now they are
smallish and rounded, fetching rather than dramatic. All

along their length they go by different names – the Adirondacks, Poconos, Catskills, Alleghenies. I was headed for the Smokies, but I intended to stop *en route* at the Biltmore Estate, just outside Asheville, North Carolina. Biltmore was built by George Vanderbilt in 1895 and was one of the biggest houses ever constructed in America – a 255-room pile of stone in the style of a Loire château, in grounds of 10,000 acres. When you arrive at Biltmore you are directed to park your car and go into a building by the gate to purchase your ticket before proceeding on to the estate. I thought this was curious until I went into the building and discovered that a gay afternoon at Biltmore would involve a serious financial commitment. The signs telling you the admission fee were practically invisible, but you could see from the ashen-faced look on people as they staggered away from the ticket windows that it must be a lot. Even so I was taken aback when my turn came and the unpleasant-looking woman at the ticket window told me that the admission fee was $17.50 for adults and $13 for children. *'Seventeen dollars and fifty cents!'* I croaked. 'Does that include dinner and a floor show?'

The woman was obviously used to dealing with hysteria and snide remarks. In a monotone she said, 'The admission fee includes admission to the George Vanderbilt house, of which fifty of the 250 rooms are open to the public. You should allow two or three hours for the self-guided tour. It also includes admission to the extensive gardens for which you should allow thirty minutes to one hour. It also includes admission and guided tour of the winery with audiovisual presentation and complimentary wine tasting. A guide to the house and grounds, available

119

for a separate charge, is recommended. Afterwards you may wish to spend further large sums of money in the Deerpark Restaurant or, if you are a relatively cheap person, in the Stable Café, as well as avail yourself of the opportunity to buy expensive gifts and remembrances in the Carriage House Gift Shop.'

But by this time I was already on the highway again, heading for the Great Smoky Mountains, which, thank God, are free.

I drove ten miles out of my way in order to spend the night in Bryson City, a modest self-indulgence. It was a small, nondescript place of motels and barbecue shacks strung out along a narrow river valley on the edge of the Great Smoky Mountains National Park. There is little reason to go there unless your name happens to be Bryson, and even then, I have to tell you, the pleasure is intermittent. I got a room in the Bennett's Court Motel, a wonderful old place that appeared not to have changed a bit since 1956, apart from an occasional light dusting. It was precisely as motels always used to be, with the rooms spread out along a covered verandah overlooking a lawn with two trees and a tiny concrete swimming pool, which at this time of year was empty but for a puddle of wet leaves and one pissed-off looking frog. Beside each door was a metal armchair with a scallop-shaped back. By the sidewalk an old neon sign thrummed with the sound of coursing neon gas and spelled out BENNETT'S COURT/VACANCY/AIR-CONDITIONED/ GUEST POOL/TV, all in green and pink beneath a tasteful blinking arrow in yellow. When I was small all motels had signs like that. Now you only see them occasionally in small forgotten towns on the edge of nowhere. Bennett's Court clearly would be the motel in Amalgam.

I took my bags inside, lowered myself experimentally on to the bed and switched on the TV. Instantly there came up a commercial for Preparation H, an unguent for haemorrhoids. The tone was urgent. I don't remember the exact words, but they were something like, 'Hey, you! Have you got haemorrhoids? Then get some Preparation H! That's an order! Remember that name, you inattentive moron! Preparation H! And even if you haven't got haemorrhoids, get some Preparation H anyway! Just in case!' And then a voice-over quickly added, 'Now available in cherry flavour.' Having lived abroad so long, I was unused to the American hard sell and it made me uneasy. I was equally unsettled by the way television stations in America can jump back and forth between commercials and programmes without hesitation or warning. You'll be lying there watching *Kojak*, say, and in the middle of a gripping shoot-out somebody starts cleaning a toilet bowl and you sit up, thinking, 'What the—' and then you realize it is a commercial. In fact, it is several minutes of commercials. You could go out for cigarettes and a pizza during commercial breaks in America, *and* still have time to wash the toilet bowl before the programme resumed.

The Preparation H commercial vanished and a micro-instant later, before there was any possibility of the viewer reflecting on whether he might wish to turn to another channel, was replaced by a clapping audience, the perky sound of steel guitars and happy but mildly brain-damaged people in sequinned outfits. This was *Grand Ole Opry*. I watched for a couple of minutes. By degrees my chin dropped onto my shirt as I listened to their singing and jesting with a kind of numb amazement. It was like a visual lobotomy. Have you ever watched an infant at play and said to yourself, 'I wonder what goes on in his little head'? Well, watch *Grand Ole Opry* for five minutes sometime and you will begin to have an idea.

After a couple of minutes another commercial break noisily intruded and I was snapped back to my senses. I switched off the television and went out to investigate Bryson City. There was more to it than I had first thought. Beyond the Swain County Courthouse was a small business district. I was gratified to note that almost everything had a Bryson City sign on it – Bryson City Laundry, Bryson City Coal and Lumber, Bryson City Church of Christ, Bryson City Electronics, Bryson City Police Department, Bryson City Fire Department, Bryson City Post Office. I began to appreciate how George Washington might feel if he were to be brought back to life and set down in the District of Columbia. I don't know who the Bryson was whom this town was so signally honouring, but I had certainly never seen my name spread around so lavishly, and I regretted that I hadn't brought a crowbar and monkey wrench because many of the signs would have made splendid keepsakes. I particularly fancied having the Bryson City Church of Christ sign beside my front gate in England and being able to put up different messages every week like 'Repent Now, Limeys.'

It didn't take long to exhaust the possibilities for diversion in downtown Bryson City, and almost before I realized it I found myself on the highway out of town leading towards Cherokee, the next town along the valley. I followed it for a little way but there was nothing to see except a couple of derelict gas stations and barbecue shacks, and hardly any shoulder to walk on so that cars shot past only inches away and whipped my clothes into a disconcerting little frenzy. All along the road were billboards and large hand-lettered signs in praise of Christ: GET A GRIP ON YOUR LIFE – PRAISE JESUS, GOD LOVES YOU, AMERICA, and the rather more enigmatic WHAT WOULD HAPPEN IF YOU DIED TOMORROW? (Well, I thought, there would be no more payments on the freezer for a start.) I turned around and went back into town. It was 5.30 in the afternoon, Bryson City was a crypt with sidewalks, and I was at a complete loss. Down a small hill, beside the rushing river, I spied an A & P supermarket, which appeared to be open, and I went down there for want of something better to do. I often used to hang out in supermarkets. Robert Swanson and I, when we were about twelve and so obnoxious that it would have been a positive mercy to inject us with something lethal, would often go to the Hinky-Dinky supermarket on Ingersoll Avenue in Des Moines during the summer because it was airconditioned, and pass the time by doing things I am now ashamed to relate – loosening the bottom of a bag of flour and then watching it pour on to the floor when some unsuspecting woman picked it up, or putting strange items like goldfish food and emetics in people's shopping carts when their backs were turned. I didn't intend to do anything like that in the A & P now – unless of course I got *really* bored – but I thought it would be comforting, in this strange place, to look at foodstuffs from my youth. And it was. It was almost like visiting old friends – Skippy Peanut Butter, Pop Tarts, Welch's Grape Juice, Sara Lee cakes. I wandered the aisles, murmuring tiny cries of joy at each sighting of an old familiar nutrient. It cheered me up no end.

Then suddenly I remembered something. Months before, in England, I had noticed an ad for panty shields in the *New York Times Magazines*. These panty shields had dimples on them and the dimples had a name that was trade-marked. This struck me as remarkable. Can you imagine being given the job of thinking up a catchy name for dimples on a panty shield? But I couldn't remember what it was. So now, for no reason other than that I had nothing better to do, I went over and had a look at the A & P's panty shield section. There was a surprising diversity of them. I would never have guessed that the market was so buoyant or indeed that there were so many panties in Bryson City that needed shielding. I had never paid much attention to this sort of thing before and it was really kind of interesting. I don't know how long I spent poking about among the various brands and reading the instructions for use, or whether I might even have started talking to myself a little, as I sometimes do when I am happily occupied. But I suppose it must have been quite some time. In any case, at the very moment that I picked up a packet of New Freedom Thins, with Funnel-Dot Protection^{TM}, and cried triumphantly, 'Aha! There you are, you little buggers!', I turned my head a fraction and noticed that at the far end of the aisle the manager and two female assistants were watching me. I blushed and clumsily wedged the packet back on the shelves. 'Just browsing!' I called in an unconvincing voice, hoping I didn't look too dangerous or insane, and made for the exit. I remembered reading some weeks before in *The Independent* that it is still against the law in twenty US states, most of them in the Deep South, for heterosexuals to engage in oral or anal intercourse. I had nothing like that in mind just now, you understand, but I think it indicates that some of these places can be doggedly unenlightened in matters pertaining to sex and could well have ordinances with respect to the unlawful handling of panty shields. It would be just my luck to pull a five to ten stretch for some unintended perversion in a place like North Carolina. At all events, I felt fortunate to make it back to my motel without being intercepted by the authorities, and spent the rest of my short stay in Bryson City behaving with the utmost circumspection.

The Great Smoky Mountains National Park covers 500,000 acres in North Carolina and Tennessee. I didn't realize it before I went there, but it is the most popular national park in America, attracting nine million visitors a year, three times as many as any other national park, and even early on a Sunday morning in October it was crowded. The road between Bryson City and Cherokee, at the park's edge, was a straggly collection of motels, junky-looking auto repair shops, trailer courts and barbecue shacks perched on the edge of a glittering stream in a cleft in the mountains. It must have been beautiful once, with dark mountains squeezing in from both sides, but now it was just squalid. Cherokee itself was even worse. It is the biggest Indian reservation in the eastern United States and it was packed from one end to the other with souvenir stores selling tawdry Indian trinkets, all of them with big signs on their roofs and sides saying MOCCASINS! INDIAN JEWELRY! TOMAHAWKS! POLISHED GEMSTONES! CRAPPY ITEMS OF EVERY DESCRIPTION! Some of the places had a caged brown bear out front – the Cherokee mascot, I gathered – and around each of these was a knot of small boys trying to provoke the animal into a show of ferocity, encouraged from a safe distance by their fathers. At other stores you could have your photograph taken with a genuine, hungover, flabby-titted Cherokee Indian in war dress for $5, but not many people seemed interested in this and the model Indians sat slumped in chairs looking as listless as the bears. I don't think I had ever been to a place quite so ugly, and it was jammed with tourists, almost all of them ugly also – fat people in noisy clothes with cameras dangling on their bellies. Why is it, I wondered idly as I nosed the car through the throngs, that tourists are always fat and dress like morons?

Then, abruptly, before I could give the question the consideration it deserved, I was out of Cherokee and in the national park and all the garishness ceased. People don't live in national parks in America as they do in Britain. They are areas of wilderness – often enforced wilderness. The Smoky Mountains were once full of hillbillies who lived in cabins up in the remote hollows, up among the clouds, but they were moved out and now the park is sterile as far as human activities go. Instead of trying to preserve an ancient way of life, the park authorities eradicated it. So the dispossessed hillbillies moved down to valley towns at the park's edge and turned them into junkvilles selling crappy little souvenirs. It seems a very strange approach to me. Now a few of the cabins are preserved as museum pieces. There was one at a visitors' centre just inside the park, which I dutifully stopped to have a look at. It was exactly like the cabins at the Lincoln village at New Salem in Illinois. I had not realized that it is actually possible to overdose on log cabins, but as I drew near the cabin I began to feel a sudden onset of brainstem death and I retreated to the car after only the briefest of looks.

The Smoky Mountains themselves were a joy. It was a perfect October morning. The road led steeply up through broad-leaved forests of dappled sunshine, full of paths and streams, and then, higher up, opened out to airy vistas. All along the road through the park there were look-out points where you could pull the car over and go 'Ooh!' and 'Wow!' at the views. They were all named after mountain passes that sounded like condominium developments for yuppies – Pigeon Gap, Cherry Cove, Wolf Mountain, Bear Trap Gap. The air was clear and thin and the views were vast. The mountains rolled away to a distant horizon, gently shading from rich green to charcoal blue to hazy smoke. It was a sea of trees – like looking out over a landscape from Colombia or Brazil, so virginal was it all. In all the rolling vastness there was not a single sign of humanity, no towns, no water-towers, no plume of smoke from a solitary farmstead. It was just endless silence beneath a bright sky, empty and clear apart from one distant bluish puff of cumulus, which cast a drifting shadow over a far-off hill.

The Oconaluftee Highway across the park is only thirty miles long, but it is so steep and winding that it took me all morning to cross it. By 10 A.M. there was a steady stream of cars in both directions, and free spaces at the look-out points were hard to find. This was my first serious brush with real tourists – retired people with trailer homes heading for Florida, young families taking off-season vacations, honeymooners. There were cars and trailers, campers and motor homes from thousands of miles away – California, Wyoming, British Columbia – and at every look-out point people were clustered around their vehicles with the doors and trunks opened, feeding from ice coolers and portable fridges. Every few yards there was a Winnebago or Komfort Motor Home – massive, self-contained dwellings on wheels that took up three parking spaces and jutted out so far that cars coming in could only barely scrape past.

All morning I had been troubled by a vague sense of something being missing, and then it occurred to me what it was. There were no hikers such as you would see in England – no people in stout boots and short pants, with knee-high tasselled stockings. No little rucksacks full of Marmite sandwiches and flasks of tea. And no platoons of cyclists in skin-tight uniforms and bakers' caps labouring breathlessly up the mountainsides, slowing up traffic. What slowed the traffic here were the massive motor homes lumbering up and down the mountain passes. Some of them, amazingly, had cars tethered to their rear bumpers, like dinghies. I got stuck behind one on the long, sinuous descent down the mountain into Tennessee. It was so wide that it could barely stay within its lane and kept threatening to nudge oncoming cars off into the picturesque void to our left. That, alas, is the way of vacationing nowadays for many people. The whole idea is not to expose yourself to a moment of discomfort or inconvenience – indeed, not to breathe fresh air if possible. When the urge to travel seizes you, you pile into your thirteen-ton tin palace and drive 400 miles across the country, hermetically sealed against the elements, and stop at a campground where you dash to plug into their water supply and electricity so that you don't have to go a single moment without air-conditioning or dishwasher and microwave facilities. These things, these 'recreational vehicles', are like life-support systems on wheels. Astronauts go to the moon with less backup. RV people are another breed – and a largely demented one at that. They become obsessed with trying to equip their vehicles with gadgets to deal with every possible contingency. Their lives become ruled by the dread thought that one day they may find themselves in a situation in which they are not entirely self-sufficient. I once went camping for two days at Lake Darling in Iowa with a friend whose father – an RV enthusiast – kept trying to press labour-saving devices on us. 'I got a great little solar-powered can opener here,' he would say. 'You wanna take that?'

'No thanks,' we would reply. 'We're only going for two days.'

'How about this combination flashlight/carving knife? You can run it off the car cigarette-lighter if you need to, and it doubles as a flashing siren if you get lost in the wilderness.'

'No thanks.'

'Well, at least take the battery-powered microwave.'

'Really, we don't want it.'

'Then how the hell are you going to pop popcorn out there in the middle of nowhere? Have you thought about that?'

A whole industry (in which no doubt the Zwingle Company of New York is actively involved) has grown up to supply this market. You can see these people at campgrounds all over the country, standing around their vehicles comparing gadgets – methane-powered ice-cube makers, portable tennis-courts, anti-insect flame-throwers, inflatable lawns. They are strange and dangerous people and on no account should be approached.

At the foot of the mountain, the park ended and

suddenly all was squalor again. I was once more struck by this strange compartmentalization that goes on in America – a belief that no commercial activities must be allowed inside the park, but permitting unrestrained development outside, even though the landscape there may be just as outstanding. America has never quite grasped that you can live in a place without making it ugly, that beauty doesn't have to be confined behind fences, as if a national park were a sort of zoo for nature. The ugliness intensified to fever pitch as I rolled into Gatlinburg, a community that had evidently dedicated itself to the endless quest of trying to redefine the lower limits of bad taste. It is the world capital of tat. It made Cherokee look decorous. There is not much more to it than a single mile-long main street, but it was packed from end to end with the most dazzling profusion of tourist clutter – the Elvis Presley Hall of Fame, Stars Over Gatlinburg Wax Museum, two haunted houses, the National Bible Museum, Hillbilly Village, Ripley's Believe It or Not Museum, the American Historical Wax Museum, Gatlinburg Space Needle, something called Paradise Island, something else called World of Illusions, the Bonnie Lou and Buster Country Music Show, Carbo's Police Museum ('See "Walking Tall" Sheriff Buford Pusser's Death Car!'), Guinness Book of Records Exhibition Centre and, not least, the Irlene Mandrell Hall of Stars Museum and Shopping Mall. In between this galaxy of entertainments were scores of parking lots and noisy, crowded restaurants, junk food stalls, ice-cream parlours, and gift shops of the sort that sell wanted posters with YOUR NAME HERE and baseball caps with droll embellishments, like a coil of realistic-looking plastic turd on the brim. Walking in an unhurried fashion up and down the street were more crowds of overweight tourists in boisterous clothes, with cameras bouncing on their bellies, consuming ice-creams, cotton candy and corn dogs, sometimes simultaneously, and wearing baseball caps with plastic turds jauntily attached to the brim.

I loved it. When I was growing up, we never got to go to places like Gatlinburg. My father would rather have given himself brain surgery with a Black and Decker drill than spend an hour in such a place. He had just two criteria for gauging the worth of a holiday attraction: was it educational, and was it free? Gatlinburg was patently neither of these. His idea of holiday heaven was a museum without an admission charge. My Dad was the most honest man I ever met, but vacations blinded him to his principles. When I had pimples scattered across my face and stubble on my chin he was still swearing at ticket booths that I was eight years old. He was so cheap on vacations that it always surprised me he didn't make us sift in litterbins for our lunch. So Gatlinburg to me was a heady experience. I felt like a priest let loose in Las Vegas with a sockful of quarters. All the noise and glitter, and above all the possibilities for running through irresponsible sums of money in a short period, made me giddy.

I wandered through the crowds, and hesitated at the entrance to the Ripley's Believe It or Not Museum. I could sense my father, a thousand miles away, beginning to rotate slowly in his grave as I looked at the posters. They told me that inside I would see a man who could hold three billiard balls in his mouth at once, a two-headed calf, a human unicorn with a horn protruding from his forehead and hundreds of other riveting oddities from all over the globe collected by the tireless Robert Ripley and crated

131

back to Gatlinburg for the edification of discerning tourists such as myself. The admission fee was $5. The pace of my father's rotating quickened as I looked into my wallet, and then sped to a whirring blur as I fished out a five-dollar bill and guiltily handed it to the unsmiling woman in the ticket booth. 'What the hell,' I thought as I went inside, 'at least it will give the old man some exercise.'

Well, it was superb. I know $5 is a lot of money for a few minutes' diversion. I could just see my father and me standing outside on the sidewalk bickering. My father would say, 'No, it's a big gyp. For that kind of money, you could buy something that would give you years of value.'

'Like what – a box of carpet tiles?' I would reply with practised sarcasm. 'Oh, please, Dad, just this once don't be cheap. There's a two-headed calf in there.'

'No, son, I'm sorry.'

'I'll be good forever. I'll take out the garbage every day until I get married. Dad, there is a guy in there who can hold three billiard balls in his mouth at once. There is a *human unicorn* in there. Dad, we could be throwing away the chance of a lifetime here.'

But he would not be moved. 'I don't want to hear any more about it. Now let's all get in the car and drive 175 miles to the Molasses Point Historical Battlefield. You'll learn lots of worthwhile things about the little-known American war with Ecuador of 1802 and it won't cost me a penny.'

So I went through the Ripley's Believe It or Not Museum and I savoured every artefact and tasteless oddity. It was outstanding. I mean honestly, where else are you going to see a replica of Columbus's flagship, the *Santa Maria*, made entirely of chicken bones? And how can you possibly put a price on seeing an eight-foot-long model of the Circus Maximus constructed of sugar cubes, or the death-mask of John Dillinger, or a room made entirely of matchsticks by one Reg Polland of Manchester, England (well done, Reg; Britain is proud of you)? We are talking lasting memories here. I was pleased to note that England was further represented by, of all things, a chimney-pot, circa 1940. Believe it or not. It was all wonderful – clean, nicely presented, sometimes even believable – and I spent a happy hour there.

Afterwards, feeling highly content, I purchased an ice-cream cone the size of a baby's head and wandered with it through the crowds of people in the afternoon sunshine. I went into a series of gift shops and tried on baseball caps with plastic turds on the brim, but the cheapest one I saw was $7.99 and I decided, out of deference to my father, that that would be just too much extravagance for one afternoon. If it came to it, I could always make my own, I thought as I returned to the car and headed for the dangerous hills of Appalachia.

Chapter ten

IN 1587, a group of 115 English settlers – men, women and children – sailed from Plymouth to set up the first colony in the New World, on Roanoke Island off what is now North Carolina. Shortly after they arrived, a child named Virginia Dare was born and thus became the first white person to arrive in America head first. Two years later, a second expedition set off from England to see how the settlers were getting on and to bring them their mail and tell them that the repairman from British Telecom had finally shown up and that sort of thing. But when the relief party arrived, they found the settlement deserted. There was no message of where the settlers had gone, nor any sign of a struggle, but just one word mysteriously scratched on a wall: 'Croatoan'. This was the name of a nearby island where the Indians were known to be friendly, but a trip to the island showed that the settlers had never arrived there. So where did they go? Did they leave voluntarily or were they spirited off by Indians? This has long been one of the great mysteries of the colonial period.

I bring this up here because one theory is that the settlers pushed inland, up into the hills of Appalachia, and settled there. No-one knows why they might have done this, but fifty years later, when European explorers arrived in Tennessee, the Cherokee Indians told them that there was a group of pale people living in the hills already, people who wore clothes and had long beards. These people, according to a contemporary account, 'had a bell which they rang before they ate their meals and had a strange habit of bowing their heads and saying something in a low voice before they ate.'

No-one ever found this mysterious community. But in a remote and neglected corner of the Appalachians, high up in the Clinch Mountains above the town of Sneedville in north-eastern Tennessee, there still live some curious people called Melungeons who have been there for as long as anyone can remember. The Melungeons (no-one knows where the name comes from) have most of the characteristics of Europeans – blue eyes, fair hair, lanky build – but a dark, almost Negroid skin colouring that is distinctly non-European. They have English family names – Brogan, Collins, Mullins – but no-one, including the Melungeons themselves, has any idea of where they come from or what their early history might have been. They are as much of a mystery as the lost settlers of Roanoke Island. Indeed, it has been suggested that they may *be* the lost settlers of Roanoke.

Peter Dunn, a colleague at *The Independent* in London, put me on to the Melungeon story when he heard that I was going to that part of the world, and kindly dug out an article he had done for the *Sunday Times Magazine* some years before. This was illustrated with remarkable photographs of Melungeons. It is impossible to describe them except to say that they were simply white people with black skin. Their appearance was, to say the least, striking. For this reason they have long been outcasts in their own county, consigned to shacks in the hills in an area called Snake Hollow. In Hancock County, 'Melungeon' is equivalent to 'Nigger'. The valley people – who are themselves generally poor and backward – regard the Melungeons as something strange and shameful, and the Melungeons as a consequence keep to themselves, coming down from the mountains only at widely-spaced intervals to buy provisions. They don't like outsiders. Neither do the valley people. Peter Dunn told me that he and the photographer who accompanied him were given a reception that ranged from mild hostility to outright intimidation. It was an uncomfortable assignment. A few months later a reporter from *Time Magazine* was actually shot near Sneedville for asking too many questions.

So you can perhaps imagine the sense of foreboding that seeped over me as I drove up Tennessee Highway 31 through a forgotten landscape of poor and scattered tobacco farms, through the valley of the twisting Clinch River, *en route* to Sneedville. This was the seventh poorest county in the nation and it looked it. Litter was adrift in the ditches and most of the farmhouses were small and unadorned. In every driveway there stood a pickup truck with a gun rack in the back window, and where there were people in the yards they stopped what they were doing to watch me as I passed. It was late afternoon, nearly dusk, when I reached. Sneedville. Outside the Hancock County Courthouse a group of teenagers were perched on the fronts of pickup trucks, talking to each other, and they too stared at me as I passed. Sneedville is so far from anywhere, such an improbable destination, that a stranger's car attracts notice. There wasn't much to the town: the courthouse, a Baptist church, some box houses, a gas station. The gas station was still open, so I pulled in. I didn't particularly need gas, but I wasn't sure when I would find another station. The guy who came out to pump the gas had an abundance of fleshy warts – a veritable crop – scattered across his face like button mushrooms. He looked like a genetic experiment that had gone horribly wrong. He didn't speak except to establish what kind of gas I wanted and he didn't remark on the fact that I was from out of state. This was the first time on the trip that a gas station attendant hadn't said in an engaging manner, 'You're a long way from home, arentcha?' or, 'What brings you all the way here from I-o-way?' or something like that. (I always told them that I was on my way east to have vital heart surgery, in the hope that they would give me extra Green Stamps.) I was very probably the first person from out of state this man had seen all year, yet he appeared resolutely uninterested in what I was doing there. It was odd. I said to him – blurted really – 'Excuse me, but didn't I read somewhere that some people called Melungeons live around here somewhere?'

He didn't answer. He just watched the pump counter spin. I thought he hadn't heard me, so I said, 'I say, excuse me, but didn't I hear that some people—'

'Don't know,' he said abruptly without looking at me. Then he looked at me. 'Don't know nothin' about that. You want your oil checked?'

I hesitated, surprised by the question. 'No thank you.'

'That's eleven dollars.' He took my money without thanks and went back inside. I was fairly dumb-founded. I don't know quite why. Through the window I could see him pick up his telephone and make a call. He looked at me as he did it. Suddenly I felt alarmed. What if he was calling the police to tell them to come out and shoot me? I laid a small patch of rubber on his driveway as I departed –

137

something you don't often see achieved with a Chevette – and made the pistons sing as I floored the accelerator and hurtled out of town at a breakneck twenty-seven miles an hour. But a mile or so later I slowed down. Partly this was because I was going up an almost vertical hill and the car wouldn't go any faster – for one breathless moment I thought it might actually start rolling backwards – and partly because I told myself not to be so jumpy. The guy was probably just calling his wife to remind her to buy more wart lotion. Even if he was calling the police to report an outsider asking impertinent questions, what could they do to me? It was a free country. I hadn't broken any laws. I had asked an innocent question, and asked it politely. How could anyone take offence at that? Clearly I was being silly to feel any sense of menace. Even so, I found myself glancing frequently into the rear-view mirror and half expecting to see the hill behind me crawling with flashing squad cars and posses of volunteer vigilantes in pickup trucks coming after me. Judiciously, I stepped up my speed from eleven to thirteen miles a hour.

High up the hill I began to encounter shacks set back in clearings in the woods, and peered at them in the hope of glimpsing a Melungeon or two. But the few people I saw were white. They stared at me with a strange look of surprise as I lumbered past, the way you might stare at a man riding an ostrich, and generally made no response to my cheerful wave, though one or two did reply with an automatic and economic wave of their own, a raised hand and a twitch of fingers.

This was real hillbilly country. Many of the shacks looked like something out of *Li'l Abner*, with sagging porches and tilting chimneys. Some were abandoned.

Many appeared to have been handmade, with rambling extensions that had clearly been fashioned from scraps of plundered wood. People in these hills still made moonshine, or stump liquor as they call it. But the big business these days is marijuana, believe it or not. I read somewhere that whole mountain villages band together and can make $100,000 a month from a couple of acres planted in some remote and lofty hollow. More than the Melungeons, that is an excellent reason not to be a stranger asking questions in the area.

Although I was clearly climbing high up into the mountains, the woods all around were so dense that I had no views. But at the summit the trees parted like curtains to provide a spectacular outlook over the valley on the other side. It was like coming over the top of the earth, like the view from an aeroplane. Steep green wooded hills with alpine meadows clinging to their sides stretched away for as far as the eye could see until at last they were consumed by a distant and colourful sunset. Before me a sinuous road led steeply down to a valley of rolling farms spread out along a lazy river. It was as perfect a setting as I had ever seen. I drove through the soft light of dusk, absorbed by the beauty. And the thing was, every house along the roadside was a shack. This was the heart of Appalachia, the most notoriously impoverished region of America, and it was just inexpressibly beautiful. It was strange that the urban professionals from the cities of the eastern seaboard, only a couple of hours' drive to the east, hadn't colonized an area of such arresting beauty, filling the dales with rusticky weekend cottages, country clubs, and fancy restaurants.

It was strange, too, to see white people living in poverty. In America, to be white and impoverished really takes some doing. Of course, this was American poverty, this was white people's poverty, which isn't like poverty elsewhere. It isn't even like the poverty in Tuskegee. It has been suggested with more than a touch of cynicism that when Lyndon Johnson launched his great War on Poverty in 1964, the focus was placed on Appalachia not because it was so destitute but because it was so white. A little-publicized survey at the time showed that forty per cent of the poorest people in the region owned a car and a third of those had been bought new. In 1964, my future father-in-law in England was, like most people there, years away from owning his first car and even now he has never owned a new one, yet no-one ever called him destitute or sent him a free sack of flour and some knitting wool at Christmas. Still, I can't deny that by American standards the scattered shacks around me were decidedly modest. They had no satellite dishes in the yard, no Weber barbecues, no station wagons standing in the drive. And I daresay they had no microwaves in the kitchen, poor devils, and by American standards that is pretty damn deprived.

Chapter eleven

I DROVE THROUGH a landscape of gumdrop hills, rolling roads, neat farms. The sky was full of those big fluffy clouds you always see in nautical paintings, and the towns had curious and interesting names: Snowflake, Fancy Gap, Horse Pasture, Meadows of Dan, Charity. Virginia went on and on. It never seemed to end. The state is nearly 400 miles across, but the twisting road must have added at least a hundred miles to that. In any case, every time I looked at the map I seemed to have moved a remarkably tiny distance. From time to time I would pass a sign that said HISTORICAL MARKER AHEAD, but I didn't stop. There are thousands of historical markers all over America and they are always dull. I know this for a fact because my father stopped at every one of them. He would pull the car up to them and read them aloud to us, even when we asked him not to. They would say something like: [SINGING TREES SACRED BURIAL SITE]

For centuries this land, known as the Valley of the Singing Trees, was a sacred burial site for the Blackbutt Indians. In recognition of this the US Government gave the land to the tribe in perpetuity in 1880. However, in 1882 oil was discovered beneath the singing trees and, after a series of skirmishes in which 27,413 Blackbutts perished, the tribe was relocated to a reservation at Cyanide Springs, New Mexico.

What am I saying? They were never as good as that. Usually they would commemorate something palpably obscure and uninteresting – the site of the first Bible college in western Tennessee, the birthplace of the inventor of the moist towelette, the home of the author of the Kansas state song. You knew before you got there that they were going to be boring because if they had been even remotely interesting somebody would have set up a hamburger stand and sold souvenirs. But Dad thrived on them and would never fail to be impressed. After reading them to us he would say in an admiring tone, 'Well, I'll be darned,' and then without fail would pull back onto the highway into the path of an oncoming truck, which would honk furiously and shed part of its load as it swerved past. 'Yes, that was really very interesting,' he would add reflectively, unaware that he had just about killed us all.

I was heading for the Booker T. Washington National Monument, a restored plantation near Roanoke where Booker T. Washington grew up. He was a remarkable man. A freed slave, he taught himself to read and write, secured an education and eventually founded the Tuskegee Institute in Alabama, the first college in America for blacks. Then, as if that were not achievement enough, he finished his career as a soul musician, churning out a series of hits in the 1960s on the Stax record label with the backup group the MGs. As I say, a remarkable man. My plan was to visit his monument and then zip over to Monticello for a leisurely look around Thomas Jefferson's home. But it was not to be. Just beyond Patrick Springs, I spied a side road leading to a place called Critz, which I calculated with a glance at the map could cut thirty miles off my driving distance. Impulsively I hauled the car around the corner, making the noise of squealing tyres as I went. I had to make the noise myself because the

Chevette couldn't manage it, though it did shoot out some blue smoke.

I should have known better. My first rule of travel is never to go to a place that sounds like a medical condition and Critz clearly was an incurable disease involving flaking skin. The upshot is that I got hopelessly lost. The road, once I lost sight of the highway, broke up into a network of unsignposted lanes hemmed in by tall grass. I drove for ages, with that kind of glowering, insane resolve that you get when you are lost and become convinced that if you just keep moving you will eventually end up where you want to be. I kept coming to towns that weren't on my map – Sanville, Pleasantville, Preston. These weren't two-shack places. They were proper towns, with schools, gas stations, lots of houses. I felt as if I should call the newspaper in Roanoke and inform the editor that I had found a lost county.

Eventually, as I passed through Sanville for the third time, I decided I would have to ask directions. I stopped an old guy taking his dog out to splash urine around the neighbourhood and asked him the way to Critz. Without batting an eyelid he launched into a set of instructions of the most breathtaking complexity. He must have talked for five minutes. It sounded like a description of Lewis and Clark's journey through the wilderness. I couldn't follow it at all, but when he paused and said, 'You with me so far?' I lied and said I was.

'Okay, well that takes you to Preston,' he went on. 'From there you follow the old drover's road due east out of town till you come to the McGregor place. You can tell it's the McGregor place because there's a sign out front saying: The McGregor Place. About a hundred yards further on there's a road going off to the left with a sign for Critz. But whatever you do don't go down there because the bridge is out and you'll plunge straight into Dead Man's Creek.' And on he went like that for many minutes. When at last he finished I thanked him and drove off without conviction in the general direction of his last gesture. Within 200 yards I had come to a T-junction and didn't have a clue which way to go. I went right. Ten minutes later, to the surprise of both of us, I was driving past the old guy and his ever-urinating dog again. Out of the corner of my eye I could see him gesturing excitedly, shouting at me that I had gone the wrong way, but as this was already abundantly evident to me, I ignored his hopping around and went left at the junction. This didn't get me any nearer Critz, but it did provide me with a new set of dead ends and roads to nowhere. At three o'clock in the afternoon, two hours after I set off for Critz, I blundered back onto Highway 58. I was 150 feet further down the road than I had been when I left it. Sourly I pulled back on to the highway and drove for many long hours in silence. It was too late to go to the Booker T. Washington National Monument or to Monticello, even assuming I could summon the intelligence to find them. The day had been a complete washout. I had had no lunch, no life-giving infusions of coffee. It had been a day without pleasure or reward. I got a room in a motel in Fredricksburg, ate at a pancake-house of ineffable crappiness and retired to my room in a dim frame of mind.

In the morning I drove to Colonial Williamsburg, a restored historic village near the coast. It is one of the most popular tourist attractions in the east and even though it was early on a Tuesday morning in October when I arrived, the car-parks were already filling up. I parked and joined a stream of people following the signs to the visitors' centre. Inside it was cool and dark. Near the door was a scale model of the village in a glass case. Oddly, there was no you-are-here arrow to help you get oriented. Indeed, the visitors' centre wasn't even shown. There was no way of telling where the village was in relation to where you were now. That seemed strange to me and I became suspicious; I stood back and watched the crowds. Gradually it became clear to me that the whole thing was a masterpiece of crowd management. Everything was contrived to leave you with the impression that the only way into Williamsburg was to buy a ticket, pass through a door ominously marked 'Processing' and then climb aboard a shuttle bus which would whisk you off to the historic site, presumably some distance away. Unless, like me, you pulled out of the river of people, you found yourself standing at the ticket counter making an instant decision on which of three kinds of ticket to buy – a Patriot's Pass for $24.50, a Royal Governor's Pass for $20 or a Basic Admission Ticket for $15.50, each allowing entrance to a different number of restored buildings. Most visitors found themselves parted from a lot of money and standing in the line to the processing doorway before they knew what had hit them.

I hate the way these places let you get all the way there before disclosing just how steep and confiscatory the admission price is. They should be required to put up roadside signs saying THREE MILES TO COLONIAL WILLIAMSBURG. GET YOUR CHEQUE-BOOKS READY! or ONE MILE TO COLONIAL

WILLIAMSBURG. IT'S PRETTY GOOD, BUT REAL EXPENSIVE. I felt that irritation, bordering on wild hate, that I generally experience when money is being tugged out of me through my nostrils. I mean honestly, $24.50 just to walk around a restored village for a couple of hours. I gave silent thanks that I had ditched the wife and kids at Manchester Airport. A day out here with the family could cost almost $75 – and that's before paying for ice-creams and soft drinks and sweat-shirts saying 'Boy, Were We Screwed at Colonial Williamsburg'.

There was something wrong with the whole set-up, something deeply fishy about the way it worked. I had lived in America long enough to know that if the only way into Williamsburg was to buy a ticket there would be an enormous sign on the wall saying YOU MUST have a ticket. don't even *think* about trying to get in without one. But there wasn't any such sign. I went outside, back out into the bright sunshine, and watched where the shuttle buses were going. They went down the driveway, joined a dual carriageway and disappeared around a bend. I crossed the dual carriageway, dodging the traffic, and followed a path through some woods. In a few seconds I was in the village. It was as simple as that. I didn't have to pay a penny. Nearby the shuttle buses were unloading ticket-holders. They had had a ride of roughly 200 yards and were about to discover that what their tickets entitled them to do was join long, ill-humoured lines of other ticket-holders standing outside each restored historic building, sweating in silence and shuffling forward at a rate of one step every three minutes. I don't think I had ever seen quite so many people failing to enjoy themselves. The glacial lines put me in mind of Disney World, which was not altogether inappropriate since Williamsburg is really a sort of Disney World of American history. All the ticket takers and street sweepers and information givers were dressed in period costumes, the women in big aprons and muffin hats, the men in tri-cornered hats and breeches. The whole idea was to give history a happy gloss and make you think that spinning your own wool and dipping your own candles must have been bags of fun. I half expected to see Goofy and Donald Duck come waddling along dressed as soldiers in the Colonial Army.

The first house I came to had a sign saying DR MCKEN-ZIE'S APOTHECARY. The door was open, so I went inside, expecting to see eighteenth-century apothecary items. But it was just a gift shop selling twee reproductions at outrageous prices – brass candle snifters at $28, reproduction apothecary jars at $35, that sort of thing. I fled back outside, wanting to stick my head in Ye Olde Village Puking Trough. But then, slowly and strangely, the place began to grow on me. As I strolled up Duke of Gloucester Street I underwent a surprising transforma-tion. Slowly, I found that I was becoming captivated by it all. Williamsburg is big – 173 acres – and the size of it alone is impressive. There are literally dozens of restored houses and shops. More than that, it really is quite lovely, particularly on a sunny morning in October with a mild wind wandering through the ash and beech trees. I ambled along the leafy lanes and broad greens. Every house was exquisite, every cobbled lane inviting, every tavern and vine-clad shoppe remorselessly a-drip with picturesque charm. It is impossible, even for a flinty-hearted jerk-off such as your narrator, not to be won over. However dubious Williamsburg may be as a historical document – and it is plenty dubious – it is at least a model town. It makes you realize what an immeasurably nice place much of America could be if only people possessed the same instinct for preservation as they do in Europe. You would think the millions of people who come to Williamsburg every year would say to each other, 'Gosh, Bobbi, this place is beautiful. Let's go home to Smellville and plant lots of trees and preserve all the fine old buildings.' But in fact that never occurs to them. They just go back and build more parking lots and Pizza Huts.

A lot of Williamsburg isn't as old as they like you to think it is. The town was the capital of colonial Virginia for eighty years, from 1699 to 1780. But when the capital was moved to Richmond, Williamsburg fell into decline. In the 1920s John D. Rockefeller developed a passion for the place and began pouring money into its restoration – $90 million so far. The problem now is that you never quite know what's genuine and what's fanciful. Take the Governor's Palace. It looks to be very old – and, as I say, no-one discourages you from believing that it is – but in fact it was only built in 1933. The original building burned down in 1781 and by 1930 had been gone for so long that nobody knew what it had looked like. It was only because somebody found a drawing of it in the Bodleian Library at Oxford that they were able to make a reasonable stab at reproducing it. But it isn't old and it may not even be all that accurate.

Everywhere you turn you are confronted, exasperatingly, with bogus touches. At the Bruton Parish Church, the gravestones were clearly faked, or at least the engravings had been reground. Rockefeller or someone else in authority had obviously been disappointed to discover that after a couple of centuries in the open air gravestones become illegible, so now the inscriptions are as fresh and deep-grooved as if they had been cut only last week, which they may well have been. You find yourself constantly wondering whether you are looking at genuine history or some Disneyesque embellishment. Was there really a Severinus Dufray and would he have had a sign outside his house saying 'Genteel Tailoring'? Possibly. Would Dr McKenzie have a note in florid lettering outside his dispensary announcing: 'Dr McKenzie begs Leave to inform the Public he has just received a large Quantity of fine Goods, viz: Tea, Coffee, fine Soap, Tobacco, etc., to be SOLD here at his shop'? Who can say?

Thomas Jefferson, a man of some obvious sensitivity, disliked Williamsburg and thought it ugly. (This is something else they don't tell you.) He called the college and hospital 'rude, mishappen piles' and the Governor's Palace 'not handsome'. He can't have been describing the same place because the Williamsburg of today is relentlessly attractive. And for that reason I liked it.

I drove on to Mount Vernon, George Washington's home for most of his life. Washington deserves his fame. What he did in running the Colonial Army was risky and audacious, not to say skilful. People tend to forget that the Revolutionary War dragged on for eight years and that Washington often didn't get a whole lot of support. Out of a populace of 5.5 million, Washington sometimes had as few as 5,000 soldiers in his army – one soldier for every

1,100 people. When you see what a tranquil and handsome place Mt Vernon is, and what an easy and agreeable life he led there, you wonder why he bothered. But that's the appealing thing about Washington, he is such an enigma. We don't even know for sure what he looked like. Almost all the portraits of him were done by, or copied from the works of, Charles Willson Peale. Peale painted sixty portraits of Washington, but unfortunately he wasn't very hot at faces. In fact, according to Samuel Eliot Morison, Peale's pictures of Washington, Lafayette and John Paul Jones all look to be more or less the same person.

Mount Vernon was everything Williamsburg should have been and was not – genuine, interesting, instructive. For well over a century it has been maintained by the Mount Vernon Ladies' Association and what a lucky thing it is we have them. Amazingly, when the house was put up for sale in 1853, neither the federal government nor the state of Virginia was prepared to buy it for the nation. So a group of dedicated women hastily formed the Mount Vernon Ladies' Association, raised the money to buy the house and 200 acres of grounds and then set about restoring it to precisely as it was in Washington's day, right down to the correct pigments of paint and patterns of wallpaper. Thank God John D. Rockefeller didn't get hold of it. Today the Association continues to run it with a dedication and skill that should be models to preservation groups everywhere, but alas are not. Fourteen rooms are open to the public and in each a volunteer provides an interesting and well-informed commentary – and is sufficiently clued-up to answer almost any question – on how the room was used and decorated. The house was very much Washington's creation. He was involved in the daintiest questions of décor, even when he was away on military campaigns. It was strangely pleasing to imagine him at Valley Forge, with his troops dropping dead of cold and hunger, agonizing over the purchase of lace ruffs and tea cosies. What a great guy. What a hero.

Chapter twelve

I SPENT THE night on the outskirts of Alexandria and in the morning drove into Washington. I remembered Washington from my childhood as hot and dirty and full of the din of jackhammers. It had that special kind of grimy summer heat you used to get in big cities in America before air-conditioning came along. People spent every waking moment trying to alleviate it – wiping their necks with capacious handkerchiefs, swallowing cold glasses of lemonade, lingering by open refrigerators, sitting listlessly before electric fans. Even at night there was no relief. It was tolerable enough outside where you might catch a puff of breeze, but indoors the heat never dissipated. It just sat, thick and stifling. It was like being inside a vacuum cleaner bag. I can remember lying awake in a hotel in downtown Washington listening to the sounds of an August night wash in through the open window: sirens, car horns, the thrum of neon from the hotel sign, the swish of traffic, people laughing, people yelling, people being shot.

We once saw a guy who had been shot, one sultry August night when we were out for a late snack after watching the Washington Senators beat the New York Yankees 4–3 at Griffith Stadium. He was a black man and he was lying among a crowd of legs in what appeared to me at the time to be a pool of oil, but which was of course the blood that was draining out of the hole in his head. My parents hustled us past and told us not to look, but we did, of course. Things like that didn't happen in Des Moines, so we gaped extensively. I had only ever seen murders on TV on programmes like *Gunsmoke* and *Dragnet*. I thought it was something they did just to keep the story moving. It had never occurred to me that shooting someone was an option available in the real world. It seemed such a strange thing to do, to stop someone's life just because you found him in some way disagreeable. I imagined my fourth grade teacher, Miss Bietlebaum, who had hair on her upper lip and evil in her heart, lying on the floor beside her desk, stilled forever, while I stood over her with a smoking gun in my hand. It was an interesting concept. It made you think.

At the diner where we went for our snack, there was yet another curious thing that made me think. White people like us would come in and take seats at the counter, but black people would place an order and then stand against the wall. When their food was ready, it would be handed to them in a paper bag and they would take it home or out to their car. My father explained to us that Negroes weren't allowed to sit at luncheon counters in Washington. It wasn't against the law exactly, but they didn't do it because Washington was enough of a Southern city that they just didn't dare. That seemed strange too and it made me even more reflective.

Afterwards, lying awake in the hot hotel room, listening to the restless city, I tried to understand the adult world and could not. I had always thought that once you grew up you could do anything you wanted – stay up all night or eat ice-cream straight out of the container. But now, on this one important evening of my life, I had discovered that if you didn't measure up in some critical way, people might shoot you in the head or make you take your food out to the car. I sat up on one elbow and asked my dad if there were places where Negroes ran lunch counters and made white people stand against the wall.

My dad regarded me over the top of a book and said he didn't think so. I asked him what would happen if a Negro tried to sit at a luncheon counter, even though he wasn't supposed to. What would they do to him? My dad said he didn't know and told me I should go to sleep and not worry about such things. I lay down and thought about it for a while and supposed that they would shoot him in the head. Then I rolled over and tried to sleep, but I couldn't, partly because it was so hot and I was confused and partly because earlier in the evening my brother had told me that he was going to come to my bed when I was asleep and wipe boogers on my face because I hadn't given him a bite of my frosted malt at the ball game, and I was frankly unsettled by this prospect, even though he seemed to be sleeping soundly now.

The world has changed a lot since those days, of course. Now if you lie awake in a hotel room at night, you don't hear the city any more. All you hear is the white sound of your air-conditioner. You could be in a jet over the Pacific or in a bathysphere beneath the sea for all you hear. Everywhere you go is air-conditioned, so the air is always as cool and clean as a freshly-laundered shirt. People don't wipe their necks much any more or drink sweating glasses of lemonade, or lay their bare arms gratefully on cool marble soda-fountains, because nowadays summer heat is something out there, something experienced only briefly when you sprint from your parking lot to your office or from your office to the luncheon counter down the block. Nowadays, black people sit at luncheon counters, so it's not as easy to get a seat, but it's more fair. And no-one goes to Washington Senators games any more because the Washington Senators no longer exist. In 1972 the owner moved the team to Texas because he could make more money there. Alas. But perhaps the most important change, at least as far as I am concerned, is that my brother no longer threatens to wipe boogers on me when I annoy him.

Washington feels like a small city. Its metropolitan population is three million, which makes it the seventh largest in America. And if you add Baltimore, right next door, it rises to over five million. But the city itself is quite small, with a population of just 637,000, less than Indianapolis or San Antonio. You feel as if you are in some agreeable provincial city, but then you turn a corner and come up against the headquarters of the FBI or the World Bank or the IMF and you realize what an immensely important place it is. The most startling of all these surprises is the White House. There you are, shuffling along downtown, looking in department store windows, browsing at cravats and négligées, and you turn a corner and there it is – the White House – right in the middle of the downtown. So handy for shopping, I thought. It's smaller than you expect. Everybody says that.

Across the street there is a permanent settlement of disaffected people and crazies, living in cardboard boxes, protesting at the Central Intelligence Agency controlling their thoughts from outer space. (Well, wouldn't you?) There was also a guy panhandling for quarters. Can you believe that? Right there in our nation's capital, right

155

where Nancy Reagan could see him from her bedroom window.

Washington's most fetching feature is the Mall, a broad, grassy strip of parkland which stretches for a mile or so from the Capitol building at the eastern end to the Lincoln Memorial at the western side, overlooking the Potomac. The dominant landmark is the Washington Monument. Slender and white, shaped like a pencil, it rises 555 feet above the park. It is one of the simplest and yet hand-somest structures I know, and all the more impressive when you consider that its massive stones had to be brought from the Nile delta on wooden rollers by Sumer-ian slaves. I'm sorry, I'm thinking of the Great Pyramids at Giza. Anyway, it is a real feat of engineering and very pleasing to look at. I had hoped to go up it, but there was a long line of people, mostly restive schoolchildren, snaked around the base and some distance into the park, all waiting to squeeze into an elevator about the size of a telephone booth, so I headed east in the direction of Capitol Hill, which isn't really much of a hill at all.

Scattered around the Mall's eastern end are the various museums of the Smithsonian Institution – the Museum of American History, the Museum of Natural History, the Air and Space Museum, and so on. The Smithsonian – which, incidentally, was donated to America by an Englishman who had never been there – used to be all in one building, but they keep splitting off sections of it and putting them in new buildings all over town. Now there are fourteen Smithsonian museums. The biggest ones are arrayed around the Mall, the others are mostly scattered around the city. Partly they had to do this because they get so much stuff every year – about a million items. In 1986, just to give you some idea, the Smithsonian's acquisitions included 10,000 moths and butterflies from Scandinavia, the entire archives of the Panama Canal Zone postal service, part of the old Brooklyn Bridge and a MiG-25 jet fighter. All of this used to be kept in a wonderful old Gothic brick building on the Mall called the Castle, but now the Castle is just used for administration and to show an introductory film.

I strolled down towards the Castle now. The park was full of joggers. I found this a little worrying. I kept thinking, 'Shouldn't they be running the country, or at least destabilizing some Central American government?' I mean to say, don't you usually have something more important to do at 10.30 on a Wednesday morning than pull on a pair of Reeboks and go sprinting around for forty-five minutes?

At the Castle I found the entrance area blocked with wooden trestles and lengths of rope. American and Japanese security men in dark suits were standing around. They all looked as if they spent a lot of time jogging. Some of them had headphones on and were talking into radios. Others had dogs on long leashes or mirrors on poles and were checking out cars parked along Jefferson Drive in front of the building. I went up to one of the American security men and asked him who was coming, but he said he wasn't allowed to tell me. I thought this was bizarre. Here I was in a country where, thanks to the Freedom of Information Act, I could find out how many suppositories Ronald Reagan's doctor had prescribed for him in 1986,* but I couldn't be told which foreign dignitary would shortly be making a public appearance on the steps of a national institution. The lady next to me said, 'It's Nakasone. President of Japan.'

* 1,472

'Oh, really,' I replied, always ready to see a celebrity. I asked the security man when he would be arriving. 'I'm not allowed to tell you that either, sir,' he said and passed on.

I stood with the crowd for a while and waited for Mr Nakasone to come along. And then I thought, 'Why am I standing here?' I tried to think of anyone I knew who would be impressed to hear that I had seen with my own eyes the Prime Minister of Japan. I imagined myself saying to my children, 'Hey, kids, guess who I saw in Washington – Yasuhiro Nakasone!' and being met with silence. So I walked on to the National Air and Space Museum, which was more interesting.

But not nearly as interesting as it ought to be, if you ask me. Back in the 1950s and 60s, the Smithsonian *was* the Castle. Everything was crammed into this one wonderfully dark and musty old building. It was like the nation's attic and, like an attic, it was gloriously random. Over here was the shirt Lincoln was wearing when he was shot, with a brown blood-stain above the heart. Over there was a diorama showing a Navajo family fixing dinner. Up above you, hanging from the gloomy rafters, were the Spirit of St Louis and the Wright Brothers' first plane. You didn't know where to look next or what you would find around each corner. Now it is as if everything has been sorted out by a fussy spinster, folded neatly and put in its proper place. You go to the Air and Space Museum and you see the Spirit of St Louis and the Wright Brothers' plane and lots of other famous planes and rocket ships and it's all highly impressive, but it is also clinical and uninspired. There is no sense of discovery. If your brother came running up to you and said, 'Hey, you'll never guess what

I found in this room over here!' you would in fact guess, more or less, because it would have to be either an aeroplane or a rocket ship. At the old Smithsonian it could have been absolutely anything – a petrified dog, Custer's scalp, human heads adrift in bottles. There's no element of surprise any more. So I spent the day trudging around the various museums dutifully and respectfully, with interest but not excitement. Still, there was so much to see that a whole day passed and I had seen only a part of it.

In the evening I came to the Mall, and walked across it to the Jefferson Memorial. I had hoped to see it at dusk, but I arrived late and the darkness fell like a blanket. Before I was very far into the park it was pitch dark. I expected to be mugged – indeed, I took it as my due, wandering into a city park like this on a dark night – but evidently the muggers couldn't see me. The only physical risk I ran was being bowled over by one of the many joggers who sprinted invisibly along the dark paths. The Jefferson Memorial was beautiful. There's not much to it, just a large marble rotunda in the shape of Monticello, with a gigantic statue of Jefferson inside and his favourite sayings engraved on the walls ('Have a nice day,' 'Keep your shirt on,' 'You could have knocked me over with a feather' etc.), but when it is lit up at night it is entrancing, with the lights of the memorial smeared across the pool of water called the Tidal Basin. I must have sat for an hour or more just listening to the rhythmic swish of the distant traffic, the sirens and car horns, the far-off sounds of people shouting, people singing, people being shot.

I lingered so long that it was too late to go to the Lincoln Memorial and I had to come back in the morning. The Lincoln Memorial is exactly as you expect it to be. He sits there in his big high chair looking grand yet kindly. There was a pigeon on his head. There is always a pigeon on his head. I wondered idly if the pigeon thought that all the people who came every day were there to look at him. Afterwards, as I strolled across the Mall, I spied yet more trestles and draped ropes, with security men hanging about. They had closed off a road across the park and had brought in two helicopters with the presidential seal on their sides and seven cannons and the Marine Corps Band. It was quite early in the morning and there were no crowds, so I went and stood beside the roped enclosure, the only spectator, and none of the security men bothered me or even seemed to notice me.

After a couple of minutes, a wailing of sirens filled the air and a cavalcade of limousines and police motor cycles drew up. Out stepped Nakasone and some other Japanese men, all in dark suits, escorted by some junior-looking Aryans from the State Department. They all stood politely while the Marine Corps Band blared a lively tune which I didn't recognize. Then there was a twenty-one-gun salute, but the cannons didn't go BOOM! as you would expect. They went puff. They were filled with some kind of noise-less powder, presumably so as not to waken the President in the White House across the way, so when the battery commander shouted, 'Ready, steady, go!' or whatever it was he shouted, there followed seven quick puff sounds and then a dense cloud of smoke drifted over us and went on a long slow waft across the park. This was done three times because there were only seven cannons. Then Nakasone gave a friendly wave to the crowd – which is to say, to me – and sprinted with his party to the presidential helicopters, whose blades were already whirring to life.

After a moment they rose up, tilted past the Washington Monument and were gone, and everyone back on the ground relaxed and had a smoke.

Weeks afterwards, back in London, I told people about my private encounter with Nakasone and the Marine Corps Band and the noiseless cannons and how the Prime Minister of Japan had waved to me alone. Most of them would listen politely, then allow a small pause and say, 'Did I tell you that Mavis has to go back into hospital next week to have her feet done?' or something like that. The English can be so crushing sometimes.

From Washington I took US 301 out past Annapolis and the US Naval Academy and over a long, low bridge across the Chesapeake Bay into eastern Maryland. Before 1952, when the bridge was built, the eastern side of the bay had enjoyed centuries of isolation. Ever since then, people have been saying that outsiders will flood in and ruin the peninsula, but it still looked pretty unspoiled to me, and my guess is that it's the outsiders who have kept it that way. It's always the outsiders who are the most fiercely opposed to shopping malls and bowling alleys, which the locals in their simple, trusting way tend to think might be kind of handy.

Chestertown, the first town of any size I came to, confirmed this. The first thing I saw was a woman in a bright pink track suit zipping past on a bicycle with a wicker basket on the front. Only an urban émigré would have a bicycle with a wicker basket. A local person would have a Subaru pickup truck. There seemed to be a lot of these bike ladies about, and between them they had clearly made Chestertown into a model community. The whole place was as neat as a pin. The sidewalks were paved with brick and lined with trees, and there was a well-tended park in the middle of the business district. The library was busy. The movie theatre was still in business and not showing a *Death Wish* movie. Everything about the place was tranquil and appealing. This was as nice a town as I had seen. This was almost Amalgam.

I drove on through the low, marshy flatlands, much taken with the simple beauty of the Chesapeake peninsula, with its high skies and scattered farms and forgotten little towns. Late in the morning I crossed into Delaware, *en route* to Philadelphia. Delaware may well be the most obscure of all the American states. I once met a girl from Delaware and couldn't think of a single thing to say to her. I said, 'So you come from Delaware? Gosh. Wow.' And she moved quickly onto someone more verbally dextrous, and also better looking. For a while it troubled me that I could live in America for twenty years, have the benefit of an expensive education and not know anything at all about one of the fifty states. I went around asking people if they had ever heard Delaware mentioned on television or seen a story pertaining to it in the newspaper or read a novel set there and they'd say, 'You know, I don't think I ever have,' and then they'd look kind of troubled too.

I determined that I would read up on Delaware so that the next time I met a girl from there I could say something droll and apposite and she might go to bed with me. But I could find almost nothing written about Delaware any-where. Even the entry in the *Encyclopaedia Britannica* was only about two paragraphs long and finished in the middle of a sentence, as I recall. And the funny thing was that as I drove across Delaware now I could feel it vanishing from my memory as I went, like those children's drawing slates on which you erase the picture by lifting the transparent sheet. It was as if a giant sheet were being lifted up behind me as I drove, expunging the experience as it unfolded. Looking back now, I can just vaguely recall some semi-industrial landscape and some signs for Wilmington.

And then I was in the outskirts of Philadelphia, the city that gave the world Sylvester Stallone and Legionnaire's disease, among other things, and was too preoccupied with the disturbing thoughts that this called up to give Delaware any further consideration.

Chapter thirteen

WHEN I WAS A CHILD, Philadephia was the third biggest city in America. What I remembered of it was driving through endless miles of ghettos, one battered block after another, on a hot July Sunday, with black children playing in the spray of fire hydrants and older people lounging around on the street corners or sitting on the front stoops. It was the poorest place I had ever seen. Trash lay in the gutters and doorways, and whole buildings were derelict. It was like a foreign country, like Haiti or Panama. My dad whistled tunelessly through his teeth the whole time, as he always did when he was uneasy, and told us to keep the windows rolled up even though it was boiling in the car. At stop lights people would stare stonily at us and Dad would whistle in double time and drum the steering wheel with his fingers and smile apologetically at anyone who looked at him, as if to say, 'Sorry, we're from out of state.'

Things have changed now, naturally. Philadelphia is no longer the third biggest city in America. Los Angeles pushed it into fourth place in the 1960s, and now there are freeways to whisk you into the heart of town without soiling your tyres in the ghettos. Even so, I managed a brief, inadvertent visit to one of the poorer neighbourhoods when I wandered off the freeway in search of a gas station. Before I could do anything about it, I found myself sucked into a vortex of one-way streets that carried me into the most squalid and dangerous-looking neighbourhood I had ever seen. It may have been, for all I know, the very ghetto we passed through all those years before – the brownstone buildings looked much the same but it was many times worse than the one I remembered. The ghetto of my childhood, for all its poorness, had the air of a street carnival. People wore colourful clothes and seemed to be having a good time. This place was just bleak and dangerous, like a war zone. Abandoned cars, old refrigerators, burnt-out sofas littered every vacant lot. Garbage cans looked as if they had been thrown to the street from the rooftops. There were no gas stations – I wouldn't have stopped anyway, not in a place like this, not for a million dollars – and most of the storefronts were boarded with plywood. Every standing object had been spray-painted with graffiti. There were still a few young people on the stoops and corners, but they looked listless and cold – it was a chilly day – and they seemed not to notice me. Thank God. This was a neighbourhood where clearly you could be murdered for a pack of cigarettes – a fact that was not lost on me as I searched nervously for a way back onto the freeway. By the time I found it, I wasn't whistling through my teeth so much as singing through my sphincter.

It really was the most uncomfortable experience I had had in many years. God, what it must be like to live there and to walk those streets daily. Do you know that if you are a black man in urban America you now stand a one in nineteen chance of being murdered? In World War II, the odds of being killed were one in fifty. In New York City there is one murder every four hours. Murder there has become the most common cause of death for people under thirty-five – and yet New York isn't even the most murderous city in America. At least eight other cities have a higher murder rate. In Los Angeles there are more murders each year on school-grounds alone than there are in the whole of London. So perhaps it is little wonder that people in American cities take violence as routine. I don't know how they do it.

On my way to Des Moines to start this trip, I passed through O'Hare Airport in Chicago where I ran into a friend who worked for the *St Louis Post Dispatch*. He told me he had been working extra hard lately because of something that had happened to his boss. The boss had been driving home from work late one Saturday night when he had stopped at some traffic lights. As he waited for the lights to change, the passenger door opened and a man with a gun got in. The gunman made the boss drive down to the riverfront, where he shot him in the head and took his money. The boss had been in a coma for three weeks and they weren't sure whether he was going to live.

My friend was telling me this not because it was such an incredible story, but simply by way of elucidating why he was having to work so damned hard lately. As for his boss, his attitude seemed to be that if you forget to lock your car doors when you're driving through St Louis late at night, well, you've got to expect to take a bullet in the head from time to time. It was very odd, his deadpan attitude, but it seems to be more and more the way in America now. It made me feel like a stranger.

I drove downtown and parked near City Hall. On top of the building is a statue of William Penn. It's the main landmark downtown, visible from all around the city, but it was covered in scaffolding. In 1985, after decades of neglect, the city fathers decided to refurbish the statue before it fell down. So they covered it in scaffolding. However, this cost so much that there was no money left to do the repairs. Now, two years later, the scaffolding was still there and not a lick of work had been done. A city engineer had recently announced with a straight face that before long the scaffolding itself would need to be refurbished. This is more or less how Philadelphia works, which is to say, not very well. No other city in America pursues the twin ideals of corruption and incompetence with quite the same enthusiasm. When it comes to asinine administration, Philadelphia is in a league of its own.

Consider: in 1985, a bizarre sect called Move barricaded itself into a tenement house on the west side of town. The police chief and mayor considered the options open to them and decided that the most intelligent use of their resources would be to blow up the house – but of course! – even though they knew there were children inside and it was in the middle of a densely-populated part of the city. So they dropped a bomb on the house from a helicopter. This started a fire that quickly grew out of control and burned down most of the neighbourhood – sixty-one houses in all – and killed eleven people, including all the children in the barricaded home.

When they aren't being incompetent, city officials like to relax with a little corruption. Just as I was driving into town I heard on the radio that a former city councillor had been sentenced to ten years in jail and his aide to eight years for attempted extortion. The judge called it a gross breach of public trust. He should know. Across town a state review board was calling for the dismissal of nine of the judge's colleagues for taking cash gifts from members of the Roofers Union. Two of those judges were already awaiting trial on extortion charges. This sort of thing is routine in Philadelphia. A few months earlier, when a state official named Bud Dwyer was similarly accused of corruption, he called a press conference, pulled out a gun and, as cameras rolled, blew his brains out. This led to an excellent local joke.

Q: What is the difference between Bud Dwyer and Bud Lite?

A: Bud Lite has a head on it.

Yet for all its incompetence and criminality, Philadelphia is a likeable place. For one thing, unlike Washington, it feels like a big city. It had skyscrapers and there was steam rising through vents in the sidewalk and on every corner stood a stainless steel hot dog stand, with a chilly-looking guy in a stocking cap bobbing around behind it. I wandered over to Independence Square – actually it's now called Independence National Historical Park – and looked respectfully at all the historic buildings. The main building is Independence Hall, where the Declaration of Independence was drawn up and the Constitution ratified. When I was first there in 1960, there was a long line stretching out of the building. There still was – in fact, it seemed not to have moved in twenty-seven years. Deep though my respect is for both the Constitution and the Declaration of Independence, I was disinclined to spend my afternoon in such a long and immobile queue. I went instead to the visitors' centre. National park visitors' centres are always the same. They have some displays in glass cases that manage to be both boring and uninformative, a locked auditorium with a board out front saying that the next showing of the free twelve-minute introductory film will be at 4 p.m. (just before 4 p.m. somebody comes and changes it to 10 a.m.), some racks of books and brochures with titles like *Pewter in History* and *Vegetables of Old Philadelphia*, which are too dull even to browse through, much less buy, and a drinking fountain and rest-rooms, which everyone makes use of because there's not much else to do. Every visitor to every national park goes into the visitors' centre, stands around kind of stupidly for a while, then has a pee and a drink of water and wanders back outside. That is what I did now.

From the visitors' centre I ambled along Independence Mall to Franklin Square, which was full of winos, many of whom had the comical idea that I might be prepared to give them twenty-five cents of my own money without their providing any product or service in return. According to my guidebook, Franklin Square had 'lots of interesting things' to see – a museum, a working book bindery, an archae-ological exhibit and 'the only post office in the United States which does not fly the American flag' (don't ask me why) – but my heart wasn't in it, especially with piteous and unwashed winos tugging at my sleeves all the while, and I fled back to the real world of downtown Philadelphia.

Late in the afternoon, I found my way to the offices of the *Philadelphia Inquirer*, where an old friend from Des Moines, Lucia Herndon, was life-style editor. The *Inquirer* offices were like newspaper offices everywhere – grubby, full of junk, littered with coffee-cups in which cigarette butts floated like dead fish in a polluted lake – and Lucia's desk, I was impressed to note, was one of the messiest in the room. This may have accounted in part for her im-pressive rise at the *Inquirer*. I only ever knew one journalist with a truly tidy desk, and he was eventually arrested for molesting small boys. Make of that what you will; but just bear it in mind the next time somebody with a tidy desk invites you camping.

We drove in my car out to the district of Mt Airy, where, conveniently for me – and for her too, come to that – Lucia lived with another old friend of mine from Des Moines, her husband, Hal. All day long I had been wondering, vaguely and intermittently, why Hal and Lucia liked Philadelphia so much – they had moved there about a year before – but now I understood. The road to Mt Airy led through the most beautiful city park I had ever been in. Called Fairmount Park and covering almost 9,000 rolling acres, it is the largest municipal park in America and it is full of trees and fragrant shrubs and bosky glades of infinite charm. It stretches for miles along the banks of the Schuylkill River. We drove through a dreamy twilight. Boats sculled along the water. It was perfection.

Mt Airy was out in the Germantown section of the city. It had a nice settled feeling to it, as if people had lived there for generations – which is in fact the case in Philadelphia, Lucia told me. The city was still full of the sort of neighbourhoods where everybody knew everybody else. Many people scarcely ever ventured more than a few hundred yards from their homes. It was not uncommon to get lost and find that hardly anybody could reliably direct you to a neighbourhood three miles away. Philadelphia also had its own vocabulary – downtown was called centre city, sidewalks were called pavements, as in Britain – and peculiarities of pronunciation.

In the evening I sat in Hal and Lucia's house, eating their food, drinking their wine, admiring their children and their house and furniture and possessions, their easy wealth and comfort, and felt a sap for ever having left America. Life was so abundant here, so easy, so convenient. Suddenly I wanted a refrigerator that made its own ice-cubes and a waterproof radio for the shower. I wanted an electric orange juicer and a room ionizer and a wristwatch that would keep me in touch with my biorhythms. I wanted it all. Once in the evening I went upstairs to go to the bathroom and walked past one of the children's bedrooms. The door was open and a bedside light was on. There were toys everywhere – on the floor, on shelves, tumbling out of a wooden trunk. It looked like Santa's workshop. But there was nothing extraordinary about this; it was just a typical middle-class American bedroom.

And you should see American closets. They are always full of yesterday's enthusiasms: golf-clubs, scuba diving equipment, tennis-rackets, exercise machines, tape recorders, darkroom equipment, objects that once excited their owner and then were replaced by other objects even more shiny and exciting. That is the great, seductive thing about America – the people always get what they want, right now, whether it is good for them or not. There is something deeply worrying, and awesomely irresponsible, about this endless self-gratification, this constant appeal to the baser instincts.

Do you want zillions off your state taxes even at the risk of crippling education?

'Oh, yes!' the people cry.

Do you want TV that would make an imbecile weep?

'Yes, please!'

Shall we indulge ourselves with the greatest orgy of consumer spending that the world has ever known?

'Sounds neat! Let's go for it!'

The whole of the global economy is based on supplying the cravings of two per cent of the world's population. If Americans suddenly stopped indulging themselves, or ran out of closet space, the world would fall apart. If you ask me, that's crazy.

I should point out that I am not talking about Hal and Lucia in all this. They are good people and lead modest and responsible lives. Their closets aren't full of scuba diving equipment and seldom-used tennis-rackets. They are full of mundane items like buckets and galoshes, ear-muffs and scouring powders. I know this for a fact because late in the night when everyone was asleep I crept out of bed and had a good look.

In the morning, I dropped Hal at his office downtown – correction, centre city – and the drive through Fairmount Park was as enchanting in the morning sunshine as it had been at dusk. All cities should have parks like this, I thought. He told me some more interesting things about Philadelphia: that it spent more money on public art than any other city in America – one per cent of the total city budget – and yet it had an illiteracy rate of forty per cent. He pointed out to me, in the middle of Fairmount Park, the palatial Philadelphia Museum of Art, which had become the city's top tourist attraction, not because of its collection of 500,000 paintings, but because its front steps were the ones Sylvester Stallone sprinted up in *Rocky*. People were actually coming to the museum in buses, looking at the steps and leaving without ever going inside to see the pictures. And he introduced me to a radio talk show hosted by a man named Howard Stern, of which Hal was a devotee. Howard Stern had a keen interest in sex and was engagingly direct with his callers. 'Good morning, Marilyn,' he would say to a caller, 'are you wearing panties?' This, we agreed, beat most early-morning talk shows hands down. Howard queried his callers with arresting candour and a measure of prurience I had not before encountered on American radio.

Unfortunately, I lost the station soon after dropping Hal off and spent the rest of the morning searching for it without success, and eventually ended up listening to a competing phone-in programme, which featured a woman who was an expert on dealing with intestinal worms in dogs. As this principally consisted of giving the dogs a tablet to make the worms die, it was not long before I felt as if I were something of an expert myself. And so the morning passed.

I drove to Gettysburg, where the decisive battle of the American Civil War was fought over three days in July 1863. There were over 50,000 casualties. I parked at the visitors' centre and went inside. It contained a small, ill-lit museum with glass cases containing bullets, brass buttons, belt buckles and that sort of thing, each with a yellowed typed caption beside it saying 'Buckle from uniform of 13th Tennessee Mountaineers. Found by Festus T. Scrubbins, local farmer, and donated by his daughter, Mrs Marinetta Stumpy.' There was precious little to give you any sense of the battle itself. It was more like the gleanings of a treasure hunt.

One interesting thing was a case devoted to the Gettysburg Address, where I learned that Lincoln was invited to speak only as an afterthought and that everyone was taken aback when he accepted. It was only ten sentences long and took just two minutes to deliver. I was further informed that he gave the address many months after the battle. I had always imagined him making it more or less immediately afterwards, while there were still bodies lying around and wraiths of smoke rising from the ruins of distant houses and people like Festus T. Scrubbins poking around among the twitching casualties to see what useful souvenirs they could extract. The truth, as so often in this life, was disappointing.

I went outside and had a look at the battlefield, which sprawls over 3,500 acres of mostly flat countryside, fringed by the town of Gettysburg with its gas stations and motels. The battlefield had the great deficiency common to all historic battlefields. It was just countryside. There was nothing much to distinguish this stretch of empty fields from that one. You had to take their word for it that a great battle was fought there. There were a lot of cannons scattered about, I'll give them that. And along the road leading to the site of Pickett's charge, the attack by Confederate troops that turned the tide of battle in the Union's favour, many of the regiments had erected obelisks and monuments to their own glory, some of them very grand. I strolled down there now. Through my dad's old binoculars I could clearly see how Pickett's troops had advanced from the direction of the town, a mile or so to the north, sweeping across the Burger King parking lot, skirting the Tastee Delite Drive-In and regrouping just outside the Crap-o-Rama Wax Museum and Gift Shop. It's all very sad. Ten thousand soldiers fell there in an hour; two out of every three Confederate soldiers didn't make it back to base. It is a pity, verging on the criminal, that so much of the town of Gettysburg has been spoiled with tourist tat and that it is so visible from the battlefield.

When I was little, my dad bought me a Union cap and a toy rifle and let me loose on the battlefield. I was in heaven. I dashed about the whole day crouching behind trees, charging over to Devil's Den and Little Round Top, blowing up parties of overweight tourists with cameras around their necks. My dad was in heaven too because the park was free and there were literally hundreds of historical plaques for him to read. Now, however, I found it difficult to summon any real excitement for the place.

I was about to depart, feeling guilty that I had come so far without getting anything much out of the experience, when I saw a sign at the visitors' centre for tours to the Eisenhower home. I had forgotten that Ike and Mamie Eisenhower lived on a farm just outside Gettysburg. Their old home was now a national historical monument and could be toured for $2.50. Impulsively I bought a ticket and went outside where a bus was just about to depart to take half a dozen of us to the farm four or five miles away down a country lane.

Well, it was great. I can't remember the last time I had such a good time in a Republican household. You are greeted at the door by a fragrant woman with a chrysanthemum on her bosom, who tells you a little about the house, about how much Ike and Mamie loved to sit around and watch TV and play canasta, and then gives you a leaflet describing each room and lets you wander off on your own so that you can linger or stride on as it pleases you. Each doorway was blocked off with a sheet of perspex, but you could lean against it and gaze into the interior. The house has been preserved precisely as it was

175

when the Eisenhowers lived there. It was as if they had simply wandered off and never come back (something that either of them was quite capable of doing towards the end). The décor was quintessentially early 1960s Republican. When I was growing up we had some neighbours who were rich Republicans and this was practically a duplicate of their house. There was a big TV console in a mahogany cabinet, table-lamps made out of pieces of driftwood, a padded leather cocktail bar, French-style telephones in every room, bookshelves containing about twelve books (usually in matching sets of three) and otherwise filled with large pieces of flowery gilt-edged porcelain of the sort favoured by homosexual French aristocrats.

When the Eisenhowers bought the place in 1950, a 200-year-old farmhouse stood on the site, but it was draughty and creaked on stormy nights, so they had it torn down and replaced with the present building, which *looks* like a 200-year-old farmhouse. Isn't that great? Isn't that just so Republican? I was enchanted. Every room contained things I hadn't seen for years – 1960s kitchen appliances, old copies of *Life Magazine*, boxy black and white portable TVs, metal alarm clocks. Upstairs the bedrooms were just as Ike and Mamie had left them. Mamie's personal effects were on her bedside table – her diary, reading glasses, sleeping-pills – and I dare say that if you knelt down and looked under the bed you would find all her old gin bottles.

In Ike's room his bathrobe and slippers were laid out and the book he had been reading on the day he died was left open on the chair beside the bed. The book was – and I ask you to remember for a moment that this was one of the most important men of this century, a man who held the world's destiny in his hands throughout much of World War II and the Cold War, a man chosen by Columbia University to be its president, a man venerated by Republicans for two generations, a man who throughout the whole of my childhood had his finger on The Button – the book was *West of the Pecos* by Zane Grey.

From Gettysburg, I headed north up US 15 towards Bloomsburg, where my brother and his family had recently moved. For years they had lived in Hawaii, in a house with a swimming-pool, near balmy beaches, beneath tropical skies and whispering palms, and now, just when I had landed a trip to America and could go anywhere I wanted, they had moved to the Rust Belt. Bloomsburg, as it turned out, was actually very nice – a bit short on balmy beaches and hula girls with swaying hips, but still nice for all that.

It's a college town, with a decidedly sleepy air. You feel at first as if you should be wearing slippers and a bathrobe. Main Street was prosperous and tidy and the surrounding streets were mostly filled with large old houses sitting on ample lawns. Here and there church spires poked out from among the many trees. It was pretty well an ideal town – one of those rare American places where you wouldn't need a car. From almost any house in town it would be a short and pleasant stroll to the library and post office and stores. My brother and his wife told me that a developer was about to build a big shopping mall outside town and most of the bigger merchants were going to move out there. People, it appeared, didn't want to stroll to do their shopping. They actually wanted to get in their cars and

177

drive to the edge of town, where they could then park and walk a similar distance across a flat, treeless parking lot. That is how America goes shopping and they wanted to be part of it. So now downtown Bloomsburg is likely to become semiderelict and another nice little town will be lost. So the world progresses.

Anyway, it was a pleasure to see my brother and his family, as you can imagine. I did all the things you do when you visit relatives – ate their food, used their bathtub, washing-machine and telephone, stood around uselessly while they searched for spare blankets and grappled with a truculent sofa bed, and of course late at night when everyone was asleep I crept out of my room and had a good look in their closets.

As it was the weekend and as they had some spare time, my brother and his wife decided to take me down to Lancaster County to show me the Amish country. It was a two-hour drive. *En route*, my brother pointed out the Three Mile Island nuclear reactor at Harrisburg, where a few years before some careless employees had very nearly irradiated the whole of the eastern seaboard, and then forty-five miles further on we passed the Peach Bottom nuclear power station, where seventeen employees had recently been dismissed after it had been revealed that they spent their working hours sleeping, taking drugs, having rubber band fights and playing video games. At some times every person in the plant was dozing, according to investigators. Allowing state utilities in Pennsylvania to run nuclear power stations is a bit like letting Prince Philip fly through London airspace. In any case, I made a mental note to bring an anti-radiation suit with me next time I came to Pennsylvania.

Lancaster County is the home of the Pennsylvania Dutch, the Amish and Mennonites. The Mennonites are named after a well-known brand of speed-stick deodorant. They aren't really. I just made that up. They are named after Menno Simons, one of their early leaders. In Europe they were called Anabaptists. They came to Lancaster County 250 years ago. Today there are 12,500 Amish people in the county, almost all of them descended from thirty original couples. The Amish split from the Mennonites in 1693, and there have been countless subdivisions since then, but the thing that they all have in common is that they wear simple clothes and shun modern contrivances. The problem is that since about 1860 they've been squabbling endlessly over just how rigorous they should be in their shunning. Every time anybody invents something they argue about whether it is ungodly or not, and the ones who don't like it go off and form a new sect. First, they argued over whether they should have steel rims or rubber rims on their buggies, then whether they should have tractors, then electricity and television. Now presumably they argue over whether they should have a frost-free refrigerator and whether their instant coffee should be powdered or freeze-dried.

The most splendid thing about the Amish is the names they give their towns. Everywhere else in America towns are named either after the first white person to get there or the last Indian to leave. But the Amish obviously gave the matter of town names some thought and graced their communities with intriguing, not to say provocative, appellations: Blue Ball, Bird in Hand, and Intercourse, to name but three. Intercourse makes a good living by attracting passers-by such as me who think it the height

179

of hilarity to send their friends and colleagues postcards with an Intercourse postal mark and some droll sentiment scribbled on the back.

Many people are so fascinated by the Amish way of life, by the idea of people living 200 years in the past, that they come quite literally by the millions to gawk. There were hundreds and hundreds of tourists thronging Intercourse when we arrived, and cars and buses choking the roads into town. Everyone hoped to see and photograph some genuine Amish. Up to five million people a year visit the county and non-Amish businessmen have erected vast souvenir palaces, replica farms, wax museums, cafeterias and gift shops to soak up the $350 million that the visitors are happy to spend each year. Now there is almost nothing left in these towns for the Amish themselves to buy, so they don't come in and the tourists have nothing to do but take pictures of each other.

Travel articles and movies like *Witness* generally gloss over this side of things, but the fact is that Lancaster County is now one of the most awful places in America, especially at weekends when traffic jams sometimes stretch for miles. Many of the Amish themselves have given up and moved to places like Iowa and upper Michigan where they are left alone. Out in the countryside, particularly on the back roads, you can still sometimes see the people in their dark clothes working in the fields or driving their distinctive black buggies down the highway, with a long line of tourist cars creeping along behind, pissed off because they can't get by and they really want to be in Bird in Hand so they can get some more funnel cakes and Sno-cones and perhaps buy a wrought-iron wine rack or combination mailbox/weather-vane to take back home to

Fartville with them. I wouldn't be surprised if a decade from now there isn't a real Amish person left in the county. It is an unspeakable shame. They should be left in peace.

In the evening, we went to one of the many barn-like family-style Pennsylvania Dutch restaurants that are scattered across the county. The parking lot was packed with buses and cars and there were people waiting everywhere, inside the building and out. We went in and were given a ticket with the number 621 on it and went with it to a tiny patch of floor-space just vacated by another party. Every few minutes a man would step to the door and call out a series of numbers ridiculously lower than ours – 220, 221, 222 – and a dozen or so people would follow him into the dining-room. We debated leaving, but a party of fat people beside us told us not to give up because it was worth the wait, even if we had to stay there until eleven o'clock. The food was that good, they said, and where food was concerned these people clearly had some experience. Well, they were right. Eventually our number was called and we were ushered into the dining-room with nine strangers and all seated together at one big trestle-table.

There must have been fifty other such tables in the room, all with a dozen or so people at them. The din and bustle were intense. Waitresses hurried back and forth with outsized trays and everywhere you looked people were shovelling food into their mouths, elbows flapping, as if they hadn't eaten for a week. Our waitress made us introduce ourselves to each other, which everybody thought was kind of dopey, and then she started bringing food, great platters and bowls of it – thick slabs of ham, mountains of fried chicken, buckets of mashed potatoes and all kinds of vegetables, rolls, soups and salads. It was incredible. You helped yourself and with two hands heaved the platter on to the next person. You could have as much of anything as you wanted – and when a bowl was empty the waitress brought back another and practically ordered you to clear it.

I've never seen so much food. I couldn't see over the top of my plate. It was all delicious and pretty soon everybody knew everybody else and was having a great time. I ate so much my armpits bulged. But still the food kept coming. Just when I thought I would have to summon a wheelchair to get me to the car, the waitress took away all the platters and bowls, and started bringing desserts – apple pies, chocolate cakes, bowls of homemade ice-cream, pastries, flans and God knows what else.

I kept eating. It was too delicious to pass up. Buttons popped off my shirt. My trousers burst open. I barely had the strength to lift my spoon, but I kept shovelling the stuff in. It was grotesque. Food began to leak from my ears. And still I ate. I ate the gross national product of Lesotho that night. Eventually, mercifully, the waitress prised the spoons from our hands and took the dessert stuff away, and we were able to stumble zombie-like into the night.

We got in the car, too full to speak, and headed towards the distant greenish glow of Three Mile Island. I lay on the back seat, my feet in the air, and moaned softly. I vowed that never again in my life would I eat a single morsel of food, and I meant it. But two hours later, when we arrived back at my brother's house, the agony had abated and my brother and I were able to begin a new cycle of gross overconsumption, beginning with a twelve-pack of beer and bucket of pretzels from his kitchen and concluding, in the early hours of the morning, with a plate of onion rings and two-foot-long submarine sandwiches, full of goo and spices, at an all-night eaterie out on Highway II.

What a great country.

Chapter fourteen

IT WAS TEN minutes to seven in the morning and it was cold. Standing outside the Bloomsburg bus station, I could see my breath. The few cars out this early trailed clouds of vapour. I was hung-over and in a few minutes I was going to climb on to a bus for a five-hour ride into New York. I would sooner have eaten cat food.

My brother had suggested that I take the bus because it would save having to find a place to park in Manhattan. I could leave the car with him and come back for it in a day or two. At two in the morning, after many beers, this had seemed a good plan. But now, standing in the early morning chill, I realized I was making a serious mistake. You only go on a long-distance bus in the United States because either you cannot afford to fly or – and this is really licking the bottom of the barrel in America – you cannot afford a car. Being unable to afford a car in America is the last step before living out of a plastic sack. As a result, most of the people on long-distance buses are one of the following: actively schizoid, armed and dangerous, in a drugged stupor, just released from prison, or nuns. Occasionally you will also see a pair of Norwegian students. You can tell they are Norwegian students because they are so pink-faced and healthy-looking and they wear little blue ankle socks with their sandals. But by and large a ride on a long-distance bus in America combines most of the shortcomings of prison life with those of an ocean crossing in a troop-ship.

So when the bus pulled up before me, heaving a pneumatic sigh, and its door flapped open, I boarded it with some misgivings. The driver himself didn't appear any too stable. He had the sort of hair that made him look as if he'd been playing with live wires. There were about half a dozen other passengers, though only two of them looked seriously insane and just one was talking to himself. I took a seat near the back and settled down to get some sleep. I had drunk far too many beers with my brother the night before, and the hot spices from the submarine sandwich were now expanding ominously inside my abdomen and drifting around like the stuff they put in lava lamps. Soon, from one end or the other, it would begin to seep out.

I felt a hand on my shoulder from behind. Through the gap in the seat I could see it was an Indian man – by that I mean a man from India, not an American Indian. 'Can I smoke on this bus?' he asked me.

'I don't know,' I said. 'I don't smoke any more, so I don't pay much attention to these things.'

'But do you *think* I can smoke on this bus?'

'I really don't know.'

He was quiet for a few minutes, then his hand was on my shoulder again, not tapping it but resting there. 'I can't find an ashtray,' he said.

'No fooling,' I responded wittily, without opening my eyes.

'Do you think that means we're not allowed to smoke?'

'I don't know. I don't care.'

'But do you *think* it means we're not allowed to smoke?'

'If you don't take your hand off my shoulder I am going to dribble vomit on it,' I said.

He removed his hand quickly and was silent for perhaps a minute. Then he said, 'Would you help me look for an ashtray?'

It was seven in the morning and I was deeply unwell. 'WILL YOU PLEASE JUST LEAVE ME ALONE!' I snapped at him, just a trifle wildly. Two seats back a pair of Norwegian students looked shocked. I gave them a look as if to say, 'And don't you try anything either, you wholesome little shits!' and sank back into my seat. It was going to be a long day.

I slept fitfully, that dissatisfying, semi-conscious sleep in which you incorporate into your dreams the things going on around you – the grinding of gears, the crying of babies, the mad swervings of the bus back and forth across the highway as the driver gropes for a dropped cigarette or lapses into a psychotic episode. Mostly I dreamt of the bus plunging over a cliff-face, sailing into a void; in my dream, we fell for miles, tumbling through the clouds, peacefully, with just the sound of air whisking past outside, and then the Indian saying to me: 'Do you think it might be all right if I smoked *now*?'

When I awoke there was drool on my shoulder and a new passenger opposite me, a haggard woman with lank grey hair who was chain-smoking cigarettes and burping prodigiously. They were the sort of burps children make to amuse themselves – rich, resonant, basso profundo burps. The woman was completely unselfconscious about it. She would look at me and open her mouth and out would roll a burp. It was amazing. Then she would take a drag on her cigarette and burp a large puff of smoke. That was amazing too. I glanced behind me. The Indian man was still there, looking miserable. Seeing me, he started to lean forward to ask a supplementary question, but I stopped him with a raised finger and he sank back. I stared out the window, feeling ill, and passed the time by trying to imagine circumstances less congenial than this. But apart from being dead or at a Bee Gees concert I couldn't think of a single thing.

We reached New York in the afternoon. I got a room in a hotel near Times Square. The room cost $110 a night and was so small I had to go out into the corridor to turn around. I had never been in a room where I could touch all four walls at once. I did all the things you do in hotel rooms – played with the lights and TV, looked in the drawers, put all the towels and ashtrays in my suitcase – and then wandered out to have a look at the city.

The last time I had been in New York was when I was sixteen and my friend Stan and I came out to visit my brother and his wife, who were then living in a strange, Kafkaesque community in Queens called Lefrak City. It consisted of about a dozen tall apartment buildings clustered around a series of lonesome quadrangles, the sort of quadrangles where rain-puddles stand for weeks and the flower-beds are littered with supermarket trolleys. Something like 50,000 people lived there. I had never conceived of so many people gathered in one place. I couldn't understand why in such a big, open country as America people would choose to live like that. But for all these people this was it. This was home. They would live out their lives never having their own back yard, never having a barbecue, never stepping out the back door at midnight to have a pee in the bushes and check out the stars. Their children would grow up thinking that supermarket trolleys grew wild, like weeds.

In the evenings, when my brother and his wife went out, Stan and I would sit with binoculars and scan the windows of the neighbouring buildings. There were hundreds of windows to choose from, each containing a ghostly glow of television. What we were looking for, of course, were naked women – and to our amazement we did actually see some, though usually this resulted in such fervent grappling for control of the binoculars that the women had dressed and gone out for the evening by the time we got their windows back in view. Mostly what we saw, however, were other men with binoculars scanning the windows of our building.

What I particularly remember was the sense of menace whenever we left the building. Groups of leather-jacketed teenagers with no place to go would sit on the walls around the complex watching anyone who passed. I always expected them to fall in behind us as we went by and to take our money and stick us with knives they had made in the prison workshop, but they never bothered us. They just stared. Even so it was frightening because we were just skinny kids from Iowa.

New York still frightened me. I felt the same sense of menace now as I walked down to Times Square. I had read so much for so long about murders and street crime that I felt a personal gratitude to everyone who left me alone. I wanted to hand out cards that said 'Thank you for not killing me'.

But the only people who assaulted me were panhandlers. There are 36,000 vagrants in New York and in two days of walking around every one of them asked me for money. Some of them asked twice. People in New York go to Calcutta to get some relief from begging. I began to regret that I didn't live in an age when a gentleman could hit such people with his cane. One guy, my favourite, came up and asked if he could borrow a dollar. That knocked me out. I wanted to say, 'Borrow a dollar? Certainly. Shall we say interest at one per cent above prime and we'll meet back here on Thursday to settle?' I wouldn't give him a dollar, of course – I wouldn't give my closest friend a *dollar* – but I pressed a dime into his grubby mitt and gave him a wink for his guile.

Times Square is incredible. You've never seen such lights, such hustle. Whole sides of buildings are given over to advertisements that blink and ripple and wave. It's like a storm on an electronic sea. There are perhaps forty of these massive inducements to spend and consume, and all but two of them were for Japanese companies: Mita Copiers, Canon, Panasonic, Sony. My mighty homeland was represented by just Kodak and Pepsi Cola. The war is over, Yankee dog, I thought bleakly.

The most riveting thing about New York is that anything can happen there. Only the week before, a woman had been eaten by an escalator. Can you beat that? She had been on her way to work, minding her own business, when suddenly the stair beneath her gave way and she was plummeted into the interior mechanism, into all the whirring cogs and gears, with the sort of consequences you can well imagine. How would you like to be the cleaner in *that* building? ('Bernie, can you come in early tonight? And listen, you'd better bring along a wire brush and a *lot* of Ajax.') New York is always full of amazing and unpredictable things. A front page story in the *New York Post* was about a pervert with AIDS who had been jailed that day for raping little boys. Can you believe that? 'What a city!' I thought. 'Such a madhouse!' For two days I walked and stared and mumbled in amazement. A large black man on Eighth Avenue reeled out of a doorway, looking dangerously disordered, and said to me, 'I been smoking ice! Big bowls of ice!' I gave him a quarter real fast, even though he hadn't asked for anything, and moved off quickly. On Fifth Avenue I went into the Trump Tower, a new sky-scraper. A guy named Donald Trump, a developer, is slowly taking over New York, building skyscrapers all over town with his name on them, so I went in and had a look around. The building had the most tasteless lobby I had ever seen – all brass and chrome and blotchy red and white marble that looked like the sort of thing that you would walk around if you saw it on the sidewalk. Here it was everywhere – on the floors, up the walls, on the ceiling. It was like being inside somebody's stomach after he'd eaten pizza. 'Incredible,' I muttered, and walked on. Next door a store sold pornographic videos, right there on Fifth Avenue. My favourite was *Yiddish Erotica, Volume 2*. What could this possibly consist of – rabbis with their trousers down, tarty women lying spread-eagled and saying, 'You wanna fuck already?' 'Superb, incredible,' I mumbled, and plodded on.

In the evening, as I strolled back along Times Square, my eye was caught by a strip-tease club with a photo-graph of the strippers in the window. They were nice-looking girls. One of the photos was of Samantha Fox. Since Ms Fox was at this time being paid something like £250,000 a year to show off her comely udders to readers of British newspapers such as the *Sun*, it seemed to me improbable, to say the least, that she would be peeling off for strangers in a smoky basement room on Times Square. In fact, I would go so far as to suggest that there was a little fraud at work here. It's a mean trick to play on a horny person.

They always used to do this to you at the Iowa State Fair. The strippers' tents behind the rides would be covered with wildly erotic paintings of the most beautiful, silky-haired, full-breasted, lithe-bodied women you ever saw – women whose moist and pouty lips seemed to be saying, 'I want you – yes, you there, with the zits and glasses. Come and fulfil me, little man.' Aged fourteen and delirious with lust, you would believe these pictures with all your heart and many of the neighbouring organs. You would hand over a crumpled dollar and go inside, into a dusty tent that smelt of horse manure and rubbing alcohol and find on stage a weary stripper looking not unlike your own mother. It was the sort of disappointment from which you never really recover, and my heart went out now to the lonely sailors and Japanese photocopier salesmen who were down there drinking sweet, warm cocktails and having a night of overpriced disappointment. 'We learn from our mistakes,' I remarked sagely to myself with a rueful smile and told a panhandler to piss off.

I went back to my room, pleased not to have been mugged, more pleased not to have been murdered. On top of my television was a card saying that for $6.50 I could have an in-room movie. There was, as I recall, a choice of four – *Friday the Thirteenth Part 19*, in which a man with a personality disorder uses knives, hatchets, Magimixes and a snow blower to kill a succession of young women just as they are about to climb in the shower; *Death Wish II*, in which Charles Bronson tracks down and kills Michael Winner; *Bimbo*, in which Sylvester Stallone as Rambo has a sex-change operation and then blows up a lot of Oriental people; and, on the adult channel, *My Panties Are Dripping*, a sensitive study of interpersonal relationships and social conflict in post-modern Denmark, with a lot of vigorous bonking thrown in for good measure. I toyed for a moment with the idea of watching a bit of the last one – just to help me relax, as they say in evangelical circles – but I was too cheap to spend $6.50 and anyway I've always suspected that if I did punch the requisite button (which was worn to a nubbin, I can tell you), the next day a bellboy would confront me with a computer print-out and tell me that if I didn't give him $50 he would send a copy of the room receipt to my mother with 'Miscellaneous charges: Deviant Porno Movie, $6.50' circled in red. So instead I lay on the bed and watched a rerun on normal television of a 1960s comedy programme called *Mr Ed*, which was about a talking horse. Judging by the quality of the jokes, I would guess that Mr Ed wrote his own material. But at least there was nothing in it that would get me blackmailed.

And thus ended my day in New York, the most exciting and stimulating city in the world. I couldn't help but reflect that I had no reason to feel superior to my fellow lonely hearts in the strip-tease club twenty floors below. I was just as lonesome as they were. Indeed, all over this big, heartless city there were no doubt tens of thousands of people just as solitary and friendless as me. What a melancholy thought.

'But I wonder how many of them can do this?' I remarked to myself and with both hands and both feet reached out and touched all four walls at once.

Chapter fifteen

I T WAS THE Columbus Day weekend and the roads were busy. Columbus has always seemed to me an odd choice of hero for a country that celebrates success as America does, because he was such a dismal failure. Consider the facts: he made four long voyages to the Americas, but never once realized that he wasn't in Asia and never found anything worthwhile. Every other explorer was coming back with exciting new products like potatoes and tobacco and nylon stockings, and all Columbus found to bring home were some puzzled-looking Indians – and he thought they were Japanese. ('Come on, you guys, let's see a little sumo.')

But perhaps Columbus's most remarkable shortcoming was that he never actually saw the land that was to become the United States. This surprises a lot of people. They imagine him trampling over Florida, saying, 'You know, this would make a nice resort.' But in fact his voyages were all spent in the Caribbean and bouncing around the swampy, bug-infested coasts of Central America. If you ask me, the Vikings would make far more worthy heroes for America. For one thing, they did actually discover it. On top of that, the Vikings were manly and drank out of skulls and didn't take any crap from anybody. Now *that's* the American way.

When I lived in America Columbus Day was one of those semi-bogus holidays that existed only for the benefit of public workers with strong unions. There was no mail on Columbus Day and if you innocently drove all the way over to the east side of the town to the Iowa State Vehicle Licensing Center to renew your driver's licence you would find the door locked and a notice hanging in the window saying 'Closed for Columbus Day Holiday. So Tough Shit To You.' But otherwise life was no different than on any other day. Now, however, it appeared that the Columbus Day holiday had spread. There were lots of cars and recreational vehicles on the highway and the radio announcers kept talking about things like the number of fatalities that were expected 'this Columbus Day weekend'. (How do they know these things anyway? Is there some kind of a secret quota?) I had been looking forward to reaching New England because I wanted to see the autumn colour. In addition, the states would be small and varied and there wouldn't be that awful rolling tedium that comes with all the other American states, even the attractive ones. But I was wrong. Of course. New England states are indubitably tiny – Connecticut is only eighty miles across; Rhode Island is smaller than London – but they are crowded with cars, people and cities. Connecticut appeared to be just one suburb. I drove up US 202 towards Litchfield, which was marked on my map as a scenic route, and it was, to be sure, more scenic than suburb, but it wasn't exactly spectacular.

Perhaps I was expecting too much. In the movies in the 1940s people were always going to Connecticut for the weekend, and it always looked wonderfully green and rustic. It was always full of empty roads and stone cottages in leafy glades. But this was just semi-suburban: ranch-houses with three-car garages and lawns with twirling

195

sprinklers and shopping centres every six blocks. Litchfield itself was very handsome, the quintessential New England town, with an old courthouse and a long sloping green with a cannon and a memorial to the war dead. On one side of the green stood pleasant shops and on the other was a tall, white steepled church, dazzling in the October sunshine. And there was colour – the trees around the green were a rich gold and lemon. This was more like it.

I parked in front of MacDonald Drug and crossed the green through a scuffle of fallen leaves. I strolled along residential streets where big houses squatted on wide lawns. Each was a variation on the same theme: rambling clapboard with black shutters. Many had wooden plaques on them pertaining to their history – 'Oliver Boardman 1785'; '1830 Col. Webb'. I spent over an hour just poking around. It was a pleasant town for poking.

Afterwards I drove east, sticking to back highways. Soon I was in the suburbs of Hartford, and then in Hartford itself, and then in the suburbs on the other side of Hartford. And then I was in Rhode Island. I stopped beside a sign saying WELCOME TO RHODE ISLAND and stared at the map. Was that really all there was to Connecticut? I considered turning back and having another sweep across the state – there had to be more to it than that – but it was getting late, so I pressed on, venturing into a deep and rather more promising pine forest. Considering Rhode Island's microscopic size it seemed to take me ages to find my way out of the forest. By the time I hit Narragansett Bay, a heavily-islanded inlet which consumes almost a quarter of the state's modest square mileage, it was almost dark, and there were lights winking from the villages scattered along the shoreline.

At Plum Point a long bridge crossed the sound to Conanicut Island, which rode low and dark on the water, like a corpse. I crossed the bridge and drove around the island a little, but by now it was too dark to see much. At one place where the shore came in near the road, I parked and walked to the beach. It was a moonless night and I could hear the sea before I could see it, coming in with a slow, rhythmic whoosh-whoosh. I went and stood at the water's edge. The waves fell on to the beach like exhausted swimmers. The wind played at my jacket. I stared for a long time out across the moody sea, the black vastness of the Atlantic, the fearsome, primordial, storm-tossed depths from which all of life has crawled and will no doubt one day return, and I thought, 'I could murder a hamburger.'

In the morning I drove into Newport, America's premier yachting community, home of the America's Cup races. The old part of town had been fixed up in recent years, by the look of it. Shops with hanging wooden signs out front lined the streets. They all had jauntily nautical names like 'The Flying Ship' and 'Shore Thing'. The harbour was almost too picturesque, with its crowds of white yachts and bare masts undulating beneath a sky in which gulls danced and reeled. But all around the fringe of the downtown there were unsightly parking lots, and a busy four-lane road, more freeway than city street, divided the waterfront from the town. Spindly trees stood along it like scrawny afterthoughts. The city had also built a little park, Perrott Park, but it was unkempt and full of graffiti. I had not encountered this kind of neglect before. Most American towns are spotless and this really surprised me, especially considering the importance of tourism to New-port. I walked up Thames Street, where some fine old sea captains' homes were fighting a losing battle with litter and dog shit and the encroachment of gas stations and car transmission places. It was all very sad. This was a place where the people didn't seem to care, or perhaps just didn't notice, how shabby they had let things grow. It reminded me of London.

I drove out to Fort Adams State Park across the bay. From there Newport looked another town altogether – a charming cut-out of needle-shaped church spires and Victorian roof-tops protruding from a parkland of trees. The bay glittered in the sunshine and its scores of sail-boats bobbed on the gentle waves. It was captivating. I drove on along the shore road, past Brenton Point, and then down Bellevue Avenue, where the most fabulous summer homes ever built line the road on both sides and spill over on to many of the streets beyond.

Between about 1890 and 1905, America's richest fa-milies – the Vanderbilts, the Astors, the Belmonts, dozens of others – tried to outdo each other by building magni-ficent homes, which they insisted on calling cottages, all along this half-mile strip of imposing cliffs. Most were loosely modelled on French châteaux and filled with furniture, marble and tapestries shipped at huge expense from Europe. Hostesses routinely spent $300,000 or more on entertainment for a season that lasted only six or eight weeks. For forty years or so this was the world head-quarters of conspicuous consumption.

Most of the houses are now run as museums. They charge an arm and a leg to get in and in any case the queues outside most of them were enormous (this was the

Columbus Day weekend, remember). You can't see much from the street – the owners didn't want common people staring at them as they sat on the lawn counting their money, so they put up dense hedges and high walls – but I discovered quite by chance that the city had built an asphalt footpath all along the cliff edge, from which I could see the backs of the grander mansions, as well as enjoy giddying views of the ocean breaking onto the rocks far below. I had the path almost to myself and walked along it in a state of quiet amazement, with my mouth open. I had never seen such a succession of vast houses, such an excess of architecture. Every house looked like a cross between a wedding-cake and a state capitol building. I knew that the grandest of all the houses was The Breakers, built by the Vanderbilts, and I kept thinking, 'Well, *this* must be it' and 'Now surely *this* must be it,' but then the next house along would be even more awesome. When at last I reached The Breakers, it was absolutely enormous, a mountain with windows. You can't look at it without thinking that nobody, with the possible exception of oneself, deserves to be that rich.

On the other side of the fence, the lawns and terraces were full of pudgy tourists in Bermuda shorts and silly hats, wandering in and out of the house, taking pictures of each other and trampling the begonias, and I wondered what Cornelius Vanderbilt would make of that, the dog-faced old prick.

I drove on to Cape Cod, another place I had never been and for which I had high expectations. It was very picturesque, with its old saltbox homes, its antique shops and wooden inns, its pretty villages with quaint names:

199

Sagamore, Sandwich, Barnstable, Rock Harbor. But it was jam-packed with tourists in overloaded cars and rumbling motor homes. Boy, do I hate motor homes! Especially on crowded peninsulas like Cape Cod where they clog the streets and block the views – and all so that some guy and his dumpy wife can eat lunch and empty their bladders without stopping.

The traffic was so dense and slow-moving that I almost ran out of gas, and just managed to limp into a two-pump station outside West Barnstable. It was run by a man who was at least ninety-seven years old. He was tall and rangy and very spry. I've never seen anybody pump gas with such abandon. First he slopped a quantity of it down the side of the car and then he got so engaged in talking about where I came from – 'Ioway, eh? We don't get many from Ioway. I think you're the first this year. What's the weather like in Ioway this time of year?' – that he let the pump run over and I had to point out to him that gasoline was cascading down the side of the car and gathering in a pool at our feet. He withdrew the nozzle, sloshing another half-gallon over the car and down his trousers and shoes, and kind of threw it back at the pump, where it dribbled carelessly.

He had a cigarette butt plugged into the side of his mouth and I was terrified he would try to light it. And he did. He pulled out a crumpled book of matches and started to fidget one of them to life. I was too stunned to move. All I could think of was a television news-reader saying, 'And in West Barnstable today a tourist from Iowa suffered third degree burns over ninety-eight per cent of his body in an explosion at a gas station. Fire officials said he looked like a piece of toast that had been left under the grill too long. The owner of the gas station has still not been found.' But we didn't explode. The little stub of cigarette sprouted smoke, which the man puffed up into a good-sized billow, and then he pinched out the match with his fingers. I suppose after all these decades of pumping gas he had become more or less incombustible, like those snake handlers who grow immune to snake venom. But I wasn't inclined to test this theory too closely. I paid him hastily and pulled straight back onto the highway, much to the annoyance of a man in a forty-foot motor home who dripped mustard on his lap in braking to avoid me. 'That'll teach you to take a building on vacation,' I muttered uncharitably, and hoped that something heavy had fallen on his wife in the back.

Cape Cod is a long, thin peninsula that sprouts out of the base of Massachusetts, runs out to sea for twenty miles or so and then curls back in on itself. It looks like an arm flexed to make a muscle – in fact, it looks remarkably like my arm because there's almost no muscle in it. There are three roads along the lower part of the peninsula – one along the north shore, one along the south shore and one up the middle – but at the peninsula's elbow at Rock Harbor, where it narrows and abruptly turns north, the three roads come together and there is just one long slow highway up the forearm to Provincetown at the fingertips. Provincetown was swarming with tourists. The town has just one route in and one route out. Only a few hundred people live there, but they get as many as 50,000 visitors a day during the summer and at holiday weekends such as this one. Parking was not allowed in the town itself – there were mean-spirited tow-away warnings everywhere – so I paid a couple of bucks to leave my car with several hundred others out in the middle of nowhere and trudged a long way into town.

Provincetown is built on sand. All around it stand rolling dunes broken only by occasional clumps of straw-coloured grass. The names of the businesses – Windy Ridge Motel, Gale Force Gift Shop – suggested that wind might be something of a local feature, and indeed there was sand drifted across the roads and piled in the doorways, and with every whipping breeze it flew in your eyes and face and dusted whatever food you happened to be eating. It must be an awful place to live. I might have disliked it less if Provincetown had tried just a little harder to be charming. I had seldom seen a place so singularly devoted to sucking money out of tourists. It was filled with ice-cream parlours and gift shops and places selling T-shirts, kites and beach paraphernalia.

I walked around for a while and had a hot dog with mustard and sand and a cup of coffee with cream and sand and had a look in a window of a real estate agency, where I noticed that a basic two-bedroom house by the beach was on offer at $190,000, though it did include a fireplace and all the sand you could eat. The beaches looked nice enough, but apart from that I couldn't see a single real attraction in the place.

Provincetown is where the pilgrim fathers first touched American soil in 1620. There's a big campanile-type tower in the middle of the town to commemorate the event. The pilgrims, curiously enough, didn't mean to land on Cape Cod at all. They were aiming for Jamestown in Virginia, but missed their target by a mere 600 miles. I think that is a considerable achievement. Here's another curious thing: they didn't bring with them a single plough or horse or cow or even a fishing line. Does that strike you as just a little bit foolish? I mean to say, if you were going to start a new life in a land far, far away, don't you think you would give some thought to how you were going to fend for yourself once you got there? Still, for all their shortcomings as planners, the pilgrim fathers were sufficiently on the ball not to linger in the Provincetown area and at the first opportunity they pushed on to mainland Massachusetts. So did I.

I had hoped to go to Hyannis Port, where the Kennedys had their summer home, but the traffic was so slow, especially around Woods Hole, where the ferry to Martha's Vineyard departs, that I dared not. Every motel I passed – and there were hundreds – said No Vacancy. I got on Interstate 93, thinking I would follow it for a few miles just to get away from Cape Cod, and start looking for a room, but before I knew it I was in Boston, caught in the evening rush-hour. Boston's freeway system is insane. It was clearly designed by a person who had spent his childhood crashing toy trains. Every few hundred yards I would find my lane vanishing beneath me and other lanes merging with it from the right or left, or sometimes both. This wasn't a road system, it was mobile hysteria. Everybody looked worried. I had never seen people working so hard to keep from crashing into each other. And this was a Saturday – God knows what it must be like on a week-day.

Boston is a big city and its outer suburbs dribble on and on all the way up to New Hampshire. So, late in the evening, without having any clear idea of how I got there, I found myself in one of those placeless places that sprout up along the junctions of interstate highways – purplishly-lit islands of motels, gas stations, shopping centres and fast food places – so brightly lit they must be visible from outer space. This one was somewhere in the region of Haverhill. I got a room in a Motel 6 and dined on greasy fried chicken and limp French fries at a Denny's Restaurant across the way. It had been a bad day, but I refused to get depressed. Just a couple of miles down the road was New Hampshire and the start of the real New England. Things could only get better.

Chapter sixteen

I HAD ALWAYS thought that New England was nothing but maple trees and white churches and old guys in checked shirts sitting around iron stoves in country general stores swapping tall tales and spitting in the cracker barrel. But if lower New Hampshire was anything to go by, clearly I had been misinformed. There was just modern commercial squalor – shopping centres, gas stations, motels. Every once in a while there would be a white church or clapboard inn standing incongruously in the midst of Burger Kings and Texacos. But far from mollifying the ugliness, it only intensified it, reminding you what had been thrown away for the sake of drive-thru burgers and cheap gasoline.

At Salisbury, I joined old Route 1, intending to follow it up the coast through Maine. Route 1, as the name suggests, is the patriarch of American roads, the first federal highway. It stretches for 2,500 miles from the Canadian border to the Florida Keys. For forty years it was the main highway along the eastern seaboard, connecting all the big cities of the North – Boston, New York, Philadelphia, Baltimore, Washington – with the beaches and citrus groves of the South. It must have been wonderful in the 1930s and 1940s to drive from Maine to Florida on vacation, going through all those big marvellous cities and then passing on to the hills of Virginia and the green mountains of the Carolinas, getting warmer with the passing miles. But by the 1960s Route 1 had become too congested to be practical – a third of all Americans live within twenty miles of it – and Interstate 95 was built to zip traffic up and down the coast with only the most fleeting sense of a changing landscape. Today Route 1 is still there, but you would need weeks to drive its entire length. Now it is just a local road, an endless city street, an epic stretch of shopping malls.

I had hoped that here in rural New England it would retain something of its former charm, but it seemed not to. I drove through a chill morning drizzle and wondered if ever I would find the real New England. At Portsmouth, an instantly forgettable little town, I crossed over into Maine on an iron bridge over the grey Piscataqua River. Seen through the rhythmic swish of windscreen wipers, Maine too looked ominously unpromising, a further sprawl of shopping centres and muddy new housing developments.

Beyond Kennebunkport the suburbs at last gave way to forest. Here and there massive brown boulders emerged eerily from the earth, like subterranean creatures coming up for air, and occasionally I caught glimpses of the sea – a grey plain, cold and bleak. I drove and drove, thinking that any moment now I would encounter the fabled Maine of lobster-pots and surf-battered shores and lonely light-houses standing on rocks of granite, but the towns I passed through were just messy and drear, and the countryside was wooded and unmemorable. Once, outside Falmouth, the road ran for a mile or so along a silvery bay with a long, low bridge leading over it to a landscape of snug farms nestled in a fold of hills, and I got briefly excited. But it was a false alarm and the landscape quickly grew dull again. The rest of the time the real Maine eluded me. It was always just over there, like the amusement parks my dad used to miss.

At Wiscasset, a third of the way up the coast to New Brunswick, I lost heart altogether. Wiscasset bills itself on the signboard at the edge of town as the prettiest village in Maine, which doesn't say a whole lot for the rest of the state. I don't mean to suggest that Wiscasset was awful, because it wasn't. It had a steep main street lined with craft shops and other yuppie emporia sloping down to a placid inlet of the Atlantic. Two old wooden ships sat rotting on the bank. It was OK. It just wasn't worth driving four hours to get there.

Abruptly I decided to abandon Route 1 and plunge northward, into the dense pine forests of central Maine, heading in an irregular line for the White Mountains, on a road that went up and down, up and down, like a rucked carpet. After a few miles I began to sense a change of atmosphere. The clouds were low and shapeless, the daylight meagre. Winter clearly was closing in. I was only seventy miles or so from Canada and it was evident that winters here were long and severe. It was written in the crumbling roads and in the huge stacks of firewood that stood outside each lonely cabin. Many chimneys were already sprouting a wintry wisp of smoke. It was barely October, but already the land had the cold and lifeless feel of winter. It was the kind of atmosphere that makes you want to turn up your collar and head for home.

Just beyond Gilead I passed into New Hampshire and the landscape became more interesting. The White Mountains rose up before me, big and round, the colour of wood-ash. Presumably they take their name from the birch trees that cover them. I drove on an empty highway through a forest of trembling leaves. The skies were still flat and low, the weather cold, but at least I was out of the monotony of the Maine woods. The road rose and fell and swept along the edge of a boulder-strewn creek. The scenery was infinitely better – but still there was no colour, none of the brilliant golds and reds of autumn that I had been led to expect. Everything from the ground to the sky was a dull, cadaverous grey.

I drove past Mt Washington, the highest peak in the north-eastern US (6,288 feet, for those of you who are keeping notes). But its real claim to fame is as the windiest place in America. It's something to do with . . . well, with the way the wind blows, of course. Anyway, the highest wind speed ever recorded anywhere on earth was logged on the top of Mt Washington in April 1934 when a gust of – pencils ready? – 231 miles an hour whistled through. That must have been an experience and a half for the meteorologists who worked up there. Can you imagine trying to describe a wind like that to somebody? 'Well, it was, you know, real . . . *windy*. I mean, *really* windy. Do you know what I'm saying?' It must be very frustrating to have a truly unique experience.

Just beyond it, I came to Bretton Woods, which I had always pictured as a quaint little town. But in fact there was no town at all, just a hotel and a ski lift. The hotel was huge and looked like a medieval fortress, but with a bright red roof. It looked like a cross between Monte Cassino and a Pizza Hut. It was here in 1944 that economists and politicians from twenty-eight nations got together and agreed to set up the International Monetary Fund and the World Bank. It certainly looked a nice place to make economic history. As John Maynard Keynes remarked at the time in a letter to his brother, Milton: 'It has been a most satisfactory week. The negotiations have been cordial, the food here is superb and the waiters are ever so pretty.'

I stopped for the night at Littleton, which, as the name suggests, was a little town near the Vermont border. I pulled into the Littleton Motel on the main street. On the office door was a sign that said 'If you want ice or advice, come before 6.30. I'm taking the wife to dinner. ("And about time too!" – wife).' Inside was an old guy on crutches who told me I was very lucky because he had just one room left. It would be $42 plus tax. When he saw me start to froth and back off, he hastily added, 'It's a real nice room. Got a brand new TV. Nice carpets. Beautiful little shower. We've got the cleanest rooms in town. We're famous for that.' He swept an arm over a selection of testimonials from satisfied customers which he displayed under glass on the counter-top. 'Our room must have been the cleanest room in town!' – A.K., Aardvark Falls, Ky. 'Boy, was our room ever clean! And such nice carpets!' – Mr and Mrs J.F., Spotweld, Ohio. That sort of thing.

Somehow I doubted the veracity of these claims, but I was too weary to return to the road, so with a sigh I said all right and signed in. I took my key and a bucket of ice (at $42 plus tax I intended to have everything that was going) and went with them to my room. And by golly it *was* the cleanest room in town. The TV was brand new and the carpet was plush. The bed was comfortable and the shower really was a beauty. I felt instantly ashamed of myself and retracted all my bad thoughts about the proprietor. ('I was a pompous little shit to have doubted you.' – Mr B.B., Des Moines, Iowa.)

BILL BRYSON

I ate fourteen ice-cubes and watched the early evening news. This was followed by an old episode of *Gilligan's Island*, which the TV station had thoughtfully put on as an inducement to its non-brain-damaged viewers to get up immediately and go do something more useful. This I did. I went out and had a look around the town. The reason I had chosen to stop for the night at Littleton was that a book I had with me referred to it as picturesque. In point of fact, if Littleton was characterized by anything it was a singular lack of picturesqueness. The town consisted principally of one long street of mostly undistinguished buildings, with a supermarket parking lot in the middle and the shell of a disused gas station a couple of doors away. This, I think we can agree, does not constitute picturesqueness. Happily, the town had other virtues. For one thing, it was the friendliest little place I had ever seen. I went into the Topic of the Town restaurant. The other customers smiled at me, the lady at the cash register showed me where to put my jacket, and the waitress, a plump and dimpled little lady, couldn't do enough for me. It was as if they had all been given some kind of marvellous tranquillizer.

The waitress brought me a menu and I made the mistake of saying thank you. 'You're welcome,' she said. Once you start this there's no stopping. She came and wiped the table with a damp cloth. 'Thank you,' I said. 'You're welcome,' she said. She brought me some cutlery wrapped in a paper napkin. I hesitated, but I couldn't stop myself. 'Thank you,' I said. 'You're welcome,' she said. Then came a placemat with Topic of the Town written on it, and then a glass of water and then a clean ashtray, and then a little basket of Saltine crackers wrapped in cellophane, and at each we had our polite exchange. I ordered the fried chicken special. As I waited I become uncomfortably aware that the people at the next table were watching me and smiling at me in a deranged fashion. The waitress was watching me too, from a position by the kitchen doorway. It was all rather unnerving. Every few moments she would come over and top up my iced water and tell me that my food would only be a minute.

'Thank you,' I'd say.

'You're welcome,' she'd say.

Eventually the waitress came out of the kitchen with a tray the size of a table-top and started setting down plates of food in front of me – soup, salad, a platter of chicken, a basket of steaming rolls. It all looked delicious. Suddenly I realized that I was starving.

'Can I get you anything else?' she said.

'No, this is just fine, thank you,' I answered, knife and fork plugged in my fists, ready to lunge at the food.

'Would you like some ketchup?'

'No thank you.'

'Would you like a little more dressing for your salad?'

'No thank you.'

'Have you got enough gravy?'

There was enough gravy to drown a horse. 'Yes, plenty of gravy, thank you.'

'How about a cup of coffee?'

'Really, I'm fine.'

'You sure there's nothing I can do for you?'

'Well, you might just piss off and let me eat my dinner,' I wanted to say, but I didn't, of course. I just smiled sweetly and said no thank you and after a while she withdrew. But she stood with a pitcher of iced water and watched me closely the whole meal. Every time I took a sip of water, she would come forward and top up my glass. Once when I reached for the pepper, she misread my intentions and started forward with the water pitcher, but then had to retreat. After that, whenever my hands left the cutlery for any reason, I would semi-mime an explanation to her of what I was about to do – 'I'm just going to butter my roll now' – so that she wouldn't rush over to give me more water. And all the while the people at the next table watched me eat and smiled encouragingly. I couldn't wait to get out of there.

When at last I finished the waitress came over and offered me dessert. 'How about a piece of pie? We've got blueberry, blackberry, raspberry, boysenberry, huckleberry, whortleberry, cherry berry, hair berry, chuckberry and berry-berry.'

'Gosh, no thanks, I'm too full,' I said placing my hands on my stomach. I looked as if I had stuffed a pillow under my shirt.

'Well, how about some ice-cream? We've got chocolate chip, chocolate fudge, chocolate ripple, chocolate-vanilla fudge, chocolate nut fudge, chocolate marshmallow swirl, chocolate mint with fudge chips, and fudge nut with or without chocolate chips.'

'Have you got just plain chocolate?'

'No, I'm afraid there's not much call for that.'

'I don't think I'll have anything then.'

'Well, how about a piece of cake. We've got—'

'Really, no thank you.'

'A cup of coffee?'

'No thank you.'

'You sure now?'

'Yes, thank you.'

'Well, I'll just get you a little more water then,' and she was off for the water jug before I could get her to give me my bill. The people at the next table watched this with interest and smiled a smile that said 'We are completely off our heads. How are you?'

Afterwards, I had a walk around the town – that is to say, I walked up one side of the street and down the other. For the size of place it was a nice town. It had two bookstores, a picture gallery, a gift shop, a movie-house. People on the sidewalk smiled at me as I passed. This was beginning to worry me. Nobody, even in America, is *that* friendly. What did they want from me? Up at the far end of the street there was a BP service station, the first one I had seen in America. Feeling vaguely homesick for Blighty, I walked up to have a look at it and was disappointed to see that there wasn't anything particularly British about it. The guy behind the counter wasn't even wearing a turban. When he saw me looking in the window he smiled at me with the same strange, unsettling smile. Suddenly I realized what it was – it was the look of someone from outer space, that odd, curiously malevolent B-movie smile of a race of interplanetary creatures who have taken over a small town in the middle of nowhere as their first step towards becoming . . . *Earth Masters*. I know this sounds improbable, but crazier things have happened – look who was in the White House, for Christ's sake. As I strolled back to the motel, I gave everyone I passed that same eerie smile, thinking I ought to keep on their good side, just in case. 'And you never know,' I remarked to myself in a low voice, 'if they do take over the planet, there might be some openings for a guy of your talents.'

*   *   *

In the morning I got up very early to a day that promised splendour. I peered out of my motel window. A pink dawn was spilled across the sky. I dressed quickly and hit the road before Littleton had even begun to stir. A few miles out of town I crossed the state line. Vermont presented an altogether greener, tidier prospect than New Hampshire. The hills were fat and soft, like a sleeping animal. The scattered farms looked more prosperous and the meadows climbed high up the rolling hillsides, giving the valleys an alpine air. The sun was soon high and warm. On a ridge overlooking an expanse of hazy foothills, I passed a sign that said PEACHAM, SETTLED 1776 and beyond that stood a village. I parked beside a red general store and got out to have a look around. There was no-one about. Presumably the people of Littleton had come in the night and taken them off to the planet Zog.

I walked past the Peacham Inn – white clapboard, green shutters, no sign of life – and wandered up a hill, past a white Congregational church and pleasant, dozing houses. At the crest of the hill stood a broad green, with an obelisk and flagpole, and beside it an old cemetery. A zephyr wind teased the flag. Down the hill, across a broad valley, a series of pale green and brown hills rolled away to the horizon, like the swells of a sea. Below me the church bell tolled the hour, but otherwise there was not a sound. This was as perfect a spot as I had ever seen. I had a look at the obelisk. COMMEMORATING PEACHAM SOLDIERS 1869, it said, and had names carved in it, good New England names like Elijah W. Sargent, Lowell Sterns, Horace Rowe. There were forty-five names in all, too many surely for a mere hamlet in the hills. But then the cemetery beside the green also looked far too large for the size of the town. It covered the hillside and the grandeur of many of the monuments suggested that this had once been a place of wealth.

I went through the gate and had a look around. My eye was caught by one particularly handsome stone, an octagonal marble column surmounted by a granite sphere. The column logged the copious deaths of Hurds and their near relatives from Capt. Nathan Hurd in 1818 to Frances H. Bement in 1889. A small panel on the back said:

Nathan H. died July 24 1852 AE. 4 Y's 1 M'o.

Joshua F. died July 31 1852 AE. 1 YR 11 M's.

Children of J. & C. Pitkin.

What could it have been, I wondered, that carried off these two little brothers just a week apart? A fever? It seemed unlikely in July. An accident in which one died and the other lingered? Two unrelated events? I pictured the parents crouched at Joshua F.'s beside, watching his life ebb, praying to God not to take him as well, and having their hopes crushed. Isn't life shitty? Everywhere I looked there was disappointment and heartbreak recorded in the stones: 'Joseph, son of Ephraim and Sarah Carter, died March 18 1846, aged 18 yrs', 'Alma Foster, daut. of Zadock and Hannah Richardson, d. May 22, 1847, AE. 17 yrs'. So many were so young. I became infected with an inexpressible melancholy as I wandered alone among these hundreds of stilled souls, the emptied lives, the row upon row of ended dreams. Such a sad place! I stood there in the mild October sunshine, feeling so sorry for all these luckless people and their lost lives, reflecting bleakly on mortality and on my own dear, cherished family so far away in England, and I thought, 'Well, fuck this,' and walked back down the hill to the car.

*   *   *

215

I drove west across Vermont, into the Green Mountains. The mountains were dark and round and the valleys looked rich. Here the light seemed softer, sleepier, more autumnal. There was colour everywhere – trees the colour of mustard and rust, meadows of gold and green, colossal white barns, blue lakes. Here and there along the roadside, produce stands brimmed with pumpkins and squash and other autumn fruits. It was like a day trip to heaven. I wandered around on back roads. There was a surprising lot of small houses, some little better than shacks. I supposed there couldn't be much work in a place like Vermont. The state has hardly any towns or industry. The biggest city, Burlington, has a population of just 37,000. Outside Groton I stopped at a roadside café for coffee and listened along with the other three customers to a fat young woman with a pair of ill-kempt children moaning in a loud voice about her financial problems to the woman behind the counter. 'I still only get four dollars an hour,' she was saying. 'Harvey, he's been at Fibberts for three years and he's only just got his first raise. You know what he gets now? Four dollars and sixty-five cents an hour. Isn't that pathetic? I told him, I said, "Harvey, they're just walkin' all over you." But he won't do nothin' about it.' She broke off here to rearrange the features on one of her children's faces with the back of her hand. 'HOW MANY TIMES HAVE I TOLD YOU NOT TO INNARUP ME WHEN I'M *TALKING*?' she enquired rhetorically of the little fellow, and then in a calmer voice turned back to the café lady and launched into a candid list of Harvey's other shortcomings, which were manifold.

Only the day before in Maine I had been in a McDonald's offering a starting wage of $5 an hour. Harvey must have been immensely moronic and unskilled – doubtless both – not to be able to keep pace with a sixteen-year-old burger jockey at McDonald's. Poor guy! And on top of that here he was married to a woman who was slovenly, indiscreet, and had a butt like a barn door. I hoped old Harvey had sense enough to appreciate all the incredible natural beauty with which God had blessed his native state because it didn't sound as if He had blessed Harvey very much. Even his kids were ugly as sin. I was half tempted to give one of them a clout myself as I went out of the door. There was just something about his nasty little face that made you itch to smack him.

I drove on, thinking what an ironic thing it was that the really beautiful places in America – the Smoky Mountains, Appalachia, and now Vermont – were always inhabited by the poorest, most under-educated people. And then I hit Stowe and realized that when it comes to making shrewd generalizations, I am a cretin. Stowe was anything but poor. It was a rich little town, full of chichi boutiques and expensive ski lodges. In fact, for most of the rest of the day, as I wandered around and through the Green Mountain ski resorts, I saw almost nothing but wealth and beauty – rich people, rich houses, rich cars, rich resorts, beautiful scenery. I drove around quite struck by it all, wandered over to Lake Champlain – also immensely beautiful – and idled down the western side of the state, just over the border from New York State.

Below Lake Champlain the landscape became more open, more rolling, as if the hills had been flattened out from the edges, like someone pulling a crease out of a bedspread. Some of the towns and villages were staggeringly pretty. Dorset, for instance, was an exquisite

BILL BRYSON

little place, standing around an oval green, full of beautiful white clapboard houses, with a summer play-house and an old church and an enormous inn. And yet. And yet there was something about these places. They were too perfect, too rich, too yuppified. At Dorset there was a picture shop called the Dorset Framery. At Bennington, just down the road, I passed a place called the Publyk House Restaurant. Every inn and lodge had a quaint and picturesque name – the Black Locust Inn, the Hob Knob, the Blueberry Inn, the Old Cutter Inn – and a hanging wooden sign out front. There was always this air of twee artifice pushing in on everything. After a while I began to find it oddly oppressive. I longed to see a bit of neon and a restaurant with a good old family name – Ernie's Chop House, Zweiker's New York Grille – with a couple of blinking beer signs in the front window. A bowling alley or drive-in movie theatre would have been most welcome. It would have made it all seem real. But this looked as if it had been designed in Manhattan and brought in by truck.

One village I went through had about four stores and one of them was a Ralph Lauren Polo Shop. I couldn't think of anything worse than living in a place where you could buy a $200 sweater but not a can of baked beans. Actually, I could think of a lot of worse things – cancer of the brain, watching every episode of a TV mini-series starring Joan Collins, having to eat at a Burger Chef more than twice in one year, reaching for a glass of water in the middle of the night and finding that you've just taken a drink from your grandmother's denture cup, and so on. But I think you get my point.

Chapter seventeen

I SPENT THE NIGHT in Cobleskill, New York, on the northern fringes of the Catskills, and in the morning drove to Cooperstown, a small resort on Lake Otsego. Cooperstown was the home of James Fenimore Cooper, from whose family the town takes its name. It was a handsome town, as handsome as any I had seen in New England, and more replete with autumn colour, with a main street of square-topped brick buildings, old banks, a movie theatre, family stores. The Cooperstown Diner, where I went for breakfast, was busy, friendly and cheap – all that a diner should be. Afterwards I went for a stroll around the residential streets, shuffling hands-in-pockets through the dry leaves, and down to the lakeside. Every house in town was old and pretty; many of the larger ones had been converted into inns and expensive B & Bs. The morning sunlight filtered through the trees and threw shadows across the lawns and sidewalks. This was as nice a little town as I had seen on the trip; it was almost Amalgam.

The only shortcoming with Cooperstown is that it is full of tourists, drawn to the town by its most famous institution, the Baseball Hall of Fame, which stands by a shady park at the far end of Main Street. I went there now, paid $8.50 admission and walked into its cathedral-like calm. For those of us who are baseball fans and agnostics, the

Hall of Fame is as close to a religious experience as we may ever get. I walked serenely through its quiet and softly-lit halls, looking at the sacred vestments and venerated relics from America's national pastime. Here, beautifully preserved in a glass case, was 'the shirt worn by Warren Spahn when registering win No. 305, which tied him with Eddie Plank for most by a left-hander.' Across the aisle was 'the glove used by Sal Maglie on September 25, 1958, no-hitter vs Phillies.' At each case people gazed reverently or spoke in whispers.

One room contained a gallery of paintings commemorating great moments in baseball history, including one depicting the first professional night game under artificial lighting played in Des Moines, Iowa, on May 2, 1930. This was exciting news to me. I had no idea that Des Moines had played a pivotal role in the history of both baseball and luminescence. I looked closely to see if the artist had depicted my father in the press-box, but then I realized that my father was only fifteen years old in 1930 and still in Winfield. This seemed kind of a pity.

In an upstairs room I suppressed a whoop of joy at the discovery of whole cases full of the baseball cards that my brother and I had so scrupulously collected and catalogued, and which my parents, in an early flirtation with senility, had taken to the dump during an attic spring-cleaning in 1981. We had the complete set for 1959 in mint condition; it is now worth something like $1,500. We had Mickey Mantle and Yogi Berra as rookies, Ted Williams from the last year he hit .400, the complete New York Yankees teams for every year between 1956 and 1962. The whole collection must have been worth something like $8,000 – enough, at any rate, to have sent

Mom and Dad for a short course of treatment at a dementia clinic. But never mind! We all make mistakes. It's only because everyone throws these things out that they grow so valuable for the lucky few whose parents don't spend their retirements getting rid of all the stuff they spent their working lives accumulating. Anyway it was a pleasure to see all the old cards again. It was like visiting a friend in hospital.

The Hall of Fame is surprisingly large, much larger than it looks from the road, and extremely well presented. I wandered through it in a state of complete contentment, reading every label, lingering at every display, reliving my youth, cocooned in a happy nostalgia, and when I stepped back out on to Main Street and glanced at my watch I was astonished to discover that three hours had elapsed.

Next door to the Hall of Fame was a shop selling the most wonderful baseball souvenirs. In my day all we could get were pennants and baseball cards and crummy little pens in the shape of baseball bats that stopped working about the second time you tried to sign your name with them. But now little boys could get everything with their team's logo on it – lamps, towels, clocks, throw rugs, mugs, bedspreads and even Christmas tree ornaments, plus of course pennants, baseball cards and pens that stop working about the second time you use them. I don't think I have ever felt such a pang of longing to be a child again. Apart from anything else, it would mean I'd get my baseball cards back and I could put them somewhere safe where my parents couldn't get at them; then when I got to my age I could buy a Porsche.

I was so taken with all the souvenirs that I began to fill my arms with stuff, but then I noticed that the store was full of Do Not Touch signs and on the counter by the cash register had been taped a notice that said 'Do Not Lean on Glass – If You Break, Cost to You Is $50.' What a jerky thing to say on a sign. How could you expect kids to come into a place full of wonderful things like this and not touch them? This so elevated my hackles that I deposited my intended purchases on the counter and told the girl I didn't want them after all. This was perhaps just as well because I'm not altogether sure that my wife would have wanted St Louis Cardinals pillowcases.

My ticket to the Hall of Fame included admission to a place on the edge of town called the Farmers Museum, where a couple of dozen old buildings – a schoolhouse, a tavern, a church and the like – have been preserved on a big site. It was about as exciting as it sounds, but having bought the ticket I felt obliged to go and have a look at it. If nothing else, the walk through the afternoon sunshine was pleasant. But I was relieved to get back in the car and hit the road again. It was after four by the time I left town. I drove on across New York State for several hours, through the Susquehanna Valley, which was very fetching, especially at this time of day and year in the soft light of an autumn afternoon: watermelon-shaped hills, golden trees, slumbering towns. To make up for my long day in Cooperstown, I drove later than usual, and it was after nine by the time I stopped at a motel on the outskirts of Elmira.

I went straight out for dinner, but almost every place I approached was closed, and I ended up eating in a restaurant attached to a bowling alley – in clear violation of Bryson's third rule of dining in a strange town. Generally, I don't believe in doing things on principle – it's kind of a principle of mine – but I do have six rules of public dining to which I try to adhere. They are:

1. Never eat in a restaurant that displays photographs of the food it serves. (But if you do, never believe the photographs.)
2. Never eat in a restaurant with flock wallpaper.
3. Never eat in a restaurant attached to a bowling alley.
4. Never eat in a restaurant where you can hear what they are saying in the kitchen.
5. Never eat in a restaurant that has live entertainers with any of the following words in their titles: Hank, Rhythm, Swinger, Trio, Combo, Hawaiian, Polka.
6. Never eat in a restaurant that has blood-stains on the walls.

In the event, the bowling-alley restaurant proved quite acceptable. Through the wall I could hear the muffled rumblings of falling bowling-pins and the sounds of Elmira's hairdressers and grease monkeys having a happy night out. I was the only customer in the restaurant. In fact, I was quite clearly the only thing standing between the waitresses and their going home. As I waited for my food, they cleared away the other tables, removed the ashtrays, sugar-bowls and table-cloths, so that after a while I found myself dining alone in a large room, with a white table-cloth and flickering candle in a little red bowl, amid a sea of barren formica table-tops.

The waitresses stood against the wall and watched me chew my food. After a while they started whispering and tittering, still watching me as they did so, which frankly I found a trifle unsettling. I may only have imagined it, but I

223

also had the distinct impression that someone was little by little turning a dimmer switch so that the light in the room was gradually disappearing. By the end of my meal I was finding my food more or less by touch and occasionally by lowering my head to the plate and sniffing. Before I was quite finished, when I just paused for a moment to grope for my glass of iced water somewhere in the gloom beyond the flickering candle, my waitress whipped the plate away and put down my bill.

'You want anything else?' she said in a tone that suggested I had better not. 'No thank you,' I answered politely. I wiped my mouth with the table-cloth, having lost my napkin in the gloom, and added a seventh rule to my list: never go into a restaurant ten minutes before closing time. Still, I never really mind bad service in a restaurant. It makes me feel better about not leaving a tip.

In the morning I woke early and experienced that sinking sensation that overcomes you when you first open your eyes and realize that instead of a normal day ahead of you, with its scatterings of simple gratifications, you are going to have a day without even the tiniest of pleasures; you are going to drive across Ohio.

I sighed and got up. I shuffled around the room in my old man posture, gathered up my things, washed, dressed and without enthusiasm hit the highway. I drove west through the Alleghenies and then into a small, odd corner of Pennsylvania. For 200 miles the border between New York and Pennsylvania is a straight line, but at its north-western corner, where I was now, it abruptly juts north, as if the draughtsman's arm had been jogged. The reason for this small cartographical irregularity was to let Pennsylvania have its own outlet on to Lake Erie so that it wouldn't have to cross New York State, and it remains today a 200-year-old reminder of how the early states weren't at all confident that the union was going to work. That it did was far more of an achievement than is often appreciated nowadays.

Just inside the Pennsylvania state line, the highway merged with Interstate 90. This is the main northern route across America, stretching 3,016 miles from Boston to Seattle, and there were lots of long-distance travellers on it. You can always tell long-distance travellers because they look as if they haven't been out of the car for weeks. You only glimpse them when they pass, but you can see that they have already started to set up home inside – there are pieces of washing hanging in the back, remnants of takeaway meals on the window-sill, and books, magazines and pillows scattered around. There's always a fat woman asleep in the front passenger seat, her mouth hugely agape, and a quantity of children going crazy in the back. You and the father exchange dull but not unsympathetic looks as the two cars slide past. You glance at each other's licence plates and feel envy or sympathy in proportion to your comparative distances from home. One car I saw had Alaska plates on it. This was unbelievable. I had never seen Alaska licence plates before. The man must have driven over 4,500 miles, the equivalent of going from London to Zambia. He was the most forlorn looking character I had ever seen. There was no sign of a wife and children. I expect by now he had killed them and put their bodies in the trunk.

A drizzly rain hung in the air. I drove along in that state of semi-mindlessness that settles over you on interstate

225

highways. After a while Lake Erie appeared on the right. Like all the Great Lakes, it is enormous, more an inland sea than a lake, stretching 200 miles from west to east and about forty miles across. Twenty-five years ago Lake Erie was declared dead. Driving along its southern shore, gazing out at its flat grey immensity, this appeared to be a remarkable achievement. It hardly seemed possible that something as small as man could kill something as large as a Great Lake. But just in the space of a century or so we managed it. Thanks to lax factory laws and the triumph of greed over nature in places like Cleveland, Buffalo, Toledo, Sandusky and other bustling centres of soot and grit, Lake Erie was transformed in just three generations from a bowl of blue water into a large toilet. Cleveland was the worst offender. Cleveland was so vile that its river, a slow-moving sludge of chemicals and half-digested solids called the Cuyahoga, once actually caught fire and burned out of control for four days. This also was a remarkable achievement, I feel. Things are said to be better now. According to a story in the *Cleveland Free Press*, which I read during a stop for coffee near Ashtabula, an official panel with the ponderous title of the International Joint Commission's Great Lakes Water Quality Board had just released a survey of chemical substances in the lake, and it had found only 362 types of chemical compared with more than a thousand the last time they had counted. That still seemed an awful lot to me and I was surprised to see a pair of fishermen standing on the shore, hunched down in the drizzle, hurling lines out on to the greenish murk with long poles. Maybe they were fishing for chemicals.

Through dull rain I drove through the outer suburbs of Cleveland, past signs for places that were all called Something Heights: Richmond Heights, Maple Heights, Garfield Heights, Shaker Heights, University Heights, Warrensville Heights, Parma Heights. Curiously the one outstanding characteristic of the surrounding landscape was its singular lack of eminences. Clearly what Cleveland was prepared to consider the heights was what others would regard as distinctly middling. Somehow this did not altogether surprise me. After a time Interstate 90 became the Cleveland Memorial Shoreway, and followed the sweep of the bay. The windscreen wipers of the Chevette flicked hypnotically and other cars threw up spray as they swished past. Outside my window the lake sprawled dark and vast until it was consumed by a distant mist. Ahead of me the tall buildings of downtown Cleveland appeared and slid towards me, like shopping on a supermarket conveyor belt.

Cleveland has always had a reputation for being a dirty, ugly, boring city, though now they say it is much better. By 'they' I mean reporters from serious publications like the *Wall Street Journal*, *Fortune* and the *New York Times Sunday Magazine*, who visit the city at five-yearly intervals and produce long stories with titles like 'Cleveland Bounces Back' and 'Renaissance in Cleveland'. No-one ever reads these articles, least of all me, so I couldn't say whether the improbable and highly relative assertion that Cleveland is better now than it used to be is wrong or right. What I can say is that the view up the Cuyahoga as I crossed it on the freeway was of a stew of smoking factories that didn't look any too clean or handsome. And I can't say that the rest of the town looked such a knock-out either. It may be improved, but all this talk of renaissance is clearly exaggerated. I somehow doubt that if the Duc d'Urbino were

227

brought back to life and deposited in downtown Cleveland he would say, 'Goodness, I am put in mind of fifteenth-century Florence and the many treasures therein.'

And then, quite suddenly, I was out of Cleveland and on the James W. Shocknessy Ohio Turnpike in the rolling rural emptiness between Cleveland and Toledo, and highway mindlessness once more seeped in. To relieve the tedium I switched on the radio. In fact, I had been switching it on and off all day, listening for a while but then giving up in despair. Unless you have lived through it, you cannot conceive of the sense of hopelessness that comes with hearing *Hotel California* by the Eagles for the fourteenth time in three hours. You can feel your brain cells disappearing with little popping sounds. But it's the disc jockeys that make it intolerable. Can there anywhere be a breed of people more irritating and imbecilic than disc jockeys? In South America there is a tribe of Indians called the Janamanos, who are so backward they cannot even count to three. Their counting system goes: 'One, two . . . oh, gosh, a whole bunch.' Obviously disc jockeys have a better dress sense and possess a little more in the way of social skills, but I think we are looking at a similar level of mental acuity.

Over and over I searched the airwaves for something to listen to, but I could find nothing. It wasn't as if I was asking for all that much. All I wanted was a station that didn't play endless songs by bouncy prepubescent girls, didn't employ disc jockeys who said 'H-e-y-y-y-y' more than once every six seconds and didn't keep telling me how much Jesus loved me. But no such station existed. Even when I did find something half-way decent, the sound would begin to fade after ten or twelve miles, and the old Beatles song that I was listening to with quiet pleasure would gradually be replaced by a semi-demented man talking about the word of God and telling me that I had a friend in the Lord.

Many American radio stations, particularly out in the hinterland, are ridiculously small and cheap. I know this for a fact because when I was a teenager I used to help out at KCBC in Des Moines. KCBC had the contract to broadcast the Iowa Oaks professional baseball games, but it was too cheap to send its sports-caster, a nice young guy named Steve Shannon, on the road with the team. So whenever the Oaks were in Denver or Oklahoma City or wherever, Shannon and I would go out to the KCBC studio – really just a tin hut standing beside a tall transmitter tower in a farmer's field somewhere south-east of Des Moines – and he would broadcast from there as if he were in Omaha. It was bizarre. Every couple of innings someone at the ballpark would call me on the phone and give me a bare summary of the game, which I would scribble into a scorebook and pass to Shannon, and on the basis of this he would give a two-hour broadcast.

It was a remarkable experience to sit there in a windowless hut on a steaming August night listening to the crickets outside and watching a man talking into a microphone and saying things like, 'Well, it's a cool evening here in Omaha, with a light breeze blowing in off the Missouri River. There's a special guest in the crowd tonight, Governor Warren T. Legless, who I can see sitting with his pretty young wife, Bobbie Rae, in a box seat just below us here in the press-box.' Shannon was a genius at this sort of thing. I remember one time the phone call from the ballpark didn't come through – the guy at the other end had gotten locked in a toilet or something – and Shannon didn't have anything to tell the listeners. So he delayed the game with a sudden downpour, having only a moment before said it was a beautiful cloudless evening, and played music while he called the ballpark and begged somebody there to let him know what was going on. Funnily enough, I later read that the exact same thing had happened to Ronald Reagan when he was a young sports-caster in Des Moines. Reagan responded by having the batter do a highly improbable thing – hit foul balls one after the other for over half an hour – while pretending that there was nothing implausible about it, which when you think about it is kind of how he ran the country as President.

Late in the afternoon, I happened on to a news broadcast by some station in Crudbucket, Ohio, or some such place. American radio news broadcasts usually last about thirty seconds. It went like this: 'A young Crudbucket couple, Dwayne and Wanda Dreary, and their seven children, Ronnie, Lonnie, Connie, Donnie, Bonnie, Johnny and Tammy-Wynette, were killed in a fire after a light airplane crashed into their house and burst into flames. Fire Chief Walter Embers said he could not at this stage rule out arson. On Wall Street, shares had their biggest one-day fall in history, losing 508 points. And the weather outlook for greater Crudbucket: clear skies with a two per cent chance of precipitation. You're listening to radio station K-R-U-D where you get more rock and less talk.' There then followed *Hotel California* by the Eagles.

I stared at the radio, wondering whether I had heard that second item right. The biggest one-day fall in shares in history? The collapse of the American economy? I twirled the dial and found another news broadcast: '. . . but Senator Poontang denied that the use of the four Cadillacs and the trips to Hawaii were in any way connected with the $120 million contract to build the new airport. On Wall Street, shares suffered their biggest one-day fall in history, losing 508 points in just under three hours. And the weather outlook here in Crudbucket is for cloudy skies and a ninety-eight per cent chance of precipitation. We'll have more music from the Eagles after this word.'

The American economy was coming apart in shreds and all I could get were songs by the Eagles. I twirled and twirled the dial, thinking that surely somebody some-where must be giving the dawn of a new Great Depression more than a passing mention – and someone was, thank goodness. It was CBC, the Canadian network, with an excellent and thoughtful programme called *As It Happens*, which was entirely devoted that evening to the crash of Wall Street. I will leave you, reader, to consider the irony in an American citizen, travelling across his own country, having to tune in to a foreign radio network to find out the details of one of the biggest domestic news stories of the year. To be scrupulously fair, I was later told that the public service network in America – possibly the most under-funded broadcast organization in the developed world – also devoted a long report to the crash. I expect it was given by a man sitting in a tin hut in a field somewhere, reading scribbled notes off a sheet of paper.

At Toledo, I joined Interstate 75, and drove north into Michigan, heading for Dearborn, a suburb of Detroit, where I intended spending the night. Almost immediately I found myself in a wilderness of warehouses and railroad tracks and enormous parking lots leading to distant car factories. The parking lots were so vast and full of cars that I half wondered if the factories were there just to produce sufficient cars to keep the parking lots full, thus eliminating any need for consumers. Interlacing all this were towering electricity pylons. If you have ever wondered what becomes of all those pylons you see marching off to the horizon in every country in the world, like an army of invading aliens, the answer is that they all join up in a field just north of Toledo, where they discharge their loads into a vast estate of electrical transformers, diodes and other contraptions that look for all the world like the inside of a television set, only on a rather grander scale, of course. The ground fairly thrummed as I drove past and I fancied I felt a crackle of blue static sweep through the car, briefly enlivening the hair on the back of my neck and leaving a strangely satisfying sensation in my armpits. I was half inclined to turn around at the next intersection and go back for another dose. But it was late and I pressed on. For some minutes I thought I smelled smouldering flesh and kept touching my head tentatively. But this may only have been a consequence of having spent too many lonely hours in a car.

At Monroe, a town halfway between Toledo and Detroit, a big sign beside the highway said WELCOME TO MONROE – HOME OF GENERAL CUSTER. A mile or so later there was another sign, even larger, saying MONROE, MICHIGAN – HOME OF LA-Z-BOY FURNITURE. Goodness, I thought, will the excitement never stop? But it did, and the rest of the journey was completed without drama.

Chapter eighteen

I SPENT THE NIGHT in Dearborn for two reasons. First, it would mean not having to spend the night in Detroit, the city with the highest murder rate in the country. In 1987, there were 635 homicides in Detroit, a rate of 58.2 per 100,000 people, or eight times the national average. Just among children, there were 365 shootings in which both the victims and gunmen were under sixteen. We are talking about a tough city – and yet it is still a rich one. What it will become like as the American car industry collapses in upon itself doesn't bear thinking about. People will have to start carrying bazookas for protection.

My second and more compelling reason for going to Dearborn was to see the Henry Ford Museum, a place my father had taken us when I was small and which I remembered fondly. After breakfast in the morning, I went straight there. Henry Ford spent his later years buying up important Americana by the truckload and crating it to his museum, beside the big Ford Motor Company Rouge Assembly Plant. The car-park outside the museum was enormous – on a scale to rival the factory car-parks I had passed the day before – but at this time of year there were few cars in it. Most of them were Japanese.

I went inside and discovered without surprise that the entrance charge was steep: $15 for adults and $7.50 for children. Americans are clearly prepared to fork out large sums for their pleasures. Grudgingly I paid the admission charge and went in. But almost from the moment I passed through the portals I was enthralled. For one thing, the scale of it is almost breathtaking. You find yourself in a great hangar of a building covering twelve acres of ground and filled with the most indescribable assortment of stuff – machinery, railway trains, refrigerators, Abraham Lincoln's rocking-chair, the limousine in which John F. Kennedy was killed (nope, no bits of brain on the floor), George Washington's campaign chest, General Tom Thumb's ornate miniature billiard-table, a bottle containing Thomas Edison's last breath. I found this last item particularly captivating. Apart from being ridiculously morbid and sentimental, how did they know which breath was going to be Edison's last one? I pictured Henry Ford standing at the death-bed shoving a bottle in his face over and over and saying, 'Is that it?'

This was the way the Smithsonian once was and still should be – a cross between an attic and a junk shop. It was as if some scavenging genius had sifted through all the nation's collective memories and brought to this one place everything from American life that was splendid and fine and deserving fondness. It was possible here to find every single item from my youth – old comic books, lunch pails, bubble gum cards, *Dick and Jane* reading books, a Hotpoint stove just like the one my mom used to have, a soda pop dispenser like the one that used to stand in front of the pool hall in Winfield.

There were even a collection of milk bottles exactly like those that Mr Morrisey, the deaf milkman, used to bring to our house every morning. Mr Morrisey was the noisiest milkman in America. He was about sixty years old and wore a large hearing-aid. He always travelled with his faithful dog Skipper. They would arrive like clockwork just before dawn. Milk had to be delivered early, you see, because in the Midwest it spoiled quickly once the sun came up. You always knew when it was 5.30 because Mr Morrisey would arrive, whistling for all he was worth, waking all the dogs for blocks around, which would get Skipper very excited and set him to barking. Being deaf, Mr Morrisey tended not to notice his own voice and you could hear him clinking around on your back porch with his rack of milk bottles and saying to Skipper, 'WELL, I WONDER WHAT THE BRYSONS WANT TODAY! LET'S SEE . . . FOUR QUARTS OF SKIMMED AND SOME COTTAGE CHEESE. WELL, SKIPPER, WOULD YOU FUCKING BELIEVE IT, I LEFT THE COTTAGE CHEESE ON THE GOD DAMN TRUCK!' And then you would look out the window to see Skipper urinating on your bicycle and lights coming on in houses all over the neighbourhood. Nobody wanted to get Mr Morrisey fired, on account of his unfortunate disability, but when Flynn Dairies discontinued home deliveries in about 1960 on economic grounds ours was one of the few neighbourhoods in the city from which there was no outcry.

I walked through the museum in a state of sudden, deep admiration for Henry Ford and his acquisitive instincts. He may have been a bully and an anti-Semite, but he sure could build a nifty museum. I could happily have spent hours picking around among the memorabilia. But the hangar is only a fractional part of it. Outside there is a whole village – a little town – containing eighty homes of famous Americans. These are the actual homes, not replicas. Ford criss-crossed the country acquiring the

residences and workshops of the people he most admired
– Thomas Edison, Harvey Firestone, Luther Burbank, the
Wright brothers and of course himself. All these he crated
up and shipped back to Dearborn where he used them to
build this 250-acre fantasy land – the quintessential American small town, a picturesque and timeless community
where every structure houses a man of genius (almost
invariably a white, Christian man of genius from the
Middle West). Here in this perfect place, with its broad
greens and pleasing shops and churches, the lucky resident
could call on Orville and Wilbur Wright for a bicycle inner
tube, go to the Firestone farm for milk and eggs (but not
for rubber yet – Harvey's still working on it!), borrow a
book from Noah Webster and call on Abraham Lincoln for
legal advice, always assuming he's not too busy with
patent applications for Charles Steinmetz or emancipating
George Washington Carver, who lives in a tiny cabin just
across the street.

It is really quite entrancing. For a start, places like
Edison's workshop and the boarding-house where his
employees lodged have been scrupulously preserved.
You can really see how these people worked and lived.
And there is a certain undeniable convenience in having
the houses all brought together. Who in a million years
would go to Columbiana, Ohio, to see the Harvey Firestone birthplace, or to Dayton to see where the Wright
brothers lived? Not me, brother. Above all, bringing these
places together makes you realize just how incredibly
inventive America has been in its time, what a genius it
has had for practical commercial innovation, often leading
to unspeakable wealth, and how many of the comforts and
pleasures of modern life have their roots in the small

towns of the American Middle West. It made me feel proud.

I drove north and west across Michigan lost in a warm after-glow of pleasure from the museum. I was past Lansing and Grand Rapids and entering the Manistee National Forest, 100 miles away, almost before I knew it. Michigan is shaped like an oven mitt and is often about as exciting. The Manistee forest was dense and dull – endless groves of uniform pine trees – and the highway through it was straight and flat. Occasionally I would see a cabin or little lake in the woods, both just glimpsable through the trees, but mostly there was nothing of note. Towns were rare and mostly squalid – scattered dwellings and ugly prefab buildings where they made and sold ugly prefab cabins, so that people could buy their own little bit of ugliness and take it out into the woods.

After Baldwin, the road became wider and emptier and the commercialism grew sparser. At Manistee, the highway ran down to Lake Michigan, and then followed the shoreline off and on for miles, going through rather more pleasant little communities of mostly boarded-up summer homes – Pierport, Arcadia, Elberta ('A Peach of A Place'), Frankfort. At Empire I stopped to look at the lake. The weather was surprisingly cold. A blustery wind blew in from Wisconsin, seventy miles away across the steely grey water, raising white caps and wavelets. I tried to go for a stroll, but I was only out for about five minutes before the wind blew me back to the car.

I went on to Traverse City, where the weather was milder, perhaps because it was more sheltered. Traverse City looked to be a wonderful old town that seemed not to have changed since about 1948. It still had a Woolworth's, a J.C. Penney, an old-fashioned movie theatre called The State and a wonderful old restaurant, the Sydney, with black booths and a long soda-fountain. You just don't see places like that any more. I had coffee and felt very pleased to be there. Afterwards I drove on north on a road running up one side of Grand Traverse Bay and down the other, so that you could always see where you were going or where you had been, sometimes veering inland past farms and cherry orchards for a couple of miles and then sweeping back down to the water's edge. As the afternoon progressed, the wind settled and the sun came out, tentatively at first, like a shy guest, and then stayed on, giving the lake bright patches of silver and blue. Far out over the water, perhaps twenty miles away, dark clouds dumped rain on the lake. It fell in a pale grey curtain. And high above a faint rainbow reached across the sky. It was inexpressibly beautiful. I drove transfixed.

In the early evening I reached Mackinaw City, on the tip of the oven mitt, the point where the shorelines of southern and northern Michigan pinch together to form the Straits of Mackinac, which separate Lake Michigan from Lake Huron. A suspension bridge, five miles long, spans the gap. Mackinaw City – they are fairly casual about how they spell the word up this way – was a scattered and unsightly little town, full of gift shops, motels, ice-cream parlours, pizzerias, carparks, and firms operating ferries to Mackinac Island. Almost every place of business, including the motels, was boarded up for the winter. The Holiday Motel, on the shore of Lake Huron, seemed to be open so I went inside and rang the desk bell. The young guy who came out looked surprised to have a customer. 'We were just about to close up for the season,' he said. 'In fact, everybody's gone out to dinner to celebrate. But we've got rooms if you want one.'

'How much?' I asked.

He seemed to snatch a figure from the air. 'Twenty dollars?' he said.

'Sounds good to me,' I said and signed in. The room was small but nice and it had heating, which was a good thing. I went out and had a walk around, to look for something to eat. It was only a little after seven, but it was dark already and the chill air felt more like December than October. I could see my breath. It was odd to be in a place so full of buildings and yet so dead. Even the McDonald's was closed, with a sign in the window telling me to have a good winter.

I walked down to the Shepler's Ferry terminal – really just a big parking lot with a shed – to see what time the ferry to Mackinac Island would depart in the morning. That was my reason for being here. There was one at eleven. I stood beside the pier, facing into the wind, and gazed for a long time out across Lake Huron. Mackinac Island was berthed a couple of miles out in the lake like a glittering cruiseship. Nearby, even larger but with no lights, was Bois Blanc Island, dark and round. Off to the left, Mackinac Bridge, lit up like a Christmas decoration, spanned the strait. Everywhere the lights shimmered on the water. It was odd that such a nothing little town could have such a wonderful view.

I ate dinner in a practically empty restaurant and then had some beers in a practically empty bar. Both places had turned on the heating. It felt good, cosy. Outside the wind beat against the plate glass windows, making a woppa-woppa sound. I liked the quiet bar. Most bars in America are dark and full of moody characters – people drinking alone and staring ahead. There's none of that agreeable coffee-house atmosphere that you find in bars in Europe. American bars are, by and large, just dark places to get drunk in. I don't like them much, but this one was OK. It was snug and quiet and well lit, so I could sit and read. Before too long I was fairly well lit myself. This was also OK.

In the morning I woke early and gave the steamy window a wipe with my hand to see what kind of day it was. The answer was: not a good one. The world was full of sleety snow, dancing about in the wind like a plague of white insects. I switched on the TV and crept back into the warm bed. The local PBS station came on. PBS is the Public Broadcasting System, what we used to call educational TV. It is supposed to show quality stuff, though because it is always strapped for funds this consists mostly of BBC melodramas starring Susan Hampshire and domestically-produced programmes that cost about $12 to make – cookery programmes, religious discussions, local high school wrestling matches. It's pretty well unwatchable most of the time, and it's getting worse. In fact, the station I was watching was holding a telethon to raise funds for itself. Two middle-aged men in casual clothes were sitting in swivel chairs, with a pair of phones on a table between them, asking for money. They were trying to look perky and cheerful, but there was a kind of desperation in their eyes.

'Wouldn't it be tragic for your children if they didn't have Sesame Street any more?' one of them was saying to the camera. 'So come on, moms and dads, give us a call and make a pledge now.' But nobody was calling. So the two talked to each other about all the wonderful programmes on PBS. They had clearly been having this conversation for some time. After a while one of them had a phone call. 'I've had my first caller,' he said as he put the phone down. 'It was from Melanie Bitowski of Traverse City and it's her fourth birthday today. So happy birthday, honey. But next time you or any of you other kids call in, why don't you get your mom or dad to pledge some money, sweetheart?' These guys were clearly begging for their jobs, and the whole of northern Michigan was turning a blind eye to their pleadings.

I showered and dressed and packed up my bag, all the while keeping an eye on the TV to see if anyone made a pledge and no-one ever did. When I switched off, one of them was saying, with just a hint of peevishness. 'Now come on, I can't believe that *nobody* out there is watching us. Somebody must be awake out there. Somebody must want to preserve quality public television for themselves and their children.' But he was wrong.

I had a large breakfast in the same place I had eaten the night before and then, because there was absolutely nothing else to do, I went and stood on the quayside, waiting for the ferry. The wind had died. The last sleet melted as it hit the ground and then stopped falling altogether. Everywhere there was the tip-tip-tip sound of dripping, off the roofs, off branches, off me. It was only ten o'clock and nothing was happening at the quayside – the Chevette, dressed with sleety snow, stood alone and forlorn in the big car park – so I went and walked around, down to the site of the original Fort Mackinac and then along

BILL BRYSON

residential streets full of treeless lawns and one-storey ranch-houses. When I returned to the ferry site, about forty minutes later, the Chevette had gained some company and there was a fair crowd of people – twenty or thirty at least – already boarding the boat.

We all sat on rows of seats in one small room. The hydroplane started up with a noise like a vacuum cleaner, then turned and slid out onto the green bleakness of Lake Huron. The lake was choppy, like a pan of water simmering on a low heat, but the ride was smooth. The people around me were strangely excited. They kept standing up to take pictures and point things out to each other. It occurred to me that many of them had never been on a ferry before, perhaps had never even seen an island, not one big enough to be inhabited anyway. No wonder they were excited. I was excited too, though for a different reason.

I had been to Mackinac Island before. My dad took us there when I was about four and I remembered it fondly. In fact, it was probably my oldest clear memory. I remembered that it had a big white hotel with a long porch and banks of flowers, positively dazzling in the July sunshine, and I could remember a big fort on a hill, and that the island had no cars, but just horse-drawn carriages, and that there was horse manure everywhere, and that I stepped in some, warm and squishy, and that my mother cleaned my shoe with a twig and a Kleenex, gagging delicately, and that as soon as she put the shoe back on my foot, I stepped backwards into some more with my other shoe, and that she didn't get cross. My mother never got cross. She didn't exactly do cartwheels, you understand, but she didn't shout or snap or look as if she were suppressing apoplexy, as I do with my children when they step in something warm and squishy, as they always do. She just looked kind of tired for a moment, and then she grinned at me and said it was a good thing she loved me, which was very true. She's a saint, my mother, especially where horse shit is concerned.

Mackinac Island is only small – about five miles long, a couple of miles wide – but like most islands it seems bigger when you are on it. Since 1901, no cars or motorized vehicles of any type have been allowed on the island, so when you step off the boat on to Main Street you find a line-up of horse-drawn carriages waiting at the kerb – a fancy one to take customers to the Grand Hotel, open phaetons to take people on expensive tours of the island, and a kind of sledge to deal with luggage and freight. Mackinac village was just as perfect as I remembered it, a string of white Victorian buildings along a sloping Main Street, snug cottages climbing up the steep hill to old Fort Mackinac, built in 1780 to defend the strait and still standing guard over the town.

I wandered off through the town, picking my way around little piles of horse manure. Without cars, the silence was almost complete. The whole island appeared to be on the brink of a six-month coma. Almost all the stores and restaurants along Main Street were shut for the season. I expect it's awful there in the summer with all the thousands of day trippers. A brochure that I picked up by the harbour listed sixty gift shops alone and more than thirty restaurants, ice-cream parlours, pizzerias and cookie stalls. But now at this time of year it all looked quaint and restful and incredibly pretty.

243

For a while, Mackinac Island was the biggest trading post in the New World – John Jacob Astor's fur trading company was based here – but its real glory dates from the late nineteenth century when wealthy people from Chicago and Detroit came to escape the city heat and enjoy the pollen-free air. The Grand Hotel, the biggest and oldest resort hotel in America, was built and the country's wealthiest industrialists constructed ornate summer houses on the bluffs overlooking Mackinac village and Lake Huron. I walked up there now. The views across the lake were fantastic, but the houses were simply breathtaking. They are some of the grandest, most elaborate houses ever built of wood, twenty-bedroomed places with every embellishment known to the Victorian mind – cupolas, towers, domes, gables, turrets, and front porches you could ride a bike around. Some of the cupolas had cupolas. They are just incredibly splendid and there are scores of them, standing side by side on the bluffs flanking Fort Mackinac. What it must be to be a child and play hide-and-seek in those houses, to have a bedroom in a tower and be able to lie in bed and gaze out on such a lake, to go bicycling on carless roads to little beaches and hidden coves, and above all to explore the woodland of beech and birch that cover the back three quarters of the island.

I wandered into them now, along one of the many paved paths that run through the dark woods, and felt like a seven-year-old on a grand adventure. Every turn in the path brought up some exotic surprise – Skull Cave, where, according to a sign beside it, an English fur trader hid from the Indians in 1763; Fort Holmes, an old British redoubt on the highest point on the island, 325 feet above Lake Huron; and two mossy old cemeteries out in the middle of nowhere, one Catholic and one Protestant. Both seemed impossibly big for such a small island, and they consisted mostly of the same few names going back generations – the Truscotts, Gables, Sawyers. I happily wandered for three hours without seeing a soul or hearing a sound made by man, and only barely sampled the island. I could easily have stayed for days. I returned to the village by way of the Grand Hotel, quite the most splendid and obnoxiously hoity-toity such institution I have ever come across. A rambling white wooden building with the biggest porch in the world (660 feet), it is indubitably swish and expensive. A single room at the time I was there cost $135 a night. A sign in the street leading down to the hotel said GRAND HOTEL – PROPER DRESS REQUIRED AT THE HOTEL AND HOTEL-OWNED STREET. GENTLEMEN AFTER 6 P.M. MUST BE ATTIRED IN A COAT AND TIE. LADIES MAY NOT BE ATTIRED IN SLACKS. This is possibly the only place in the world where you are told how to dress just to walk down the street. Another sign said a charge would be levied on anyone coming in to the hotel just to gawp. Honestly. I suppose they have a lot of trouble with day trippers. I walked stealthily down the road towards the hotel, half expecting to see a sign saying 'Anyone Passing Beyond This Point Wearing Plaid Trousers or White Shoes Will Be Arrested.' But there wasn't anything. I had it in my mind to put my head in the front door, just to see what life is like for really rich people, but there was a liveried doorman standing guard, so I had to beat a retreat.

I caught the afternoon ferry back to the mainland, and drove over the Mackinac Bridge to the chunk of land Michigan people call the upper peninsula. Before the bridge was built in 1957, this bit of Michigan was pretty well cut off from its own state, and even now it has an overwhelming sense of remoteness. It is mostly just a bleak and sandy peninsula, 150 miles long, squeezed between three of the Great Lakes, Superior, Huron and Michigan. Once again, I was almost in Canada. Sault Sainte Marie was just to the north. Its great locks connect Lake Huron and Lake Superior and are the busiest in the world, carrying a greater volume of tonnage than the Suez and Panama canals combined, believe it or not.

I was on Route 2, which follows the northern shoreline of Lake Michigan for most of its length. It is impossible to exaggerate the immensity of the Great Lakes. There are five of them, Erie, Huron, Michigan, Superior and Ontario, and they stretch 700 miles from top to bottom, 900 miles from east to west. They cover 94,500 square miles, making them almost precisely the size of the United Kingdom. Together they form the largest expanse of fresh water on earth.

More squally storms were at work far out on the lake, though where I was it was dry. About twenty miles off-shore was a group of islands – Beaver Island, High Island, Whiskey Island, Hog Island and several others. High Island was once owned by a religious sect called the House of David, whose members all had beards and specialized, if you can believe it, in playing baseball. In the 1920s and 30s they toured the country taking on local teams wherever they went and I guess they were just about unbeatable. High Island was reputedly a kind of penal colony for members of the sect who committed serious infractions – struck out too often or something. It was said that people were sent there and never heard from again. Now, like all the other islands in the group except Beaver, it is uninhabited. I felt a strange pang of regret that I couldn't go over and explore them. In fact, the whole of the Great Lakes was exerting a strange hold on me, which I couldn't begin to understand. There was something alluring about the idea of a great inland sea, about the thought that if you had a boat you could spend years just bouncing around from one Great Lake to another, chugging from Chicago to Buffalo, Milwaukee to Montreal, pausing *en route* to investigate islands, bays and towns with curious names like Deadman's Point, Egg Harbor, Summer Island. A lot of people do just that, I guess – buy a boat and disappear. I can see why.

All over the peninsula I kept encountering roadside food stands with big signs on them saying PASTIES. Most of them were closed and boarded up, but at Menominee, the last town before I crossed into Wisconsin, I passed one that was open and impulsively I turned the car around and went back to it. I had to see if they were real Cornish pasties or something else altogether but with the same name. The guy who ran the place was excited to have a real Englishman in his store. He had been making pasties for thirty years but he had never seen a real Cornish pasty or a real Englishman, come to that. I didn't have the heart to tell him that actually I came from Iowa, the next state over. Nobody ever gets excited at meeting an Iowan. The pasties were the real thing, brought to this isolated corner of Michigan by nineteenth-century Cornishmen who came to work in the local mines. 'Everybody eats them up here in the upper peninsula,' the man told me. 'But nobody's ever heard of them anywhere else. You cross the state line into Wisconsin, just over the river, and people don't know what they are. It's kind of strange.'

The man handed me the pasty in a paper bag and I went with it out to the car. It did seem to be a genuine Cornish pasty except that it was about the size of a rugby ball. It came on a styrofoam platter with a plastic fork and some sachets of ketchup. Eagerly I tucked into it. Apart from anything else I was starving.

It was awful. There wasn't anything wrong with it exactly – it was a genuine pasty, accurate in every detail – it was just that after more than a month of eating American junk food it tasted indescribably bland and insipid, like warmed cardboard. 'Where's the grease?' I thought. 'Where's the melted cheese patty and pan-fried chicken gravy? Where, above all, is the chocolate fudge frosting?' This was just meat and potatoes, just natural unenhanced flavour. 'No wonder it's never caught on over here,' I grumbled and pushed it back into the bag.

I started the car and drove on into Wisconsin, looking for a motel and a restaurant where I could get some real food – something that would squirt when I bit into it and run down my chin. That, of course, is the way food should be.

Chapter nineteen

'AT NORTHERN WISCONSIN GENERAL HOSPITAL, we'll help you to achieve your birthing goals,' said a voice on the radio. Oh, God, I thought. This was yet another new development since I had left America – the advent of hospital advertising. Everywhere you go you now encounter hospital ads. Who are they for? A guy gets hit by a bus, does he say, 'Quick, take me to Michigan General. They've got a magnetic resonance imager there.' I don't understand it. But then I don't understand anything to do with American health care.

Just before I left on this trip, I learned that a friend was in Mercy Hospital in Des Moines. So I looked up the number in the phone book and under Mercy Hospital there were ninety-four telephone numbers listed. The phone numbers started with Admitting and proceeded alphabetically through Biofeedback, Cancer Hotline, Impotency Program, Infant Apnea Hotline, Osteoporosis Program, Public Relations, Sleep Referral Services, something called Share Care Ltd, Smoke Stoppers and on and on. Health care in America is now a monolithic industry and it is completely out of control.

The person I was visiting, an old family friend, had just learned that she had ovarian cancer. As a complication arising from this, she also had pneumonia. As you might imagine, she looked a little under the weather. While I was with her, a social worker came in and gently explained to her some of the costings involved in her treatment. My friend could, for instance, have Medicine A, which would cost $5 a dose, but which she would have to take four times a day, or she could have Medicine B, which would cost $18 a dose, but which she would have to take only once a day. That was the social worker's job, to act as a liaison between the doctor, the patient and the insurance company, and to try to see to it that the patient wasn't hit with a lot of bills that the insurance company wouldn't pay. My friend would, of course, be billed for this service. It seemed so crazy, so unreal, to be watching an old friend sucking air from an oxygen mask, all but dead, and giving weak yes-or-no nods to questions concerning the continuance of her own life based on her ability to pay.

Contrary to popular belief abroad, it is possible, indeed quite easy, to get free treatment in America by going to a county hospital. They aren't very cheery places, in fact they are generally pretty grim, but they are no worse than any NHS hospital. There has to be free treatment because there are 40 million people in America without hospital insurance. God help you, however, if you try to sneak into a county hospital for a little free health care if you've got money in the bank. I worked for a year at the county hospital in Des Moines and I can tell you that they have batteries of lawyers and debt collectors whose sole job is to dig into the backgrounds of the people who use their facilities and make sure they really are as destitute as they claim to be.

Despite the manifest insanities of private health care in America, there is no denying that the quality of treatment is the best in the world. My friend received superb and unstinting care (and, not incidentally, they cured both her cancer and her pneumonia). She had a private room, with a private bath, a remote control television and video recorder, her own telephone. The whole hospital was carpeted and full of exotic palms and cheerful paintings. In government hospitals in Britain, the only piece of carpet or colour TV you find is in the nursing officers' lounge. I worked in an NHS hospital years ago and once late at night I sneaked into the nursing officers' lounge just to see what it was like. Well, it was like the Queen's sitting-room. It was all velvety furniture and half-eaten boxes of Milk Tray chocolates.

The patients, in the meantime, slept beneath bare light bulbs in cold and echoing barrack halls, and spent their days working on jigsaw puzzles that had at least a fifth of the pieces missing, awaiting a fortnightly twenty-second visit by a swift-moving retinue of doctors and students. Those were, of course, the good old days of the NHS. Things aren't nearly so splendid now.

Forgive me. I seem to have gone off on a little tangent there. I was supposed to be guiding you across Wisconsin, telling you interesting facts about America's premier dairy state, and instead I go off and make unconstructive re-marks about British and American health care. This was unwarranted.

Anyway, Wisconsin is America's premier dairy state, producing seventeen per cent of the nation's cheese and milk products, by golly, though as I drove across its rolling pleasantness I wasn't particularly struck by an abundance of dairy cows. I drove for long hours, south past Green Bay, Appleton and Oshkosh and then west towards Iowa. This was quintessential Mid-western farming country, a study in browns, a landscape of low wooded hills, bare trees, faded pastures, tumbledown corn. It all had a kind of muted beauty. The farms were large, scattered and prosperous-looking. Every half mile or so I would pass a snug-looking farmhouse, with a porch swing and a yard full of trees. Standing nearby would be a red barn with a rounded roof and a tall grain silo. Everywhere corn cribs were packed to bursting. Migrating birds filled the pale sky. The corn in the fields looked dead and brittle, but often I passed large harvesters chewing up rows and spitting out bright yellow ears.

I drove through the thin light of afternoon along back highways. It seemed to take forever to cross the state, but I didn't mind because it was so fetching and restful. There was something uncommonly alluring about the day, about the season, the sense that winter was drawing in. By four o'clock the daylight was going. By five the sun had dropped out of the clouds and was slotting into the distant hills, like a coin going into a piggy bank. At a place called Ferryville, I came suddenly up against the Mississippi River. It fairly took my breath away, it was so broad and beautiful and graceful lying there all flat and calm. In the setting sun it looked like liquid stainless steel.

On the far bank, about a mile away, was Iowa. Home. I felt a strange squeeze of excitement that made me hunch up closer to the wheel. I drove for twenty miles down the eastern side of the river, gazing across to the high dark bluffs on the Iowa side. At Prairie du Chien I crossed the river on an iron bridge full of struts and crossbars. And then I was in Iowa. I actually felt my heart quicken. I was home. This was my state. My licence plate matched everyone else's. No-one would look at me as if to say, 'What are you doing here?' I belonged.

In the fading light, I drove almost randomly around north-east Iowa. Every couple of miles I would pass a farmer on a tractor juddering along the highway, heading home to dinner on one of the sprawling farms up in these sheltered hills above the Mississippi. It was Friday, one of the big days of the farmer's week. He would wash his arms and neck and sit down with his family to a table covered with great bowls of food. They would say grace together. After dinner the family would drive into Hooterville and sit out in the cold October air and through their steamy breath watch the Hooterville High Blue Devils beat Kraut City 28–7 at football. The farmer's son, Merle Jr, would score three of the touchdowns. Afterwards Merle senior would go to Ed's Tavern to celebrate (two beers, never more) and receive the admiration of the community for his son's prowess. Then it would be home to bed and up early in the frosty dawn to go out hunting for deer with his best friends, Ed and Art and Wally, trudging across the fallow fields, savouring the clean air and the companionship. I was seized with a huge envy for these people and their unassuming lives. It must be wonderful to live in a safe and timeless place, where you know everyone and everyone knows you, and you can all count on each other. I envied them their sense of community, their football games, their bring-and-bake sales, their church socials. And I felt guilty for mocking them. They were good people.

I drove through the seamless blackness, past Millville, New Vienna, Cascade, Scotch Grove. Every once in a while I would pass a distant farmhouse whose windows were pools of yellow light, warm and inviting. Occasionally there would be a larger town, with a much larger pool of light scooped out of the darkness – the high school football field, where the week's game was in progress. These football fields lit up the night; they were visible from miles off. As I drove through each town, it was clear that everybody was out at the game. There was nobody on the streets. Apart from one forlorn teenaged girl standing behind the counter in the local Dairy Queen, waiting for the post-game rush, everyone in town was at the football game. You could drive in with a fleet of trucks and strip the town during a high school football game in Iowa. You could blow open the bank with explosives and take the money out in wheelbarrows and no-one would be there to see it. But of course nobody would think of such a thing because crime doesn't exist in rural Iowa. Their idea of a crime in these places would be to miss the Friday football game. Anything worse than that only exists on television and in the newspapers, in a semi-mythic distant land called the Big City.

I had intended to drive on to Des Moines, but on an impulse I stopped at Iowa City. It's a college town, the home of the University of Iowa, and I still had a couple of friends living there – people who had gone to college there and then never quite found any reason to move on. It was nearly ten o'clock when I arrived, but the streets were packed with students out carousing. I called my old friend John Horner from a street corner phone and he told me to meet him in Fitzpatrick's Bar. I stopped a passing student and asked him the way to Fitzpatrick's Bar, but he was so drunk that he had lost the power of speech. He just gazed numbly at me. He looked to be about fourteen years old. I stopped a group of girls, similarly intoxicated, and asked them if they knew the way to the bar. They all said they did and pointed in different directions, and then became so convulsed with giggles that it was all they could do to stand up. They moved around in front of me like passengers on a ship in heavy seas. They looked about fourteen years old too.

'Are you girls always this happy?' I asked.

'Only at homecoming,' one of them said.

Ah, that explained it. Homecoming. The big social event of the college year. There are three ritual stages attached to homecoming celebrations at American universities: (1) get grossly intoxicated; (2) throw up in a public place; (3) wake up not knowing where you are or how you got there and with your underpants on backwards. I appeared to have arrived in town somewhere between stages one and two, though in fact a few of the more committed revellers were already engaged in gutter serenades. I picked my way through the weaving throngs in downtown Iowa City asking people at random if they knew the way to Fitzpatrick's Bar. No-one seemed to have heard of it – but then many of the people I encountered probably could not have identified themselves in a roomful of mirrors. Eventually I stumbled on the bar myself. Like all bars in Iowa City on a Friday night, it was packed to the rafters. Everybody looked to be fourteen years old, except one person – my friend John Horner, who was standing at the bar looking all of his thirty-five years. There is nothing like a college town to make you feel old before your time. I joined Horner at the bar. He hadn't changed a lot. He was now a pharmacist and a respectable member of the community, though there was still a semi-wild glint in his eye. In his day, he had been one of the most committed drug-takers in the community. Indeed, although he always strenuously denied it, everyone knew that his motive for studying pharmacology was to be able to create a more exotic blend of hallucinogenic drugs. We had been friends almost forever, since first grade at least. We exchanged broad smiles and warm handshakes and tried to talk, but there was so much noise and throbbing music that we were just two men watching each other's mouths move. So we gave up trying to talk and instead had a beer and stood smiling inanely at each other, the way you do with someone you haven't seen for years, and watching the people around us. I couldn't get over how young and fresh-looking they all seemed. Everything about them looked brand new and unused – their clothes, their faces, their bodies. When we had drained our beer bottles, Horner and I stepped out on to the street and walked to his car. The fresh air felt wonderful. People were leaning against buildings everywhere and puking. 'Have you ever seen so many twerpy little assholes in all your life?' Horner asked me rhetorically.

'And they're all just fourteen years old,' I added.

'Physically they are fourteen years old,' he corrected me, 'but emotionally and intellectually they are still somewhere shy of their eighth birthday.'

'Were we like that at their age?'

'I used to wonder that, but I don't think so. I may have been that stupid once, but I was never that shallow. These kids wear button-down collar shirts and penny loafers. They look like they're on their way to an Osmonds concert. And they don't know *anything*. You talk to them in a bar and they don't even know who's running for President. They've never heard of Nicaragua. It's scary.'

We walked along thinking about the scariness of it all. 'But there's something even worse,' Homer added. We were at his car. I looked at him across the top of it. 'What's that?' I asked.

'They don't smoke dope. Can you believe that?'

Well, I couldn't. The idea of students at the University of Iowa not smoking dope is . . . well, simply inconceivable. On any list of reasons for going to the University of Iowa, smoking dope took up at least two of the first five places. 'Then what are they here for?'

'They're getting an *education*,' Horner said in a tone of wonder. 'Can you believe that? They *want* to be insurance salesmen and computer programmers. That's their dream in life. They want to make a lot of money so they can go out and buy more penny loafers and Madonna albums. It terrifies me sometimes.'

We got in his car and drove through dark streets to his house. Horner explained to me how the world had changed. When I left America for England, Iowa City was full of hippies. Difficult as it may be to believe, out here amid all these cornfields, the University of Iowa was for many years one of the most radical colleges in the country, at its peak exceeded in radicalness only by Berkeley and Columbia. Everybody there was a hippie, the professors as much as the students. It wasn't just that they smoked dope and frequently rioted; they were also open-minded and intellectual. People cared about things like politics and the environment and where the world was going. Now, from what Horner was telling me, it was as if all the people in Iowa City had had their brains laundered at the Ronald McDonald Institute of Mental Readjustment.

'So what happened?' I asked Horner when we were

settled at his house with a beer. 'What made everyone change?'

'I don't know exactly,' he said. 'The main thing, I guess, is that the Reagan Administration has this obsession with drugs. And they don't distinguish between hard drugs and soft drugs. If you're a dealer and you're caught with pot, you get sent away for just as long as if it were heroin. So now nobody sells pot. All the people who used to sell it have moved on to crack and heroin because the risk is no worse and the profits are a lot better.'

'Sounds crazy,' I said.

'Of course it's crazy!' Horner answered, a little hotly. Then he calmed down. 'Actually a lot of people just stopped dealing in pot altogether. Do you remember Frank Dortmeier?'

Frank Dortmeier was a guy who used to ingest drugs by the sackful. He would snort coke through a garden hose given half a chance. 'Yeah, sure,' I said.

'I used to get my pot from him. Then they brought in this law that if you are caught selling dope within a thousand yards of a public school they put you in jail for ever. It doesn't matter that you may only be selling one little reefer to your own mother, they still put you away for eternity just as if you were standing on the school steps shoving it down the throats of every snivelling little kid who passed by. Well, when they brought this law in, Dortmeier started to get worried because there was a school up the street from him. So one night under cover of darkness, he goes out with a hundred-foot tape measure and measures the distance from his house to the school and damn me but it's 997 yards. So he just stops selling dope, just like that.' Horner drank his beer sadly. 'It's really frustrating. I mean, have you ever tried to watch American TV without dope?'

'It must be tough,' I agreed.

'Dortmeier gave me the name of his supplier so I could go and get some myself. Well, this guy was in Kansas City. I had no idea. So I drove all the way down there, just to buy a couple of ounces of pot, and it was crazy. The house was full of guns. The guy kept looking out the window like he was expecting the police to tell him to come out with his hands up. He was half convinced that I was an undercover narcotics officer. I mean here I am, a thirty-five-year-old family man, with a college education and a respectable job, I'm 180 miles from home and I'm wondering if I'm going to get blown away, and all so that I can just have a little something to help me get through *Love Boat* reruns on TV. It was too crazy for me. You need somebody like Dortmeier for a situation like that – somebody with a lust for drugs and no brain.' Horner shook the beer can by his ear to confirm that it was empty and then looked at me. 'You wouldn't by any wild chance have any dope with you?' he asked.

'I'm sorry, John,' I said.

'Shame,' said Horner and went out to the kitchen to get us more beers.

I spent the night in Horner's spare room and in the morning stood with him and his pleasant wife in the kitchen drinking coffee and chatting while small children swirled about our legs. Life is odd, I thought. It seemed so strange for Horner to have a wife and children and a paunch and a mortgage and to be, like me, approaching the cliff-face of middle age. We had been boys for so long together that I suppose I had thought the condition was permanent. I realized with a sense of dread that the next time we met we would probably talk about gallstone operations and the relative merits of different brands of storm windows. It put me in a melancholy mood and kept me there as I reclaimed my car from its parking space downtown and returned to the highway.

I drove along old Route 6, which used to be the main highway to Chicago, but now, with Interstate 80 just three miles to the south, it is all but forgotten, and I hardly saw a soul along its length. I drove for an hour and a half without much of a thought in my head, just a weary eagerness to get home, to see my mom, to have a shower, and not to touch a steering wheel for a long, long time.

Des Moines looked wonderful in the morning sunshine. The dome on the state capitol building gleamed. The trees were still full of colour. They've changed the city completely – downtown now is all modern buildings and bubbling fountains and whenever I'm there now I have to keep looking up at the street signs to get my bearings – but it felt like home. I suppose it always will. I hope so. I drove through the city, happy to be there, proud to be part of it.

On Grand Avenue, near the governor's mansion, I realized I was driving along behind my mother, who had evidently borrowed my sister's car. I recognized her because the right turn signal was blinking pointlessly as she proceeded up the street. My mother generally puts the turn signal on soon after pulling out of the garage and then leaves it on for pretty much the rest of the day. I used to point this out to her, but then I realized it is actually a good thing because it alerts other motorists that they are approaching a driver who may not be entirely on top of matters. I followed along behind her. At Thirty-First Street the blinking turn signal jumped from the right side of the car to the left – I had forgotten that she likes to move it around from time to time – as we turned the corner for home, but then it stayed cheerily blinking on the left for the last mile, down Thirty-First Street and up Elmwood Drive.

I had to park a fair distance from the house and then, despite a boyish eagerness to see my mother, I took a minute to log the final details of the trip in a notebook I had been carrying with me. It always made me feel oddly important and professional, like a jumbo jet pilot at the end of a transatlantic flight. It was 10.38 a.m., and I had driven 6,842 miles since leaving home thirty-four days earlier. I circled this figure, then got out, grabbed my bags from the trunk, and walked briskly to the house. My mother was already inside. I could see her through the back window, moving around in the kitchen, putting away groceries and humming. She is always humming. I opened the back door, dropped my bags and called out those four most all-American words: 'Hi, Mom, I'm home!'

She looked real pleased to see me. 'Hello, dear!' she said brightly and gave me a hug. 'I was just wondering when I'd be seeing you again. Can I get you a sandwich?'

'That would be great,' I said even though I wasn't really hungry.

It was good to be home.

PART TWO

West

Chapter twenty

I WAS HEADED FOR Nebraska. Now there's a sentence you don't want to have to say too often if you can possibly help it. Nebraska must be the most unexciting of all the states. Compared with it, Iowa is paradise. Iowa at least is fertile and green and has a hill. Nebraska is like a 75,000-square-mile bare patch. In the middle of the state is a river called the Platte, which at some times of the year is two or three miles wide. It looks impressive until you realize that it is only about four inches deep. You could cross it in a wheelchair. On a landscape without any contours or depressions to shape it, the Platte just lies there, like a drink spilled across a table-top. It is the most exciting thing in the state.

When I was growing up, I used to wonder how Nebraska came to be lived in. I mean to say, the original settlers, creaking across America in their covered wagons, must have passed through Iowa, which is green and fertile and has, as I say, a hill, but stopped short of Colorado, which is green and fertile and has a mountain range, and settled instead for a place that is flat and brown and full of stubble and prairie-dogs. Doesn't make a lot of sense, does it? Do you know what the original settlers made their houses of? Dried mud. And do you know what happened to all those mud houses when the rainy season came every year? That's correct, they slid straight into the Platte River.

For a long time I couldn't decide whether the original settlers in Nebraska were insane or just stupid, and then I saw a stadium full of University of Nebraska football fans in action on a Saturday and realized that they must have been both. I may be a decade or so out of touch here but when I left America, the University of Nebraska didn't so much play football as engage in weekly ritual slaughters. They were always racking up scores of 58–3 against hapless opponents. Most schools, when they get a decent lead, will send in a squad of skinny freshmen in unsoiled uniforms to let them run around a bit and get dirty and, above all, to give the losers a sporting chance to make the score respectable. It's called fair play.

Not Nebraska. The University of Nebraska would send in flamethrowers if it were allowed. Watching Nebraska play football every week was like watching hyenas tearing open a gazelle. It was unseemly. It was unsporting. And of course the fans could never get enough of it. To sit among them with the score 66–0 and watch them bray for more blood is a distinctly unnerving experience, particularly when you consider that a lot of these people must work at Strategic Air Command in Omaha. If Iowa State ever upset Nebraska, I wouldn't be at all surprised if they nuked Ames. All of these thoughts percolated through my mind on this particular morning and frankly left me troubled.

I was on the road again. It was a little after 7.30 a.m. on a bright but still wintry Monday morning in April. I drove west out of Des Moines on Interstate 80, intending to zip across the western half of Iowa and plunge deep into Nebraska. But I couldn't face Nebraska just yet, not this early in the morning, and abruptly at De Soto, just fifteen miles west of Des Moines, I pulled off the interstate and started wandering around on back roads. Within a couple of minutes I was lost. This didn't altogether surprise me. Getting lost is a family trait.

My father, when behind the wheel, was more or less permanently lost. Most of the time he was just kind of lost, but whenever we got near something we were intent on seeing he would become seriously lost. Generally it would take him about an hour to realize that he had gone from the first stage to the second. All during that time, as he blundered through some unfamiliar city, making sudden and unpredictable turns, getting honked at for going the wrong way down one-way streets or for hesitating in the middle of busy intersections, my mother would mildly suggest that perhaps we should pull over and ask directions. But my father would pretend not to hear her and would press on in that semi-obsessional state that tends to overcome fathers when things aren't going well.

Eventually, after driving the wrong way down the same one-way street so many times that merchants were beginning to come and watch from their doorways, Dad would stop the car and gravely announce, 'Well, I think we should ask directions', in a tone suggesting that this had been his desire all along.

This was always a welcome development, but seldom more than a partial breakthrough. Either my mom would get out and stop a patently unqualified person – a nun on an exchange visit from Costa Rica, usually – and come back with directions that were hopelessly muddled, or my father would go off to find somebody and then not come back. The problem with my dad was that he was a great talker. This is always a dangerous thing in a person who gets lost a lot. He would go into a café to ask the way to

Giant Fungus State Park and the next thing you knew he would be sitting down having a cup of coffee and a chat with the proprietor or the proprietor would be taking him out back to show him his new septic tank or something. In the meantime the rest of us would have to sit in a quietly baking car, with nothing to do but sweat and wait and listlessly watch a pair of flies copulate on the dashboard.

After a very long time my father would reappear, wiping crumbs from around his mouth and looking real perky. 'Darnedest thing,' he would say, leaning over to talk to my mom through the window. 'Guy in there collects false teeth. He's got over 700 sets down in his basement. He was so pleased to have someone to show them to that I just couldn't say no. And then his wife insisted that I have a piece of blueberry pie and see the photographs from their daughter's wedding. They'd never heard of Giant Fungus State Park, I'm afraid, but the guy said his brother at the Conoco station by the traffic lights would know. *He* collects fanbelts, of all things, and apparently has the largest collection of pre-war fanbelts in the upper Midwest. I'm just going down there now.' And then, before anybody could stop him, he'd be gone again. By the time he finally returned my father would know most of the people in town and the flies on the dashboard would have a litter of infants.

Eventually I found what I was looking for: Winterset, birthplace of John Wayne. I drove around the town until I found his house – Winterset is so small that this only took a minute – and slowed down to look at it from the car. The house was tiny and the paint was peeling off it. Wayne, or Marion Morrison as he then was, only lived there for a year or so before his family moved to California. The house is run as a museum now, but it was shut. This didn't surprise me, as pretty much everything in the town was shut, quite a lot of it permanently from the look of things. The Iowa Movie Theater on the square was clearly out of business, its marquee board blank, and many of the other stores were gone or just hanging on. It was a depressing sight because Winterset was really quite a nice-looking little town with its county courthouse and square and long streets of big Victorian houses. I bet, like Winfield, it was a different place altogether fifteen or twenty years ago. I drove back out to the highway past the Gold Buffet ('Dancing Nitely') feeling an odd sense of emptiness.

Every town I came to was much the same – peeling paint, closed businesses, a deathly air. South-west Iowa has always been the poorest part of the state and it showed. I didn't stop because there was nothing worth stopping for. I couldn't even find a place to get a cup of coffee. Eventually, much to my surprise, I blundered on to a bridge over the Missouri River and then I was in Nebraska City, in Nebraska. And it wasn't at all bad. In fact, it was really quite pleasant – better than Iowa by a long chalk, I was embarrassed to admit. The towns were more prosperous-looking and better maintained, and the roadsides everywhere were full of bushes from which sprang a profusion of creamy flowers. It was all quite pretty, though in a rather monotonous way. That is the problem with Nebraska. It just goes on and on, and even the good bits soon grow tedious. I drove for hours along an undemanding highway, past Auburn, Tecumseh, Beatrice (a town of barely 10,000 people but which produced two Hollywood stars, Harold Lloyd and Robert Taylor), Fairbury, Hebron, Deshler, Ruskin.

At Deshler I stopped for coffee and was surprised at how cold it was. Where the weather is concerned, the Midwest has the worst of both worlds. In the winter the wind is razor-sharp. It skims down from the Arctic and slices through you. It howls and swirls and buffets the house. It brings piles of snow and bone-cracking cold. From November to March you walk leaning forward at a twenty-degree angle, even indoors, and spend your life waiting for your car to warm up, or digging it out of drifts or scraping futilely at ice that seems to have been applied to the windows with Superglue. And then one day spring comes. The snow melts, you stride about in shirt-sleeves, you incline your face to the sun. And then, just like that, spring is over and it's summer. It is as if God has pulled a lever in the great celestial powerhouse. Now the weather rolls in from the opposite direction, from the tropics far to the south, and it hits you like a wall of heat. For six months, the heat pours over you. You sweat oil. Your pores gape. The grass goes brown. Dogs look as if they could die. When you walk downtown you can feel the heat of the pavement rising through the soles of your shoes. Just when you think you might very well go crazy, autumn comes and for two or three weeks the air is mild and nature is friendly. And then it's winter and the cycle starts again. And you think, 'As soon as I'm big enough, I'm going to move far, far away from here.'

At Red Cloud, home of Willa Cather, I joined US 281 and headed south towards Kansas. Just over the border is Smith Center, home of Dr Brewster M. Higley, who wrote the words to *Home on the Range*. Wouldn't you just know that *Home on the Range* would be written by somebody with a name like Brewster M. Higley? You can see the log cabin where he wrote the words. But I was headed for something far more exciting – the geographical centre of the United States. You reach it by turning off the highway just outside the little town of Lebanon and following a side road for about a mile through the wheat fields. Then you come to a forlorn little park with picnic tables and a stone monument with a wind-whipped flag atop it and a plaque saying that this is the centremost point in the continental United States, by golly. Beside the park, adding to the sense of forlornness, was a closed-down motel, which had been built in the evident hope that people would want to spend the night in this lonely place and send postcards to their friends saying, 'You'll never guess where we are.' Clearly the owner had misread the market.

I climbed onto a picnic table and could instantly see for miles across the waving fields. The wind came at me like a freight train. I felt as if I were the first person to come there for years. It was a strange feeling to think that of all the 230 million people in the United States I was the most geographically distinctive. If America were invaded, I would be the last person captured. This was it, the last stand, and as I climbed down off the table and returned to the car I felt an uneasy sense of guilt for leaving the place undefended.

I drove into the gathering evening gloom. The clouds were low and swift. The landscape was a sea of white grass, fine as a child's hair. It was strangely beautiful. By the time I reached Russell, it was dark and rain was falling. The headlights swept over a sign that said WELCOME TO BOB DOLE COUNTRY. Russell is the home town of Bob Dole, who was at this time running for the Republican nomination for

President. I stopped and got a room for the night, figuring that if Dole were elected President, I could tell my children that I had once spent the night in his home town and perhaps thereby deepen their respect for me. Also, every time Russell was shown on TV over the next four years I could say, 'Hey, I was there!' and make everybody in the room stop talking while I pointed out things I had seen. In the event, Dole dropped out of the race two days later, primarily because nobody could stand him, apart from his family and some other people around Russell, and the town, alas, lost its chance at fame.

I awoke to a more promising day. The sun was bright and the air was clear. Bugs exploded colourfully against the windscreen, a sure sign of spring in the Midwest. In the sunshine Kansas seemed an altogether more agreeable place, which surprised me a little. I had always thought one of the worst things anyone could say to you was, 'We're transferring you to Kansas, son.' Kansas calls itself 'the Wheat State'. That kind of says it all, don't you think? It really makes you want to cancel that Barbados trip, doesn't it? But in fact Kansas was OK. The towns I went through all looked trim and prosperous and quintessentially American. But then Kansas is the most quintessential of American states. It is, after all, where Superman and Dorothy from the Wizard of Oz grew up, and all the towns I went through had a cosy, leafy, timeless air to them. They looked like the sort of places where you could still have your groceries delivered by a boy on a bike and people would still say things like 'By golly' and 'Gee willickers'. At Great Bend, I stopped on the square beside the Barton County Courthouse and had a look around. It was like passing through a time warp. The place appeared not to have changed a fraction since 1965. The Crest Movie Theater was still in business. Nearby stood the *Great Bend Daily Tribune* and the Brass Buckle Clothing Store, with a big sign on it that said FOR GUYS AND GALS. Gee willickers. A man and his wife passed me on the sidewalk and said good morning like old friends. The man even tipped his hat. From a passing car came the sound of the Everly Brothers. This was almost too eerie. I half expected Rod Serling to step out from behind a tree and say, 'Bill Bryson doesn't know it, but he's just driven into a community that doesn't exist in time or space. He's just embarked on a one-way trip into . . . The Twilight Zone.'

I had a look in the window of the Family Pharmacy and Gift Shop, which had an interesting and unusual display that included a wheelchair, a packet of disposable absorbent underpants (it isn't often you find a store catering for the incontinent impulse shopper), teddy bears, coffee-mugs bearing wholesome sentiments like World's Best Grandma, mother's day cards and a variety of porcelain animals. In one corner of the window was a poster for a concert by – you are never going to believe this – Paul Revere and the Raiders. Can you beat that? There they were, still dressed up like Continental soldiers, prancing about and grinning, just like when I was in junior high school. They would be performing at the Civic Auditorium in Dodge City in two weeks. Tickets started at $10.75. This was all becoming too much for me. I was glad to get in the car and drive on to Dodge City, which at least is intentionally unreal.

Somewhere during the seventy miles between Great Bend and Dodge City you leave the Midwest and enter the

BILL BRYSON

West. The people in the towns along the way stop wearing baseball caps and shuffling along with that amiable dopeyness characteristic of the Midwest and instead start wearing cowboy hats and cowboy boots, walking with a lope and looking vaguely suspicious and squinty, as if they think they might have to shoot you in a minute. People in the West like to shoot things. When they first got to the West they shot buffalo.* Once there were 70 million buffalo on the plains and then the people of the West started blasting away at them. Buffalo are just cows with big heads. If you've ever looked a cow in the face and seen the unutterable depths of trust and stupidity that lie within, you will be able to guess how difficult it must have been for people in the West to track down buffalo and shoot them to pieces. By 1895, there were only 800 buffalo left, mostly in zoos and touring Wild West shows. With no buffalo left to kill, Westerners started shooting Indians. Between 1850 and 1890 they reduced the number of Indians in America from 2 million to 90,000.

Nowadays, thank goodness, both have made a recovery. Today there are 30,000 buffalo and 300,000 Indians, and of course you are not allowed to shoot either, so all the Westerners have left to shoot at are road signs and each other, both of which they do rather a lot. There you have a capsule history of the West.

* Many people will tell you that you mustn't call them buffalo, that they are really bison. Buffalo, these people will tell you, actually live in China or some other distant country and are a different breed of animal altogether. These are the same people who tell you that you must call geraniums pelargoniums. Ignore them.

274

When they weren't shooting things, the people of the West went into towns like Dodge City for a little social and sexual intercourse. At its peak, Dodge City was the biggest cow town and semen sink in the West, full of drifters, drovers, buffalo hunters and the sort of women that only a cowboy could find attractive. But it was never as tough and dangerous as you were led to believe on *Gunsmoke* and all those movies about Bat Masterson and Wyatt Earp. For ten years it was the biggest cattle market in the world; that's all.

In all those years, there were only thirty-four people buried in Boot Hill Cemetery and most of those were just vagrants found dead in snowdrifts or of natural causes. I know this for a fact because I paid $2.75 to go and see Boot Hill and the neighbouring 'Historic Front Street', which has been rebuilt to look like it did when Dodge City was a frontier town and Bat Masterson and Wyatt Earp were the sheriffs. Matt Dillon never existed, I was distressed to learn, though Bat Masterson and Wyatt Earp were both real enough. Bat Masterson ended his life as sports editor on the *New York Morning Telegraph*. Isn't that interesting? And here's another interesting fact, which I didn't tell you about earlier because I've been saving it: Wyatt Earp was from Pella, the little Iowa town with the windmills. Isn't that great?

Fifty miles beyond Dodge City is Holcomb, Kansas, which gained a small notoriety as the scene of the murders described with lavish detail in the Truman Capote book *In Cold Blood*. In 1959, two small-time crooks broke into the house of a wealthy Holcomb rancher named Herb Clutter because they had heard he had a safe full of money. In fact he didn't. So, chagrined, they tied Clutter's wife and two teenaged children to their beds and took Clutter down to the basement and killed them all. They slit Clutter's throat (Capote described his gurglings with a disturbing relish) and shot the others in the head at point-blank range. Because Clutter had been prominent in state politics, the *New York Times* ran a small story about the murders. Capote saw the story, became intrigued and spent five years interviewing all the main participants – friends, neighbours, relatives, police investigators and the murderers themselves. The book, when it came out in 1965, was considered an instant classic, largely because Capote told everyone it was. In any case, it was sufficiently seminal, as we used to say in college, to have made a lasting impact and it occurred to me that I could profitably re-read it and then go to Holcomb and make a lot of trenchant observations about crime and violence in America.

I was wrong. I quickly realized there was nothing typical about the Clutter murders: they would be as shocking today as they were then. And there was nothing particularly seminal about Capote's book. It was essentially just a grisly and sensational murder story that pandered, in a deviously respectable way, to the reader's baser instincts. All that a trip to Holcomb would achieve would be to provide me with the morbid thrill of gawping at a house in which a family had long before been senselessly slaughtered. Still, that's about all I ask out of life, and it was bound, at the very least, to be more interesting than Historic Front Street in Dodge City.

In Capote's book, Holcomb was a tranquil, dusty hamlet, full of intensely decent people, a place whose citizens didn't smoke, drink, lie, swear or miss church, a place in which sex outside marriage was unforgivable and sex before marriage unthinkable, in which teenagers were home at eleven on a Saturday night, in which Catholics and Methodists didn't mingle if they could possibly help it, in which doors were never locked, and children of eleven or twelve were allowed to drive cars. For some reason I found the idea of children driving cars particularly astonishing. In Capote's book, the nearest town was Garden City, five miles down the highway. Things had clearly changed. Now Holcomb and Garden City had more or less grown together, connected by an umbilicus of gas stations and fast food places. Holcomb was still dusty, but no longer a hamlet. On the edge of town was a huge high school, obviously new, and all around were cheap little houses, also new, with barefooted Mexican children running around in the front yards. I found the Clutter house without too much trouble. In the book it stood apart from the town, down a shady lane. Now the lane was lined with houses. There was no sign of occupancy at the Clutter house. The curtains were drawn. I hesitated for a long time and then went and knocked at the front door, and frankly was relieved that no-one answered. What could I have said? Hello, I'm a stranger passing through town with a morbid interest in sensational murders and I just wondered if you could tell me what it's like living in a house in which several people have had their brains splattered on to the walls? Do you ever think about it at meal-times, for instance?

I got back in the car and drove around, looking for anything that was familiar from the book, but the shops and cafés all seemed to have gone or been renamed. I stopped at the high school. The main doors were locked –

it was four in the afternoon – but some students from the track team were drifting about on the playing fields. I accosted two of them standing along the perimeter and asked them if I could talk to them for a minute about the Clutter murders. It was clear that they didn't know what I was talking about.

'You know,' I prompted. 'In Cold Blood. The book by Truman Capote.'

They looked at me blankly.

'You've never heard of In Cold Blood? Truman Capote?' They hadn't. I could scarcely believe it. 'Have you ever heard of the Clutter murders – a whole family killed in a house over there beyond that water-tower?'

One of them brightened. 'Oh, yeah,' he said. 'Whole family just wiped out. It was, you know, weird.'

'Does anybody live in the house now?'

'Dunno,' said the student. 'Somebody used to live there, I think. But now I think maybe they don't. Dunno really.' Talking was clearly not his strongest social skill, though compared with the second student he was a veritable Cicero. I thought I had never met two such remarkably ignorant young men, but then I stopped three others and none of them had heard of In Cold Blood either. Over by the pole-vaulting pit I found the coach, an amiable young social sciences teacher named Stan Kennedy. He was supervising three young athletes as they took turns sprinting down a runway with a long pole and then crashing with their heads and shoulders into a horizontal bar about five feet off the ground. If knocking the hell out of a horizontal bar was a sport in Kansas, these guys could be state champions. I asked Kennedy if he thought it odd that so many of the students had never heard of In Cold Blood.

'I was surprised at that myself when I first came here eight years ago,' he said. 'After all, it was the biggest thing that ever happened in the town. But you have to realize that the people here hated the book. They banned it from the public library and a lot of them even now won't talk about it.'

This surprised me. A few weeks before I had read an article in an old *Life* magazine about how the townspeople had taken Truman Capote to their hearts even though he was a mincing little poof who talked with a lisp and wore funny caps. In fact, it turns out, they disdained him not only as a mincing little poof, but as a meddler from the big city who had exploited their private grief for his own gain. Most people wanted to forget the whole business and discouraged their children from developing an interest in it. Kennedy had once asked his brightest class how many of the students had read the book, and three quarters of them had never even looked at it.

I said I thought that was surprising. If I had grown up in a place where something famous had happened I would want to read about it. 'So would I,' Kennedy said. 'So would most people from our generation. But kids these days are different. A lot of them can barely read. And you just can't teach them anything. There's no spark of enthusiasm there. It's as if years of watching TV have hypnotized them. Some of them can hardly speak a coherent sentence.'

We agreed that this was, you know, weird.

There is nothing much to be said for the far west of Kansas except that the towns are small and scattered and the highways mostly empty. Every ten miles or so there is a side road, and at every side road there is an old pickup truck stopped at a stop sign. You can see them from a long way off – in Kansas you can see everything from a long way off – glinting in the sunshine. At first you think the truck must be broken down or abandoned, but just as you get within thirty or forty feet of it, it pulls out onto the highway in front of you, causing you to make an immediate downward adjustment in your speed from sixty miles an hour to about twelve miles an hour and to test the resilience of the steering wheel with your forehead. This happens to you over and over. Curious to see what sort of person could inconvenience you in this way in the middle of nowhere, you speed up to overtake it and see that sitting at the wheel is a little old man of eighty-seven, wearing a cowboy hat three sizes too large for him, staring fixedly at the empty road as if piloting a light aircraft through a thunderstorm. He is of course quite oblivious of you. Kansas has more drivers like this than any other state in the nation, more than can be accounted for by simple demographics. Other states must send them their old people, perhaps by promising them a free cowboy hat when they get there.

Chapter twenty-one

I SHOULD HAVE known better, but I had it in my mind that Colorado was nothing but mountains. Somehow I thought that the moment I left Kansas I would find myself amid the snow-tipped Rockies, in lofty meadows of waving buttercups, where the skies were blue and the air was as crisp as fresh celery. But it was nothing like that at all. It was just flat and brown and full of remote little towns with charmless names: Swink, Ordway, Manzanola. They in turn were all full of poor-looking people and mean-looking dogs nosing around on the margins of liquor stores and gas stations. Broken bottles glittered among the stubble in the road-side ditches and the signs along the way were pocked from shotgun blasts. This sure wasn't the Colorado John Denver was forever yodelling on about.

I was imperceptibly climbing. Every town along the highway announced its elevation, and each was several hundred feet higher than the previous one, but it wasn't until I had nearly reached Pueblo, 150 miles into the interior, that I at last saw mountains. Suddenly there they were, blue and craggy and heavy with snow.

My plan was to take State Highway 67 north up to Victor and Cripple Creek, two old gold-mining towns. The road was marked on my map as scenic. What I didn't realize was that it was unpaved and that it led through a mountain pass ominously called Phantom Canyon. It was the most desolate and bone-shaking road I have ever been on, full of ruts and rocks – the kind of road that makes everything in the car dance about and doors fly open. The problem was that there was no way to turn around. One side of the road hugged a wall of rock, rising up and up, like the side of a skyscraper; the other fell sharply away to a creek of excited water. Meekly I pressed on, driving at a creeping pace and hoping that things would improve in a while. But of course they didn't. The road grew even steeper and more perilous. Here and there the two sides of the canyon would narrow and I would be hemmed in for a while by walls of fractured stone that looked as if they had been struck with a hammer, and then suddenly it would open out again to reveal hair-raising views down to the twisting canyon floor far, far below.

Everywhere above me house-sized boulders teetered on pin-heads of rock, just waiting to tumble down the mountainside and make a doormat of me. Rockslides were evidently common. The valley floor was a graveyard of boulders. I prayed that I would not meet another vehicle coming down the hill and have to reverse all the way to the valley floor. But I needn't have worried because of course not a single other person in the whole of North America was sufficiently moronic to drive through Phantom Valley at this time of year, when a sudden storm could turn the road to mud and bog the car down for months, or send it slipping and sliding over the void. I wasn't used to dealing with landscapes that can kill you. Cautiously I pressed on.

High up in the mountains I crossed a wooden bridge of laughable ricketyness over a deep chasm. It was the sort of bridge on which, in the movies, a slat always breaks, causing the heroine to plunge through up to her armpits with her pert legs wiggling helplessly above the chasm, until the hero dashes back to save her, spears falling all around them. When I was twelve years old, I could never understand why the hero, operating from this position of superiority, didn't say to the lady, 'OK, I'll save your life, but later you have to let me see you naked. Agreed?'

Beyond the bridge wet snow began to fly about. It mixed with the hundreds of insects that had been flinging themselves into the windscreen since Nebraska (what a senseless waste of life!) and turned it into a brown sludge. I attacked it with window washer solution, but this just converted it from a brown sludge to a creamy sludge and I still couldn't see. I stopped and jumped out to wipe at the window with my sleeve, certain that at any moment a bobcat, seeing the chance of a lifetime, would drop onto my shoulders and rip off my scalp with a sound like two strips of Velcro being parted. I imagined myself, scalpless, stumbling down the mountainside with the bobcat nipping at my heels. This formed such a vivid image in my mind that I jumped back into the car, even though I had only created a small rectangle of visibility about the size of an envelope. It was like looking out of a tank turret.

The car wouldn't start. Of course. Drily I said, 'Oh, thank you, God.' Up here in the thin air, the Chevette just gasped and wheezed and quickly became flooded. While I waited for the flooding to subside, I looked at the map and was dismayed to discover that I still had twenty miles to go. I had only done eight miles so far and I had been at it for well over an hour. The possibility that the Chevette might not make it to Victor and Cripple Creek took root in my skull. For the first time it occurred to me that perhaps no-one ever came along this road. If I died out here, I reflected bleakly, it could be years before anyone found me or the Chevette, which would obviously be a tragedy. Apart from anything else the battery was still under warranty.

But of course I didn't die out there. In fact, to tell you the truth, I don't intend ever to die. The car started up; I crept up over the last of the high passes and thence into Victor without further incident. Victor was a wonderful sight, a town of Western-style buildings perched incongruously in a high green valley of the most incredible beauty. Once it and Cripple Creek, six miles down the road, were boom towns to beat all boom towns. At their peak, in 1908, they had 500 gold mines between them and a population of 100,000. Miners were paid in gold. In twenty-five years or so the mines produced $800 million worth of gold and made a lot of people rich. Jack Dempsey lived in Victor and started his career there.

Today only a couple of working mines are left and the population is barely a thousand. Victor had the air of a ghost town, though at least the streets were paved. Chipmunks darted among the buildings and grass was growing through cracks in the sidewalk. The town was full of antique stores and craft shops, but almost all of them were closed, evidently waiting for the summer season. Quite a few were empty and one, the Amber Inn, had been seized for non-payment of taxes. A big sign in the window said so. But the post office was open and one café, which was full of old men in bib overalls and younger men with beards and pony tails. All the men wore baseball caps, though here they advertised brands of beer – Coors, Bud Lite, Olympia – rather than brands of fertilizer.

I decided to drive on to Cripple Creek for lunch, and then wished I hadn't. Cripple Creek stands in the shadows of Mt Pisgah and Pikes Peak and was far more touristy than Victor. Most of the stores were open, though they weren't doing much business. I parked on the main street in front of the Sarsaparilla Saloon and had a look around. Architecturally, Cripple Creek was much the same as Victor, but here the businesses were almost all geared to tourists: gift shops, snack bars, ice-cream parlours, a place where children could pan for gold in an artificial creek, a miniature golf-course. It was pretty awful, and made worse by the bleakening weather. Flurries of snow were still swirling about. It was cold and the air was thin. Cripple Creek is nearly two miles up. At that altitude, if you're not used to it, you feel uncomfortably breathless a lot of the time and vaguely unwell all of the time. Certainly the last thing I wanted was an ice-cream or a game of miniature golf, so I returned to the car and pressed on.

At the junction of US 24, I turned left and headed west. Here the weather was superb. The sun shone, the sky was blue. Out of the west, a flotilla of clouds sailed in, fluffy and benign, skimming the peaks. The highway was of pink asphalt; it was like driving along a strip of bubble gum. The road led up and over the Wilkerson Pass and then down into a long valley of rolling meadows with glittering streams and log cabins set against a backdrop of muscular mountains. It looked like a scene out of a deodorant commercial. It was glorious, and I had it almost all to myself. Near Buena Vista the land dramatically dropped away to reveal a plain and beyond it the majestic Collegiate Peaks, the highest range in the United States, with sixteen peaks of over 14,000 feet along a thirty-mile stretch. I fell with the highway down the mountainside and crossed the plain towards the Collegiate range, tall

285

and blue and snow-peaked. It was like driving into the opening credits of a Paramount movie.

I had intended to make for Aspen, but at the turning at Twin Lakes I found a white barrier barring the way and a sign saying that the highway to Aspen over Independence Pass was closed because of snow. Aspen was just twenty miles down the closed road, but to reach it by the alternative northern route would have required a detour of 150 miles. Disappointed, I looked for some place else to go for the night and drove on to Leadville, a place about which I knew nothing and indeed had never even heard.

Leadville was outstanding. The outskirts of the town were ragged and shabby – there's a surprising amount of poverty in Colorado – but the main street was broad and lined with sturdy Victorian buildings, many of them with turrets and towers. Leadville was another gold and silver mining town; it was here that the Unsinkable Molly Brown got her start, as did Meyer Guggenheim. Like Cripple Creek and Victor, it now catered to tourists – every place in the Rockies caters to tourists – but it had a much more genuine feel to it. Its population was 4,000, enough to give it an independent life apart from what the tourists brought it.

I got a room in the Timberline Motel, had a stroll around the town and a creditable meal at the Golden Burro Café – not the greatest food in the world, or even possibly in Leadville, but at $6 for soup, salad, chicken fried steak, mashed potatoes, green beans, coffee and pie, who's bitching? – followed by a moonlight stroll back to the motel, a hot shower and a little TV. If only life could always be so simple and serene. I was asleep by ten, dreaming happy dreams in which I manfully dealt with pouncing bobcats, swaying wooden bridges and windscreens full of sticky insects. The heroine even let me see her with her clothes off. It was a night to remember.

Chapter twenty-two

IN THE MORNING, the weatherman on the TV said that a 'frunnal system' was about to dump many inches of snow on the Rockies. This seemed to please him a lot. You could see it in his twinkling eyes. His map showed a band of unpleasantness sitting like a curse over almost the whole of the West. Roads would be shut, he said, a hint of a grin tugging at the corners of his mouth, and travel advisories would be issued. Why are television weathermen always so malicious? Even when they are trying to be sincere, you can see that it's a front – that just under the surface there lurks a person who spent his childhood pulling the wings off insects and snickering whenever another child fell under the wheels of a passing vehicle.

Abruptly, I decided to head south for the arid mountains of New Mexico, over which the weather-map showed nothing much in particular happening. I had a niece at a small, exclusive college in Santa Fe whom I hadn't seen for a long time and I was sure she would be delighted for all her friends on campus to witness a slobby, overweight man pull up in a cheap, dusty car, leap out and embrace her, so I decided to drive straight there.

I headed south on US 285, which runs along the line of the continental divide. All around me was the most incredible natural beauty, but the landscape was constantly blemished by human intrusions – ugly trailer parks, untidy homesteads, even junk yards. Every town was mostly a collection of fast food places and gas stations, and all along the road for many miles stood signs the size of barns saying CAMPGROUND, MOTEL, RAFTING.

The further south I went the more barren the landscape grew, and after a while the signs disappeared. Beyond Saguache the wide plain between the mountains became a sweep of purple sage, interspersed with dead brown earth. Here and there a field of green had been snatched from the scrub with the aid of massive wheeled water-sprinklers. In the middle of these oases would stand a neat farmhouse. But otherwise the landscape between the distant mountain ranges was as featureless as a dried seabed. Between Saguache and Monte Vista lies one of the ten or twelve longest stretches of straight road in America: almost forty miles without a single bend or kink. That may not sound such a lot on paper, but it feels endless on the road. There is nothing like a highway stretching off to an ever-receding vanishing-point to make you feel as if you are going nowhere. At Monte Vista, the road takes a left turn – this makes you perk up and grip the wheel – and then there is another twenty-mile stretch as straight as a ruler's edge. And so it goes. Two or three times in an hour you zip through a dusty little town – a gas station, three houses, one tree, a dog – or encounter a fractional bend in the road which requires you to move the steering wheel three centimetres to the right or left for two seconds, and that's your excitement for the hour. The rest of the time you don't move a muscle. Your buttocks grow numb and begin to feel as if they belong to another person.

In the early afternoon I crossed over into New Mexico – one of the high points of the day – and sighed at the discovery that it was just as unstimulating as Colorado had been. I switched on the radio. I was so far from anywhere that I could only pick up scattered stations, and those were all Spanish-speaking ones playing that kind of aye-yi-yi Mexican music that's always sung by strolling musicians with droopy moustaches and big sombreros in the sort of restaurants where high school teachers take their wives for their thirtieth wedding anniversaries – the sort of places where they like to set your food alight to impress you. It had never once occurred to me in thirty-six years of living that anyone listened to Mexican music for pleasure. Yet here there were a dozen stations blaring it out. After each song, a disc jockey would come on and jabber for a minute or two in Spanish in the tone of a man who has just had his nuts slammed in a drawer. There would then be a break for an advertisement, read by a man who sounded even more urgent and excited – he clearly was having his nuts repeatedly slammed in a drawer – and then there would be another song. Or rather, it would be the same song again, as far as I could tell. That is the unfortunate thing about Mexican musicians. They only seem to know one tune. This may explain why they have difficulty finding work anywhere other than at second-rate restaurants.

At a hamlet called Tres Piedras – almost every place in New Mexico has a Spanish name – I took Highway 64 to Taos, and things began to improve. The hills grew darker and the sage became denser and lusher. Everyone always talks about the sky around Taos, and it is astonishing. I had never seen a sky so vivid and blue, so liquid. The air in this part of the desert is so clear that you can some-times see for 180 miles, or so my guidebook said. In any case, you can certainly see why Taos has always attracted artists and writers – or at least you can until you get to Taos itself. I had expected it to be a sweet little artists' colony, full of people with smocks and easels, and it was just a tourist trap, with slow-moving traffic and stores selling ugly Indian pottery and big silver belt buckles and postcards. There were a couple of interesting galleries, but mostly it was hot and dusty and full of silver-haired hippies. It was mildly amusing to see that hippies still existed – indeed were now grandparents – but it was scarcely worth the bother of getting there. So I drove on to Santa Fe, fearful that it would be much the same. But it was not. In fact, it was quite beautiful, and I was instantly charmed.

The first nice thing about Santa Fe is that it has trees. It has trees and grass and shade and cool plazas full of flowers and plants and the soothing burble of running water. After days of driving across the barren wastes of the West this is a treat beyond dimension. The air is warm and clean and the reddish Sangre de Cristo mountains at the city's back are just sensational, especially at sunset when they simply glow, as if lit from within, like jack-o'-lanterns. The town itself is just too rich and pretty for words. It is the oldest continuously inhabited city in America – it was founded in 1610, a decade before the pilgrims set off from Plymouth – and takes great pride in its age. Everything in Santa Fe, and I mean everything, is made out of adobe. There's an adobe Woolworth's, an adobe multi-storey parking lot, an adobe six-storey hotel. When you pass your first adobe gas station and adobe supermarket, you think, 'Hey, let's get out of here,' but then you realize that it isn't something laid on for the tourists. Adobe is simply the indigenous building material, and using it everywhere gives the town a uniformity of appearance few other places achieve. Besides, Santa Fe is filthy rich, so everything is done tastefully and well.

I drove up into the hills looking for St John's College, where my niece was a student. It was four in the afternoon and the streets were full of long shadows. The sun was settling onto the mountains and the adobe houses on every hillside were lit with a rich orange-brown glow. St John's is a small college perched high up in the hills, with the finest view in town, looking down over Santa Fe and the rolling mountains beyond. It has only 300 students on its sleepy campus, but my niece, on this fine spring afternoon, was not among them. No-one knew where she was, but everyone promised to let her know that a slobby, overweight person with dusty shoes and tropical armpits had come looking for her and would call back in the morning.

I went back into town, got a room, had a deep, hot bath, changed into clean clothes and spent the evening shambling happily around the tranquil streets of downtown Santa Fe, gazing admiringly at the window displays in the expensive galleries and boutiques, savouring the warm evening air, and disconcerting people in the more exclusive restaurants by pressing my face up against the windows and looking critically at their food. The heart of Santa Fe is the Plaza, a Spanish-style square with white benches and a tall obelisk commemorating the battle of Valverde, whatever

THE LOST CONTINENT

that was. On the base was an engraved inscription in which
February had been misspelled as Febuary; this pleased me
very much. Another pleasing thing about the Plaza was a
place on the corner called the Ore House. Downstairs it is a
restaurant, but upstairs there is a bar with an open porch
where you can sit – where indeed I did sit – for many
tranquil hours drinking beers brought to your table by a
pleasant waitress with a nice bottom, enjoying the mild
evening and watching the stars fill the pale blue desert sky.
Through the open door into the bar I could also watch the
pianist, a well-groomed young man who played a seemingly endless series of chords and tinkling arpeggios that
never really developed into anything you could call a song.
But he cruised suavely up and down the keyboard and he
had a winning smile and excellent teeth, which I suppose is
the main thing in a cocktail bar pianist. Anyway, the ladies
clearly liked him.

I don't know how many beers I had, but – I will be frank
here – it was too many. I had not allowed for the fact that
in the thin mountain air of Santa Fe you get drunk much
faster. In any case, I was surprised to discover as I stood up
a couple of hours after entering that the relationship
between my mind and legs, which was normally quite a
good one, had broken down. More than that, my legs now
didn't seem to be getting on at all well with each other.
One of them started for the stairs, as instructed, but the
other, in a burst of petulance, decided to make for the rest-
room. The result was that I lurched through the bar like a
man on stilts, grinning inanely as if to say, 'Yes, I know I
look like an asshole. Isn't this amusing?'

En route, I bumped into the table of a party of middle-
aged rich people, slopping their drinks, and could only

293

broaden my brainless smile and burble that I was ever so sorry. I patted one of the ladies affectionately on the shoulder with that easy familiarity that overcomes me when I am drunk and used her as a kind of springboard to propel myself towards the stairs, where I smiled a farewell to the room – everyone was by now watching me with interest – and descended the stairs in one fluid motion. I didn't exactly fall, but then again I didn't exactly walk down. It was more like surfing on the soles of my shoes, and was, I believe, not unimpressive. But then I often perform my best stunts while intoxicated. Once, many years ago during a party at John Horner's house, I fell backwards out of an upstairs window and bounced to my feet with an *élan* that is still widely talked about south of Grand Avenue.

In the morning, chastened with a hangover, I drove back to the campus of St John's, found my niece and embarrassed her – possibly even grossed her out – with a hug. We went to breakfast in a fancy restaurant downtown and she told me all about St John's and Santa Fe and afterwards showed me the sights of the town: St Francis's Cathedral (very beautiful), the Palace of the Governors (very boring, full of documents about territorial governors) and the famous staircase at the Loretto Chapel. This is a wooden staircase that rises twenty-one and a half feet in a double spiral up to a choir loft. The remarkable thing about it is that it is not supported by anything except its own weight. It looks as if it ought to fall down. The story is that the nuns of the chapel prayed for someone to build them a staircase and an anonymous carpenter turned up, worked on the staircase for six months and then disappeared without payment as mysteriously as he had arrived. For a hundred years the nuns milked this story for all it was worth, and then one day a few years ago they abruptly sold the chapel to a private company, which now runs it for a profit and charges you 50¢ to get in. This kind of soured me on the place, and it didn't do a whole lot for my respect for nuns.

Generally speaking – which is of course always a dangerous thing to do, generally speaking – Americans revere the past only as long as there is some money in it somewhere and it doesn't mean going without airconditioning, free parking and other essential conveniences. Preserving the past for its own sake doesn't come into it much. There is little room for sentiment. When somebody comes along and offers a group of nuns good money for their staircase, they don't say, 'Certainly not, it is a hallowed shrine, built for us by a mysterious and rather hunky-looking courier of Jesus.' They say, 'How much?' And if the offer is good enough they sell it and use the money to build a new convent on a bigger site, with airconditioning, lots of parking space and a games room. I don't mean to suggest for a moment that nuns are worse than other Americans in this regard. They are simply behaving in the customary American way. I find that very sad. It is no wonder that so few things last for more than a generation in America.

I left Santa Fe and drove west along Interstate 40. This used to be Route 66. Everybody loved Route 66. People used to write songs about it. But it was only two lanes wide, not at all suitable for the space age, hopelessly inadequate for people in motor homes, and every fifty miles or so it would pass through a little town where you might encounter a stop sign or a traffic light – what a drag! – so they buried it under the desert and built a new superhighway that shoots across the landscape like a four-lane laser and doesn't stop for anything, even mountains. So something else that was nice and pleasant is gone forever because it wasn't practical – like passenger trains and milk in bottles and corner shops and Burma Shave signs. And now it's happening in Britain, too. They are taking away all the nice things there because they are impractical, as if that were reason enough – the red phone-boxes, the pound note, those open London buses that you can leap on and off. There is almost no experience in life that makes you look and feel more suave than jumping on or off a moving London bus. But they aren't practical. They require two men (one to drive and one to stop thugs from kicking the crap out of the Pakistani gentleman at the back) and that is uneconomical, so they have to go. And before long there will be no more milk in bottles delivered to the doorstep or sleepy rural pubs and the countryside will be mostly shopping centres and theme parks. Forgive me. I don't mean to get upset. But you are taking my world away from me, piece by little piece, and sometimes it just pisses me off. Sorry.

I drove west along Interstate 40, through an impoverished landscape. Habitations were few. Such towns as existed were mostly just scatterings of trailer homes dumped along the roadside, as if dropped from a great height. They had no yards, no fences, nothing to separate them from the desert. Much of the land was given over to Indian reservations. Every twenty or thirty miles I would pass a lone hitch-hiker, sometimes an Indian but usually a white person, alone and with bags. I had seen hardly any hitch-hikers before now, but here there were many, the men looking dangerous, the women looking crazy. I was entering a land of drifters: dreamers, losers, vagrants, crazy people – they all always go west in America. They all have this hopeless idea that they will get to the coast and make a fortune as a movie star or rock musician or game show contestant or something. And if things don't work out they can always become a serial murderer. It's strange that no-one ever goes east, that you never encounter anyone hitch-hiking to New York in pursuit of some wild and crazy dream to be a certified public accountant or make a killing in leveraged buy-outs.

The weather worsened. Dust began to blow across the road. I was driving into the storm that the weatherman had spoken of on television the morning before. Beyond Albuquerque the skies darkened and a sleety rain began to dart about. Tumbleweeds bounced across the desert and over the highway, and the car was knocked sharply side-ways with each gust of wind.

I had always thought that deserts were hot and dry the year around. I can tell you now that they are not. I suppose because we always took our vacations between June and August it implanted in me the idea that everywhere in America outside the Midwest was hot the year around. Wherever you went in the summer in America it was murder. It was always ninety degrees. If you closed the windows you baked, but if you left them open everything blew everywhere – comic books, maps, loose articles of clothing. If you wore shorts, as we always did, the bare skin on your legs became part of the seat, like cheese melted onto toast, and when it was time to get up, there was a ripping sound and a screaming sensation of agony as the two parted. If in your sun-baked delirium you carelessly leaned your arm against the metal part of the door on to which the sun had been shining, the skin where it made contact would shrivel and disappear, like a plastic bag in a flame. This would always leave you speechless. It was a truly amazing, and curiously painless, spectacle to watch part of your body just vanish. You didn't know whether to shriek at your mother as if you had been gravely wounded, or do it again, in a spirit of scientific enquiry. In the end, usually, you would do nothing, but just sit listlessly, too hot to do anything else.

So I was surprised to find myself in wintry weather, in a landscape as cold as it was bleak. The darting sleet thickened as the highway climbed up and into the Zuni Mountains. Beyond Gallup it turned to snow. Wet and heavy, it fell from the sky like scattered feathers, and the afternoon became like night.

Twenty miles beyond Gallup, I entered Arizona and the further I drove into that state the more evident it became that I was entering a storm of long standing. The snow along the roadside became ankle-deep and then knee-deep. It was odd to think that only a couple of hours before I had been strolling around Santa Fe in bright sunshine and shirtsleeves. Now the radio was full of news of closed roads and atrocious weather – snow in the mountains, torrential rain elsewhere. It was the worst spring storm in decades, the weatherman said with ill-disguised glee. The Los Angeles Dodgers had been rained out at home for the third day in a row – the first time this had happened since they moved to the coast from Brooklyn thirty years before. There was nowhere I could turn to escape this storm. Bleakly, I pushed on towards Flagstaff, 100 miles to the west.

'And there's fourteen inches of snow on the ground at Flagstaff – with more expected,' the weatherman said, sounding very pleased.

Chapter twenty-three

NOTHING PREPARES you for the Grand Canyon. No matter how many times you read about it or see it pictured, it still takes your breath away. Your mind, unable to deal with anything on this scale, just shuts down and for many long moments you are a human vacuum, without speech or breath, but just a deep, inexpressible awe that anything on this earth could be so vast, so beautiful, so silent.

Even children are stilled by it. I was a particularly talkative and obnoxious child, but it stopped me cold. I can remember rounding a corner and standing there agog while a mouthful of half-formed jabber just rolled backwards down my throat, forever unuttered. I was seven years old and I'm told it was only the second occasion in all that time that I had stopped talking, apart from short breaks for sleeping and television. The one other thing to silence me was the sight of my grandfather dead in an open coffin. It was such an unexpected sight – no-one had told me that he would be on display – and it just took my breath away. There he was all still and silent, dusted with powder and dressed in a suit. I particularly remember that he had his glasses on (what did they think he was going to do with those where he was going?) and that they were crooked. I think my grandmother had knocked them askew during her last blubbery embrace and then everyone else had been too squeamish to push them back into place. It was a shock to me to realize that never again in the whole of eternity would he laugh over *I Love Lucy* or repair his car or talk with his mouth full (something for which he was widely noted in the family). It was awesome.

But not nearly as awesome as the Grand Canyon. Since, obviously, I could never hope to relive my grandfather's funeral, the Grand Canyon was the one vivid experience from my childhood that I could hope to recapture, and I had been looking forward to it for many days. I had spent the night at Winslow, Arizona, fifty miles short of Flagstaff, because the roads were becoming impassable. In the evening the snow had eased to a scattering of flakes and by morning it had stopped altogether, though the skies still looked dark and pregnant. I drove through a snow-whitened landscape towards the Grand Canyon. It was hard to believe that this was the last week of April. Mists and fog swirled about the road. I could see nothing at the sides and ahead of me except the occasional white smear of oncoming headlights. By the time I reached the entrance to Grand Canyon National Park, and paid the $5 admission, snow was dropping heavily again, thick white flakes so big that their undersides carried shadows.

The road through the park followed the southern lip of the canyon for thirty miles. Two or three times I stopped in laybys and went to the edge to peer hopefully into the silent murk, knowing that the canyon was out there, just beyond my nose, but I couldn't see anything. The fog was everywhere – threaded among the trees, adrift on the roadsides, rising steamily off the pavement. It was so thick I could kick holes in it. Glumly I drove on to the Grand Canyon village, where there was a visitors' centre and a rustic hotel and a scattering of administrative buildings. There were lots of tour buses and recreational vehicles in the parking lots and people hanging around in entrance-ways or picking their way through the slushy snow, going from one building to another. I went and had an over-priced cup of coffee in the hotel cafeteria and felt damp and dispirited. I had really been looking forward to the Grand Canyon. I sat by the window and bleakly watched the snow pile up.

Afterwards, I trudged towards the visitors' centre, per-haps 200 yards away, but before I got there I came across a snow-spattered sign announcing a look-out point half a mile away along a trail through the woods, and impul-sively I went down it, mostly just to get some air. The path was slippery and took a long time to traverse, but on the way the snow stopped falling and the air felt clean and refreshing. Eventually I came to a platform of rocks, marking the edge of the canyon. There was no fence to keep you back from the edge, so I shuffled cautiously over and looked down, but could see nothing but grey soup. A middle-aged couple came along and as we stood chatting about what a dispiriting experience this was, a miraculous thing happened. The fog parted. It just silently drew back, like a set of theatre curtains being opened, and suddenly we saw that we were on the edge of a sheer, giddying drop of at least a thousand feet. 'Jesus!' we said and jumped back, and all along the canyon edge you could hear people saying 'Jesus!', like a message being passed down a long line. And then for many moments all was silence, except for the tiny fretful shiftings of the snow, because out there in front of us was the most awesome, most silencing sight that exists on earth.

The scale of the Grand Canyon is almost beyond comprehension. It is ten miles across, a mile deep, 180 miles long. You could set the Empire State Building down in it and still be thousands of feet above it. Indeed you could set the whole of Manhattan down inside it and you would still be so high above it that buses would be like ants and people would be invisible, and not a sound would reach you. The thing that gets you – that gets everyone – is the silence. The Grand Canyon just swallows sound. The sense of space and emptiness is overwhelming. Nothing happens out there. Down below you on the canyon floor, far, far away, is the thing that carved it: the Colorado River. It is 300 feet wide, but from the canyon's lip it looks thin and insignificant. It looks like an old shoelace. Everything is dwarfed by this mighty hole.

And then, just as swiftly, just as silently as the fog had parted, it closed again and the Grand Canyon was a secret once more. I had seen it for no more than twenty or thirty seconds, but at least I had seen it. Feeling semi-satisfied, I turned around and walked back towards the car, content now to move on. On the way, I encountered a young couple coming towards the edge. They asked me if I'd had any luck and I told them all about how the fog had parted for a few seconds. They looked crushed. They said they had come all the way from Ontario. It was their honeymoon. All their lives they had wanted to see the Grand Canyon. Three times every day for the past week they had put on their moonboots and honeymoon winterwear and walked hand in hand to the canyon's edge, but all they had seen so far was an unshifting wall of fog.

'Still,' I said, trying to help them look on the bright side, 'I bet you've gotten in a lot of good shagging.' I didn't really say that. Even *I* wouldn't say that. I just made sympathetic noises and said what a shame it was about the weather and wished them luck. I walked on in a reflective mood to the car, thinking about the poor honeymooners. As my father always used to tell me, 'You see, son, there's always someone in the world worse off than you.'

And I always used to think, 'So?'

I headed north on Highway 89 towards Utah. The radio was full of more news of bad weather in the Rockies and Sierra Nevadas, and of roads closed by rockslides and heavy snow, though here in northern Arizona there was no snow at all. Absolutely none. Ten miles beyond the Grand Canyon it just disappeared and a few miles after that it was like spring. The sun came out. The world was warm. I rolled the window down a little.

I drove and drove. That is what you do in the West. You drive and you drive and you drive, advancing from one scattered town to the next, creeping across a landscape like Neptune. For long, empty hours your one goal in life is to get to Dry Gulch or Cactus City or wherever. You sit there watching the highway endlessly unfurl and the odometer advancing with the speed of centuries and all you think about is getting to Dry Gulch and hoping by some miracle it will have a McDonald's or at least a coffee shop. And when at last you get there, all there is is a two-pump gas station and a stall with an old Indian woman selling Navajo trinkets and you realize that you have to start the process all over again with another impossibly isolated hamlet with a depressingly unpromising name: Coma, Doldrum, Dry Well, Sunstroke.

The distances are almost inconceivable. There is often thirty miles between houses and a hundred miles or more between towns. What would it take to make you live in a place where you had to drive seventy-five miles just to buy a pair of shoes – and even then they would look as if they came from a funeral home?

The answer to my question, of course, is that not many people do want to live in such a place, except for Indians, who were never given much choice. I was now driving across the largest Indian reservation in America – a Navajo reservation stretching for 150 miles from north to south and 200 miles from east to west – and most of the few cars along the highway were driven by Indians. Almost without exception these were big old Detroit cars in dreadful condition, with all the trim gone or flopping loosely, and with at least one mismatched door and important-looking pieces hanging from the undercarriage, clattering on the highway, shooting sparks or dense smoke. They never seemed to be able to get over about forty miles an hour, but they were always difficult to pass because of the way they drifted around on the highway.

Occasionally they would drift far off to the right, some-times even kicking up desert dust, and I would shoot past. Always it was the same sight: a car packed with Indian men and boys and a driver drunk beyond repair, sitting there with a wet-dream look on his face – the look of a man who is only barely conscious but having a splendid time none the less.

At Page, Arizona, home of the Glen Canyon Dam, I passed into Utah and almost immediately the landscape improved. The hills grew purplish and red and the desert took on a blush of colour. After a few miles, the sage-brush

305

BILL BRYSON

thickened and the hills became darker and more angular. It all looked oddly familiar. Then I consulted my Mobil guidebook and discovered that this was where all the Hollywood westerns were made. More than a hundred film and television companies had used Kanab, the next town down the road, as their headquarters for location shooting.

This excited me, and when I got to Kanab, I stopped and went into a café to see if I could find out more. A voice from the back called out that she would be just a minute, so I had a look at the menu on the wall. It was the strangest menu I had ever seen. It was full of foods I had never heard of: potato logs ('small, medium and family size'), cheese sticks for 89c, pizza pockets for $1.39, Oreo shakes for $1.25. The special offer was '8oz log, roll and slaw, $7.49'. I decided I would have coffee. After a moment the woman who ran the café came out wiping her hands on a towel. She told me some of the films and TV shows that had been shot around Kanab: *Duel at Diablo*, *Butch Cassidy and the Sundance Kid*, *My Friend Flicka*, *The Rifleman*, some Clint Eastwood movies. I asked her whether any Hollywood stars ever came in for some potato logs or cheese sticks. She shook her head wistfully and said no. Somehow this didn't altogether surprise me.

I spent the night at Cedar City and in the morning drove to Bryce Canyon National Park, which was invisible on account of fog and snow, and then, in a surly mood, to Zion National Park, where it was like summer. This was very odd because the two parks are only about forty miles apart, and yet they seemed to inhabit different continents

306

as far as the weather went. If I live forever I will not begin to understand the weather of the West.

Zion was incredibly beautiful. Whereas at the Grand Canyon you are on the top looking down, at Zion you are at the bottom looking up. It is just a long, lush canyon, dense with cottonwood trees along the valley floor, hemmed in by towering copper-coloured walls of rock – the sort of dark, forbidding valley you would expect to pass through in a hunt for the lost city of gold. Here and there long, thin waterfalls emerged from the rock face and fell a thousand feet or more down to the valley, where the water collected in pools or tumbled onward into the swirling Virgin River. At the far end of the valley the high walls squeezed together until they were only yards apart. In the damp shade, plants grew out of cracks in the rock, giving the whole the appearance of hanging gardens. It was very picturesque and exotic.

The sheer walls on either side looked as if they might rain boulders at any moment – and indeed they sometimes do. Half-way along the path the little river was suddenly littered with rocks, some of them the size of houses. A sign said that on July 16, 1981, more than 15,000 tons of rock fell 1,000 feet into the river here, but it didn't say whether there were any people squashed beneath them. I dare say there were. Even now in April there were scores of people all along the path; in July there must have been hundreds. At least a couple of them must have got caught. When the rocks came tumbling down, there would be no place to run.

I was standing there reflecting on this melancholy thought when I became aware of a vaguely irritating whirring noise beside me. It was a man with a video camera, taking footage of the rocks. It was one of the early, primitive models, so he had all kinds of power packs and auxiliary paraphernalia strapped to his body, and the camera itself was enormous. It must be like going on vacation with your vacuum cleaner. Anyway, it served him right. My first rule of consumerism is never to buy anything you can't make your children carry. The man looked exhausted, but having spent a ridiculously inflated sum to buy the camera, he was now determined to film everything that passed before his eyes, even at the risk of acquiring a hernia (and when that happened he would of course get his wife to film the operation).

I can never understand these people who rush to buy new gadgets; surely they must see that they are going to look like idiots in about a year when the manufacturers come up with tiny lightweight versions of the same thing at half the price? Like the people who paid £200 for the first pocket calculators and then a few months later they were giving them away at gas stations. Or the people who bought the first colour televisions.

One of our neighbours, Mr Sheitelbaum, bought a colour TV in 1958 when there were only about two colour programmes a month. We used to peek through his window when we knew one was coming on, and it was always the same – people with orange faces and clothes that kept changing hue. Mr Sheitelbaum kept bobbing up to fiddle with the many little knobs with which the thing was equipped while his wife shouted encouragement from across the room.

For a few moments the colour would be pretty fair – not accurate exactly, but not too disturbing – and then just as Mr Sheitelbaum placed his butt back on the sofa it would all go haywire and we would have green horses and red clouds, and he'd be back at the control panel again. It was hopeless. But having spent such a huge amount of money on this thing, Mr Sheitelbaum would never give up on it, and for the next fifteen years whenever you walked past his living-room window you would see him fiddling with the controls and muttering.

In the late afternoon, I drove on to St George, a small city not far from the state line. I got a room in the Oasis Motel and dined at Dick's Café. Afterwards, I went for a stroll. St George had a nice old-town feel about it, though in fact most of the buildings were new except for the Gaiety Movie Theater ('All Seats $2') and Dixie Drugstore next door. The drugstore was closed, but I was brought up short by the sight of a soda-fountain inside, a real marble-topped soda-fountain with twirly stools and straws in paper wrappers – the sort in which you tear off one end and then blow, sending the wrapper on a graceful trajectory into the cosmetics department.

I was crushed. This must be just about the last genuine drugstore soda-fountain in America and the place was closed. I would have given whole dollars to go in and order a green river or a chocolate soda and send a few straw wrappers wafting about and then challenge the next person along to a stool-twirling contest. My personal best is four full revolutions. I know that doesn't sound much, but it's a lot harder than it looks. Bobby Wintermeyer did five once and then threw up. It's a pretty hairy sport, believe me.

On the corner was a big brick Mormon church, or temple or tabernacle or whatever they call them. It was dated 1871 and looked big enough to hold the whole town – and indeed it probably often does since absolutely everybody in Utah is a Mormon. This sounds kind of alarming until you realize that it means Utah is the one place on the planet where you never have to worry about young men coming up to you and trying to convert you to Mormonism. They assume you are one of them already. As long as you keep your hair cut fairly short and don't say, 'Oh, shit!' in public when something goes wrong, you may escape detection for years. It makes you feel a little like Kevin McCarthy in *Invasion of the Body Snatchers*, but it is also strangely liberating.

Beyond the Mormon church things became mostly residential. Everything was green and fresh after the recent rains. The town smelled of spring, of lilacs and fresh-mown grass. The evening was creeping in. It was that relaxed time of day when people have finished their dinners and are just pootling about in the yard or garage, not doing much of anything in preparation for shortly doing even less.

The streets were the widest I've ever seen in any town, even out here in the residential neighbourhoods. Mormons sure do love wide streets. I don't know why. Wide streets and lots of wives for bonking, those are the foundation stones of Mormonism. When Brigham Young founded Salt Lake City one of the first things he did was decree that the streets be 100 feet wide, and he must have said something similar to the people of St George. Young knew the town well – he had his winter home there – so if the townspeople ever tried anything slack with the streets he'd have been on to them right away.

Chapter twenty-four

HERE'S A RIDDLE for you. What is the difference between Nevada and a toilet? Answer: You can flush a toilet.

Nevada has the highest crime rate of any state, the highest rape rate, the second highest violent crime rate (it's just pipped by New York), the highest highway fatality rate, the second highest rate of gonorrhoea (Alaska is the trophy-holder), and the highest proportion of transients – almost eighty per cent of the state's residents were born elsewhere. It has more prostitutes than any other state in America. It has a long history of corruption and strong links with organized crime. And its most popular entertainer is Wayne Newton. So you may understand why I crossed the border from Utah with a certain sense of disquiet.

But then I got to Las Vegas and my unease vanished. I was dazzled. It's impossible not to be. It was late afternoon, the sun was low, the temperature was in the high eighties, and the Strip was already thronged with happy vacationers in nice clean clothes, their pockets visibly bulging with money, strolling along in front of casinos the size of airport terminals. It all looked fun and oddly wholesome. I had expected it to be nothing but hookers and high rollers in stretched Cadillacs, the sort of people who wear white leather shoes and drape their jackets over their shoulders, but these were just ordinary folks like you and me, people who wear a lot of nylon and Velcro.

I got a room in a motel at the cheaper end of the Strip, showered lavishly, danced through a dust storm of talcum powder, pulled on my cleanest T-shirt, and went straight back out, tingling with clean skin and child-like excitation. After days of driving across the desert you are ready for a little stimulation, and Las Vegas certainly provides it. Now, in the oven-dry air of early evening, the casino lights were coming on – millions and millions of them, erupting into walls of bilious colour and movement, flashing, darting, rippling, bursting, all of them competing for my attention, for the coins in my pocket. I had never seen such a sight. It is an ocular orgasm, a three-dimensional hallucination, an electrician's wet dream. It was just as I had expected it to be but multiplied by ten.

The names on the hotels and casinos were eerily familiar: Caesar's Palace, the Dunes, the Sands, the Desert Inn. What most surprised me – what most surprises most people – is how many vacant lots there were. Here and there among the throbbing monoliths there were quarter-mile squares of silent desert, little pockets of dark calm, just waiting to be developed. When you have been to one or two casinos and seen how the money just pours into them, like gravel off a dump truck, it is hard to believe that there could be enough spare cash in the world to feed still more of them, yet more are being built all the time. The greed of mankind is practically insatiable, mine included.

I went into Caesar's Palace. It is set well back from the street, but I was conveyed in on a moving sidewalk, which rather impressed me. Inside the air was thick with unreality. The décor was supposed to be like a Roman temple or something. Statues of Roman gladiators and statesmen were scattered around the place and all the cigarette girls and ladies who gave change were dressed in skimpy togas, even if they were old and overweight, which most of them were, so their thighs wobbled as they walked. It was like watching moving Jell-O. I wandered through halls full of people intent on losing money – endlessly, single-mindedly feeding coins into slot machines or watching the clattering dance of a steel ball on a roulette wheel or playing games of blackjack that had no start or finish but were just continuous, like time. It all had a monotonous, yet anxious rhythm. There was no sense of pleasure or fun. I never saw anyone talking to anyone else, except to order a drink or cash some money. The noise was intense – the crank of one-armed bandits, the spinning of thousands of wheels, the din of clattering coins when a machine paid out.

A change lady Jell-O'd past and I got $10 worth of quarters from her. I put one in a one-armed bandit – I had never done this before; I'm from Iowa – pulled the handle and watched the wheels spin and thunk into place one by one. There was a tiny pause and then the machine spat six quarters into the pay-out bucket. I was hooked. I fed in more quarters. Some-times I would lose and I would put in more quarters. Sometimes the machine would spit me back some quarters and I would put those in as well. After about five minutes I had no quarters left. I flagged down another amplehipped vestal virgin and got $10 more. This time I won $12 worth of quarters straight off. It made a lot of noise. I looked around proudly, but no-one paid any attention to me. Then I won $5 more. Hey, this is all right, I thought. I put all my quarters in a little plastic bucket that said Caesar's Palace on it. There seemed to be an awful lot of them, gleaming up at me, but in about twenty minutes the bucket was empty. I went and got another $10 worth of quarters, and started feeding them in. I won some and lost some. I was beginning to realize that there was a certain pattern to it: for every four quarters I put in, I would on average get three back, sometimes in a bunch, sometimes in dribbles. My right arm began to ache a little. It was boring really, pulling the handle over and over, watching the wheels spin and thunk, thunk, thunk, spin and thunk, thunk, thunk. With my last quarter I won $3 worth of quarters, and was mildly disappointed because I had been hoping to go for dinner and now here I had a mittful of quarters again. So I dutifully fed the quarters into the machine and won some more money. This really was getting tiresome. Finally, after about thirty minutes I got rid of the last quarter and was able to go and look for a restaurant.

On the way out my attention was caught by a machine making a lot of noise. A woman had just won $600. For ninety seconds the machine just poured out money, a waterfall of silver. When it stopped, the woman regarded the pile without pleasure and began feeding it back into the machine. I felt sorry for her. It was going to take her all night to get rid of that kind of money.

I wandered through room after room trying to find my way out, but the place was clearly designed to leave you disoriented. There were no windows, no exit signs, just endless rooms, all with subdued lighting and with carpet that looked as if some executive had barked into a telephone, 'Gimme 20,000 yards of the ugliest carpet you got.' It was like woven vomit. I wandered for ages without knowing whether I was getting closer to or further from an exit. I passed a little shopping centre, restaurants, a buffet, cabarets, dark and silent bars where people brooded, bars with live music and astonishingly untalented entertainers

('And gimme some astonishingly untalented entertainers while you're at it'), and one large room in which the walls were covered with giant TV screens showing live sporting events – major league baseball, NBA basketball, boxing matches, a horse race. A whole wallful of athletes were silently playing their hearts out for the benefit of the room's lone spectator, and he was asleep.

I don't know how many gaming rooms there were, but there were many. It was often hard to tell whether I was seeing a new room or an old room from another angle. In each one it was the same – long ranks of people dully, mechanically losing money. It was as if they had been hypnotized. None of them seemed to see that everything was stacked against them. It is all such an incredible con. Some of the casinos make profits of $100 million a year – that's the kind of money many large corporations make – and without having to do anything but open their doors. It takes almost no skills, no intelligence, no class to run a casino. I read in *Newsweek* that the guy who owns the Horseshoe casino downtown has never learned how to read and write. Can you believe that? That gives you some idea of the sort of level of intellectual attainment you need to be a success in Vegas. Suddenly, I hated the place. I was annoyed with myself for having been taken in by it all, the noise and sparkle, for having so quickly and mindlessly lost thirty dollars. For that kind of money I could have bought a baseball cap with a plastic turd on the brim *and* an ashtray in the shape of a toilet saying 'Place Your Butt Here. Souvenir of Las Vegas, Nevada.' This made me deeply gloomy.

I went and ate in the Caesar's Palace buffet, hoping that some food would improve my outlook. The buffet cost $8, but you could eat all you wanted, so I took a huge amount of everything, determined to recoup some of my loss. The resultant plate was such a mixture of foods, gravies, barbecue sauces and salad creams that it was really just a heap of tasteless goo. But I shovelled it all down and then had an outsized platter of chocolate goo for dessert. And then I felt very ill. I felt as if I had eaten a roll of insulation. Clutching my distended abdomen, I found my way to an exit. There was no moving sidewalk to return me to the street – there's no place in Las Vegas for losers or quitters – so I had to make a long weaving walk down the floodlit driveway to the Strip. The fresh air helped a little, but only a little. I limped through the crowds along the Strip, looking like a man doing a poor imitation of Quasimodo, and went into a couple of other casinos, hoping they would re-excite my greed and make me forget my swollen belly. But they were practically identical to Caesar's Palace – the same noise, the same stupid people losing all their money, the same hideous carpets. It all just gave me a headache. After a while, I gave up altogether. I plodded back to my motel and fell heavily on the bed and watched TV with that kind of glazed immobility that overcomes you when your stomach is grossly overloaded and there's no remote control device and you can't quite reach the channel switch with your big toe.

So I watched the local news. Principally this consisted of a run-down of the day's murders in Las Vegas accompanied by film from the various murder scenes. These always showed a house with the front door open, some police detectives shuffling around, a group of neighbourhood children standing on the fringes, waving happily at the camera and saying hi to their moms. In between each report the anchorman and anchorwoman would trade witless quips and then say in a breezy tone something like, 'A mother and her three young children were hacked to death by a crazed axeman at Boulder City today. We'll have a filmed report after these words.' Then there would be many long minutes of commercials, mostly for products to keep one's bowels sleek, followed by filmed reports on regional murders, house fires, light airplane crashes, multiple car pile-ups on the Boulder Highway and other bits of local carnage, always with film of mangled vehicles, charred houses, bodies under blankets, and a group of children standing on the fringes, waving happily at the cameras and saying hi to their moms. It may only have been my imagination, but I would almost swear that it was the same children in every report. Perhaps American violence had bred a new kind of person – the serial witness.

Finally there was a special report about a man awaiting release from prison who ten years before had raped a young woman and then, for reasons of obscure gratification, had sawn off her arms at the elbows. No kidding. This was so shocking even to the hardened sensibilities of Nevadans that a mob was expected to be waiting for the man when he was released at 6 a.m. the next day, according to the TV reporter, who then gave all the details necessary to enable viewers to go down and join in. The police, the reporter added with a discernible trace of pleasure, were refusing to guarantee the man's safety. The report concluded with a shot of the reporter talking to camera in front of the prison gate. Behind her a group of children were jumping up and down and waving hi to their moms. This was all becoming too bizarre for me. I got

317

up heavily and switched the TV to *Mr Ed*. At least you know where you are with *Mr Ed*.

In the morning I took Interstate 15 south out of Las Vegas, a long, straight drive through the desert. It's the main route between Las Vegas and Los Angeles, 272 miles away, and it's like driving across an oven hob. After about an hour I passed over into California, into a shimmering landscape of bleached earth and patchy creosote bushes called the Devils Playground. The sunlight glared. The far-off Soda Mountains quivered and distant cars coming towards me looked like balls of fire, so brilliant was their reflection, and always ahead on the road there was a slick smear of mirage that disappeared as I drew near and reappeared further on. Along the shoulder of the road, sometimes out on the desert itself, were cars that had failed to complete the journey. Some of them looked to have been there for a long time. What an awful place to break down. In the summer, this was one of the hottest spots on earth. Off to the right, over the parched Avawatz Mountains, was Death Valley, where the highest temperature ever recorded in America, 134 degrees Fahrenheit, was logged in 1913 (the world record, in 1922 in Libya, is just two degrees higher). But that was the shade temperature. A thermometer lying on the ground in the sun has gone over 200 degrees. Even now in April the temperature was nudging ninety and it was very unpleasant. It was impossible to imagine it almost half as hot again. And yet people live out there, in awful little towns like Baker and Barstow, where the temperature often stays over ninety degrees for 100 days in a row and where they can go ten years without a drop of rain. I pressed on, longing for clear water and green hills.

One good thing about California is that it doesn't take long to find a complete contrast. The state has the strangest geography. At Death Valley you have the lowest point in America – 282 feet below sea level – and yet practically overlooking it is the highest point in the country (not counting Alaska) – Mt Whitney, at 14,494 feet. You could, if you wished, fry an egg on the roof of your car in Death Valley, then drive thirty miles into the mountains and quick-freeze it in a snowbank. My original intention was to cross the Sierra Nevadas by way of Death Valley (breaking off from time to time to perform experiments with eggs), but a weather lady on the radio informed me that the mountain passes were all still closed on account of the recent nasty weather. So I had to make a long and unrewarding detour across the Mojave Desert, on old Highway 58. This took me past Edwards Air Force Base, which runs for almost forty miles along the highway behind a seemingly endless stretch of chain-link fence. It was at Edwards that the Space Shuttle used to land and that Chuck Yeager broke the sound barrier, so it's really quite a hotshot place, but from the highway I couldn't see anything at all – no planes, no hangars, just mile after mile of tall chain-link fence.

Beyond the little town of Mojave, the desert ended and the landscape erupted in smooth hills and citrus groves. I crossed the Los Angeles Aqueduct, which carries water from northern California to Los Angeles; fifty miles to the south. Even out here the city's smog was threaded through the hills. Visibility was no more than a mile. Beyond that there was just a wall of brownish-grey haze. On the other side of it the sun was a bleary disc of light. Everything seemed to be bled of colour. Even the hills looked jaundiced. They were round and covered with

319

boulders and low-growing trees. There was something strangely familiar about them – and then I realized what it was. These were the hills that the Lone Ranger and Zorro and Roy Rogers and the Cisco Kid used to ride around on in the TV shows of the 1950s. I had never noticed until now that the West of the movies and the West of television were two quite different places. Movie crews had obviously gone out into the real West – the West of buttes and bluffs and red river valleys – while television companies, being cheap, had only just driven a few miles into the hills north of Hollywood and filmed on the edges of orange groves.

Here clearly were the very boulders that Tonto, the Lone Ranger's faithful sidekick, used to creep around on. Every week the Lone Ranger would send Tonto off to creep around on some boulders in order to spy on an encampment of bad guys and every week Tonto would get captured. He was hopeless. Every week the Lone Ranger would have to ride in and save Tonto, but he didn't mind doing that because he and Tonto were very close. You could see it in the way they looked at each other.

Those were the days all right. Now children sit and watch people having their vitals sprayed around the room with a chain-saw and think nothing of it. I know that makes me sound very old and crotchety to all you youngsters out there, but I think it's a pity that we can't have some good wholesome entertainment like we had when I was a boy, when the heroes wore masks and capes, and carried whips, and liked other men a whole bunch. Seriously, have you ever stopped to think what strange role models we were given when we were children? Like Superman. Here's a guy who changes his clothes in public. Or Davy Crockett, a man who conquered the frontier, fought valiantly at the Alamo and yet never noticed that he had a dead squirrel on his head. It's no wonder people my age grew up confused and got heavily involved with drugs. My favourite hero of all was Zorro, who whenever he was peeved with someone would whip out his sword and with three deft strokes carve a Z in the offending party's shirt. Wouldn't you just love to be able to do that?

'Waiter, I specifically asked for this steak rare.'

Slash, slash, slash!

'Excuse me, but I believe I was here before you.'

Slash, slash, slash!

'What do you mean, you don't have it in my size?'

Slash, slash, slash!

For weeks, my friend Robert Swanson and I tried to master this useful trick by practising with his mother's kitchen knives, but all we had to show for it were some torn shirts and ragged wounds across our chests, and after a time we gave it up as both painful and impossible, a decision that even now I rue from time to time.

As I was close to Los Angeles, I toyed with the idea of driving on in, but I was put off by the smog and the traffic and above all by the thought that in Los Angeles someone might come up to me and carve a Z in my chest for real. I think it's only right that crazy people should have their own city, but I cannot for the life of me see why a sane person would want to go there. Besides, Los Angeles is *passé*. It has no surprises. My plan was to drive up through the hidden heart of California, through the fertile San Joaquin Valley. Nobody ever goes there. There is a simple reason for this, as I was about to discover. It is really boring.

Chapter twenty-five

I WOKE UP quietly excited. It was a bright clear morning and in an hour or two I was going to go to Sequoia National Park and drive through a tree. This excited me, in a calm, unshowy sort of way. When I was five, my Uncle Frank and Aunt Fern from Winfield went to California on vacation – this was, of course, before it turned out that Frank was a homo, the old devil, and ran off to Key West with his barber, which rather shocked and upset a lot of people in Winfield, especially when they realized that from now on they would have to drive all the way to Mount Pleasant to get their hair cut – and they sent us a postcard showing a redwood tree of such enormous girth that a road had been cut right through the base of it. The postcard pictured a handsome young couple in a green Studebaker convertible driving through the tree and look-ing as if they were having something approximating a wholesome orgasm. It made an immediate impression on me. I went to my dad and asked him if we could go to California on our next vacation and drive through a tree and he looked at the card and said, 'Well . . . maybe one day,' and I knew then that I had about as much chance of seeing the road through a tree as I had of sprouting pubic hair.

Every year my father would call a family powwow (can you believe this?) to discuss where we were going on vacation and every year I would push for going to California and the tree with a road through it, and my brother and sister would sneer cruelly and say that that was a really mega-dumb idea. My brother always wanted to go to the Rocky Mountains, my sister to Florida and my mother said she didn't care where we went as long as we were all together. And then my dad would pull out some brochures with titles like 'Arkansas – Land of Several Lakes' and 'Arkansas – the Sho' Nuff State' and 'Important Vacation Facts about Arkansas' (with a foreword by Governor Luther T. Smiley), and suddenly it would seem altogether possible that we might be going to Arkansas that year, whatever our collective views on the matter might be.

When I was eleven, we went to California, the very state that housed my dream tree, but we only went to places like Disneyland and Hollywood Boulevard and Beverly Hills. (Dad was too cheap to buy a map showing the homes of the movie stars, so we just drove around and speculated.) A couple of times at breakfast I asked if we could drive up and see the tree with a road through it, but everybody was so dismissive – it was too far away, it would be too stupendously boring for words, it would probably cost a lot of money – that I lost heart and stopped asking. And in fact I never asked again. But it stayed at the back of my mind, one of my five great unfulfilled dreams from childhood. (The others, it goes without saying, were the ability to stop time, to possess the gift of X-ray vision, to be able to hypnotize my brother and make him be my slave, and to see Sally Ann Summerfield without a stitch of clothing on.)

Not surprisingly, none of these dreams came true. (Which is perhaps just as well. Sally Ann Summerfield is a blimp now. She turned up at my high school reunion two years ago and looked like a shipping hazard.) But now here at last I was about to fulfil one of them. Hence the tingle of excitement as I slung my suitcase in the trunk and headed up Highway 63 for Sequoia National Park.

I had spent the night in the little city of Tulare, in the heart of the San Joaquin Valley. This is the richest and most fertile farming country in the world. They grow over 200 kinds of crop in the San Joaquin Valley. That very morning, on the local news on TV, they reported that the farming income for Tulare Country for the previous year was $1.6 billion – that's the sort of money Austin Rover turns over – and yet it was only the second highest figure for the state. Fresno County, just up the road, was richer still. Even so, the landscape didn't look all that brilliant. The valley was as flat as a tenniscourt. It stretched for miles in every direction, dull and brown and dusty, and a permanent haze hung on the horizon, like a dirty window. Perhaps it was the time of year, or perhaps it was the drought that was just beginning to choke central California, but it didn't look rich or fruitful. And the towns that speckled the plain were equally dull. They looked like towns from anywhere. They didn't look rich or modern or interesting. Except that there were oranges the size of grapefruits growing on trees in the front yards, I could have been in Indiana or Illinois or anywhere. That surprised me. On our family trip to California it had been like driving into the next decade. It had all looked sleek and modern. Things that were still novelties in Iowa – shopping centres, drive-in banks, McDonald's restaurants, miniature golf-courses, kids on skate-boards – were old and long-established in California. Now they just looked older. The rest of the country had caught up. The California of 1988 had nothing that Iowa didn't have. Except smog. And beaches. And oranges growing in front yards. And trees you could drive through.

I joined Highway 198 at Visalia and followed it as it shot through fragrant lemon groves, ran along the handsome shoreline of Lake Kaweah and climbed up into the foothills of the Sierra Nevada mountains. Just beyond Three Rivers I entered the park, where a ranger in a wooden booth charged me a $5 entrance fee and gave me a brochure detailing the sights beyond. I looked quickly through it for a photograph of a road through a tree, but there weren't any pictures, just words and a map bearing colourful and alluring names: Avalanche Pass, Mist Falls, Farewell Gap, Onion Valley, Giant Forest. I made for Giant Forest.

Sequoia National Park and Kings Canyon National Park are contiguous. Effectively they are one national park and, like all national parks in the West, it is a good-sized one – seventy miles from top to bottom, thirty miles across. Because of the twisting roads as I climbed up into the mountains, progress was slow, though splendidly scenic.

I drove for two hours on lofty roads through boulder-strewn mountains. Snow was still lying about in broad patches. At last I entered the dark and mysterious groves of the giant sequoia (Sequoiadendron giganteum, according to my brochure). The trees were tall, no doubt about it, and fat around the base, though not fat enough to take a highway. Presumably they would get fatter as I moved deeper into the forest. Sequoias are ugly trees. They soar up and up and up, but their branches are sparse and stubby, so they look silly, like the sort of trees three-year-olds draw. In the middle of the Giant Forest stands the General Sherman Tree – the biggest living thing on Earth. Surely the General Sherman was the one I was looking for.

'Oh boy, Chevette, have I got a treat for you!' I called out and patted the steering wheel fondly. When at last I neared the General Sherman, I found a small parking lot and a path leading to the tree through the woods. Evidently it was no longer possible to drive through the tree. This was a disappointment – name me something in life that isn't – but never mind, I thought. I'll walk through it; the pleasure will last longer. Indeed, I'll walk through it severally. I will stroll and saunter and glide, and if there aren't too many people about, I might well dance around it in the light-footed manner of Gene Kelly splashing through puddles in *Singin' in the Rain*.

So I banged the car door shut and walked up the trail to the tree and there it was, with a little fence around it to keep people from getting too close. It was big all right – tall and fat – but not *that* tall, not *that* fat. And there was no hole through its base. You might just about have managed to cut a modest road through it, but – and here's the important thing – no-one ever had. Beside the tree was a large wooden board with an educational message on it. It said 'The giant General Sherman is not only the biggest tree in the world, but also the biggest living thing. It is at least 2,500 years old, and thus also one of the oldest living things. Even so, it is surprisingly boring, isn't it? That is because it isn't all that tall and all that fat. What sets it apart from other redwoods is that it doesn't taper very much. It stays pretty fat all the way up. Hence it has a greater bulk than any other tree. If you want to see really impressive redwoods – ones with roads driven through their bases –

you have to go to Redwood National Park, way up near the Oregon border. Incidentally, we've erected a fence around the base of the tree to keep you well back from it and intensify your disappointment. As if that were not enough, there is a party of noisy young Germans coming up the path behind you. Isn't life shitty?'

As you will appreciate, this is somewhat paraphrased, but that was the gist of it. The Germans came and were obnoxious and unthoughtful, as adolescents tend to be, and stole the tree from me. They perched on the fence and started taking pictures. I derived some small pleasure from wandering in front of the cameraman whenever he was about to click the shutter, but this is an activity from which it is difficult to extract sustained amusement, even with Germans, and after a minute or two I left them there jabbering away about *die Pop Musik* and *das Drugs Scene* and their other adolescent preoccupations.

In the car I looked at the map and was disheartened to discover that Redwood National Park was almost 500 miles away. I could hardly believe it. Here I was 300 miles north of Los Angeles and yet I could drive another 500 miles and *still* be in California. It is 850 miles from top to bottom – about the distance between London and Milan. It would take me a day and a half to get to Redwood National Park, plus a day and a half to get back to where I was now. I didn't have that kind of time. Gloomily, I started the car and drove on to Yosemite National Park, seventy miles up the highway.

And what a disappointment that proved to be. I'm sorry to moan, I truly am, but Yosemite was a let-down of monumental proportions. It is incredibly, mouth-gawpingly beautiful. Your first view of the El Capitan valley, with its towering mountains and white waterfalls spilling hundreds of feet down to the meadows of the valley floor, makes you think that surely you have expired and gone to heaven. But then you drive on down into Yosemite village and realize that if this is heaven you are going to spend the rest of eternity with an awful lot of fat people in Bermuda shorts.

Yosemite is a mess. The National Parks Service in America – let's be candid here – does a pretty half-assed job of running many of the national parks. This is surprising because in America most leisure-time activities are about a million times better than anywhere else. But not national parks. The visitors' centres are usually dull, the catering is always crappy and expensive, and you generally come away having learned almost nothing about the wildlife, geology and history of the places you've driven hundreds of miles to see. The national parks are supposed to be there to preserve a chunk of America's wilderness, but in many of them the number of animals has actually fallen. Yellowstone has lost all its wolves, mountain lions and white-tailed deer, and the numbers of beaver and bighorn sheep are greatly depleted. These animals are thriving outside Yellowstone, but as far as the Parks Service itself is concerned they are extinct.

I don't know why it should be, but the National Parks Service has a long history of incompetence. In the 1960s, if you can believe it, the Parks Service invited the Walt Disney Corporation to build a development in Sequoia National Park. Mercifully, that plan was quashed. But others have succeeded, most notably in 1923 when, after a long fight between conservationists and businessmen, the Hetch Hetchey Valley in the northern part of Yosemite

– which was said to be even more spectacularly beautiful than Yosemite Valley itself – was flooded to create a reservoir to provide drinking water for San Francisco, 150 miles to the west. So for the last sixty years one of the half-dozen or so most breathtaking stretches of landscape on the planet has lain under water for commercial reasons. God help us if they ever find oil there.

The great problem at Yosemite today is simply finding your way around. I've never seen a place so badly signposted. It's as if they are trying to hide the park from you. At most parks the first thing you want to do is go to the visitors' centre and have a look at the big map to get your bearings and decide what you want to see. But at Yosemite the visitors' centre is almost impossible to find. I drove around Yosemite village for twenty-five minutes before I discovered a parking lot and then it took me a further twenty minutes, and a long walk in the wrong direction, to find the visitors' centre. By the time I found it I knew my way around and didn't need it any more.

And everything is just hopelessly, depressingly crowded – the cafeterias, the post office, the stores. This was in April; what it must be like in August doesn't bear guessing at. I have never been anywhere that was simultaneously so beautiful and so awful. In the end, I had a nice long walk and a look at the waterfalls and the scenery and it was outstanding. But I cannot believe that it can't be better run.

In the evening I drove on to Sonora, through a tranquil sunset, along sinuous mountain roads. I reached the town after dark and had difficulty finding a room. It was only the middle of the week, but most places were full. The motel I finally found was grossly overpriced and the TV reception was terrible. It was like watching people moving around in front of fun-house mirrors. Their bodies would proceed across the screen and their heads would follow a moment later, as if connected by elastic. I was paying $42 for this. The bed was like a pool table with sheets. And the toilet seat didn't have a 'Sanitized For Your Protection' wrapper on it, denying me my daily ritual of cutting it with my scissors and saying, 'I now declare this toilet open.' These things become important to you when you have been alone on the road for a while. In a sour mood I drove into town and went to a cheap restaurant for dinner. The waitress made me wait a long time before she came and took my order. She looked tarty and had an irritating habit of repeating everything I said to her.

'I'd like the chicken fried steak,' I said.

'You'd like the chicken fried steak?'

'Yes. And I would like French fries with it.'

'You want French fries with it?'

'Yes. And I would like a salad with Thousand Island dressing.'

'You want a salad with Thousand Island dressing?'

'Yes, and a Coke to drink.'

'You want a Coke to drink?'

'Excuse me, miss, but I've had a bad day and if you don't stop repeating everything I say, I'm going to take this ketchup bottle and squirt it all down the front of your blouse.'

'You're going to take that ketchup bottle and squirt it all down the front of my blouse?'

I didn't really threaten her with ketchup – she might have had a large boy-friend who would come and pummel me; also, I once knew a waitress who told me that whenever a customer was rude to her she went out to the kitchen and spat in his food, and since then I have never spoken sharply to a waitress or sent under-cooked food back to the kitchen (because then the cook spits in it, you see) – but I was in such a disagreeable mood that I put my chewing-gum straight into the ashtray without wrapping it in a piece of tissue first, as my mother always taught me to do, and pressed it down with my thumb so that it wouldn't fall out when the ashtray was turned over, but would have to be prised out with a fork. And what's more – God help me – it gave me a tingle of satisfaction.

In the morning I drove north from Sonora along Highway 49, wondering what the day would bring. I wanted to head east over the Sierra Nevadas, but many of the passes were still closed. Highway 49, as it turned out, took me on an agreeably winding journey through hilly country. Groves of trees and horse pastures over-looked the road, and occasionally I passed an old farmhouse, but there was little sign that the land was used for anything productive. The towns I passed through – Tuttletown, Melones, Angel's Camp – were the places where the California Gold Rush took place. In 1848, a man named James Marshall found a lump of gold at Sutter Creek, just up the road, and people went crazy. Almost overnight, 40,000 prospectors poured into the state and in a little over a decade, between 1847 and 1860, California's population went from 15,000 to nearly 400,000. Some of the towns have been preserved as they were at the time – Sonora is not too bad in this regard – but mostly there's not much to show that this was once the scene of the greatest gold rush in history. I suppose this is largely because most of the people lived in tents and when the gold ran out so did they. Now most of the little towns offered the customary stretch of gas stations, motels and hamburger emporia. It was Anywhere, USA.

At Jackson, I found that Highway 88 was open through the mountains – the first open passage through the Sierras in almost 300 miles – and I took it. I had expected that I would have to take the next but one pass along, the infamous Donner Pass, where in 1846 a party of settlers became trapped by a blizzard for several weeks and survived by eating each other, an incident that caused a great sensation at the time. The leader of the group was named Donner. I don't know what became of him, but I bet he took some ribbing whenever he went into a restaurant after that. At any rate, it got his name on the map. The Donner Pass was also the route taken by the first transcontinental railroad, the Southern Pacific, and first transcontinental highway, old Route 40, the Lincoln Highway, on their 3,000-mile journey from New York to San Francisco. As with Route 66 further south, Route 40 had been callously dug up and converted into a dull interstate highway, so I was pleased to find a back road open through the mountains.

And it was very pleasant. I drove through pine-forested scenery, with occasional long views across unpeopled valleys, up and over Mokelumne Peak (9,332 feet), heading in the general direction of Lake Tahoe and Carson City. The road was steep and slow and it took me much of the afternoon to drive the hundred or so miles to the Nevada border. Near Woodfords I entered the Toiyabe National Forest, or at least what once had been the Toiyabe National Forest. For miles and miles there was nothing but charred land, mountainsides of dead earth and stumps of trees. Occasionally I passed an undamaged house around which a firebreak had been dug. It was an odd sight, a house with swings and a paddling-pool in the middle of an ocean of blackened stumps. A year or so before the owners must have thought they were the luckiest people on the planet, to live in the woods and mountains, amid the cool and fragrant pines. And now they lived on the surface of the moon. Soon the forest would be replanted and for the rest of their lives they could watch it grow again, inch by annual inch.

I had never seen such devastation – miles and miles of it – and yet I had no recollection of having read about it. That's the thing about America. It's so big that it just absorbs disasters, muffles them with its vastness. Time and again on this trip I had seen news stories that would elsewhere have been treated as colossal tragedies – a dozen people killed by floods in the South, ten crushed when a store roof collapsed in Texas, twenty-two dead in a snowstorm in the east – and each of them treated as a brief and not terribly consequential diversion between ads for haemorrhoid unguents and cottage cheese. Partly it is a consequence of that inane breeziness common to local TV newsreaders in America, but mostly it is just the scale of the country. A disaster in Florida is regarded in California in the same way that a disaster in Italy is regarded in Britain – as something briefly and morbidly diverting, but too far away to be tragic in any personal sense.

I entered Nevada about ten miles south of Lake Tahoe. Las Vegas had so put me off that I had no desire to go to another sink of iniquity, though I was later told that Tahoe is a really nice place and not at all like Las Vegas. Now I shall never know. I can tell you, however, that Carson City was just about the most nothing little city you could ever hope to zip through. It's the state capital, but mostly it was just Pizza Huts and gas stations and cheap-looking casinos.

I headed out of town on US 50, past Virginia City and towards Silver Springs. This was more or less the spot where the map used to burst into flames on *Bonanza*. Remember that? It has been many years since I've seen the programme, but I recall Pa and Hoss and Little Joe and the surly-looking one whose name I forget all living in a landscape that was fruitful and lush, in a Western, high chaparral sort of way. But out here there was nothing but cement-coloured plains and barren hills and almost no habitations at all. Everything was grey, from the sky to the ground. This was to remain the pattern for the next two days.

It would be difficult to conceive of a more remote and cheerless state than Nevada. It has a population of just 800,000 in an area about the size of Britain and Ireland combined. Almost half of that population is accounted for by Las Vegas and Reno, so most of the rest of the state is effectively just empty. There are only seventy towns in the entire state – the British Isles have 40,000, just to give you some comparison – and some of them are indescribably remote. For instance, Eureka, a town of 1,200 in the middle of the state, is 100 miles in any direction from the nearest town. Indeed, the whole of Eureka County has just three towns and a total population of under 2,500 – and this in an area of a couple of thousand square miles.

I drove for a while across this fearsome emptiness,

taking a back highway between Fallon and a spot on the map called Humboldt Sink, where I gratefully joined Interstate 80. This was a cowardly thing to do, but the car had been making odd noises off and on for the past couple of days – a sort of faint clonk clonk oh god help me clonk I'm dying oh god oh god clonk noise – which wasn't covered in the trouble-shooting section of the owner's manual. I couldn't face the prospect of breaking down and being stranded for days in some Godforsaken dust-hole while waiting for an anti-clonk device to be shipped in from Reno on the weekly Greyhound. In any case, Highway 50, the nearest alternative road, would have taken me 150 miles out of my way and into Utah. I wanted to go a more northerly route across Montana and Wyoming – the 'Big Sky' country. So it was with some relief that I joined the interstate, though even this was remarkably empty – usually I could see one car in the distance far ahead and one in the distance far behind – considering it was the main artery across the country. Indeed, with a sufficiently capacious fuel tank and bladder, you could drive the whole way between New York and San Francisco without stopping.

At Winnemucca I pulled off for gas and coffee and called my mother to let her know that I hadn't been killed yet and was doing all right for underwear – a matter of perennial concern to my mother. I was able to reassure her on this score and she reassured me that she hadn't willed her money to the International Guppy Institute or anything similarly rash (I just like to check!), so we were able to continue our respective days with light hearts.

In the phone booth was a poster with a photograph of a young woman on it under the caption 'Have you seen this girl?' She was attractive and looked youthful and happy. The poster said she was nineteen years old and had been driving from Boston to San Francisco on her way home for Christmas when she disappeared. She had called her parents from Winnemucca to tell them to expect her the next afternoon and that was the last anyone had heard of her. Now she was almost certainly dead, somewhere out there in that big empty desert. Murder is terrifyingly easy in America. You can kill a stranger, dump the body in a place where it will never be found and be 2,000 miles away before the murdered person is even missed. At any given time there are an estimated twelve to fifteen serial murderers at large in the country, just drifting around, snatching random victims and then moving on, leaving behind few clues and no motives. A couple of years earlier in Des Moines, some teenaged boys were cleaning out an office downtown for one of their fathers on a Sunday afternoon when a stranger came in, took them into a back room and shot each of them once in the back of the head. For no reason. That guy was caught, as it happens, but he could as easily have gone off to another state and done the same thing again. Every year in America 5,000 murders go unsolved. That is an incredible number.

I spent the night in Wells, Nevada, the sorriest, seediest, most raggedy-assed town I've ever seen. Most of the streets were unpaved and lined with battered-looking trailer homes. Everyone in town seemed to collect old cars. They sat rusting and windowless in every yard. Almost everything in town appeared to exist on the edge of dereliction. Such economic life as Wells could muster came from the passing traffic of Interstate 80. A number of truck stops and motels were scattered around, though many of these were closed down and those that remained were evidently struggling. Most of the motel signs had letters missing or burnt out, so that they said 'Lone St r Mot I – V can y'. I had a walk around the business district before dinner. This consisted mostly of closed-down stores, though a few places appeared still to be in business: a drugstore, a gas station, a Trailways Bus depot, the Overland Hotel – sorry, H tel – and a movie-house called The Nevada, though this proved upon closer inspection also to be deceased. There were dogs everywhere, sniffing in doorways and peeing on pretty much everything. It was cold, too. The sun was setting behind the rough, distant peaks of the Jackson Mountains and there was a decided chill in the air. I turned up my collar and trudged the half-mile from the town proper to the interstate junction with US 93, where the most prosperous-looking truck stops were gathered, forming an oasis of brightness in the pinkish dusk.

I went into what looked to be the best of them, a large café, consisting of a gift shop, restaurant, casino and bar. The casino was small, just a room with a couple of dozen slot-machines, mostly nickel ones, and the gift shop was about the size of a closet. The café was crowded and dense with smoke and chatter. Steel-guitar music drifted out of the juke-box. I was the only person in the room who didn't have a cowboy hat on, apart from a couple of the women.

I sat in a booth and ordered fried chicken. The waitress was real friendly, but she had little open sores all over her hands and arms and only about three teeth, and her apron looked as if she had spent the afternoon butchering piglets. This put me off my dinner a bit, to tell you the

337

truth, and then she brought my dinner and that put me off eating altogether.

It was absolutely the worst food I have ever had in America, at any time, under any circumstances, and that includes hospital food, gas station food and airport coffee shop food. It even includes Greyhound Bus Station food and Woolworth's luncheon counter food. It was even worse than the pastries they used to put in the food-dispensing machines at the Register and Tribune Building in Des Moines and those tasted like somebody had been sick on them. This food was just plain terrible, and yet everybody in the room was shovelling it away as if there were no tomorrow. I picked at it for a while – bristly fried chicken, lettuce with blackened veins, French fries that had the appearance and appeal of albino slugs – and gave up, despondent. I pushed the plate away and wished that I still smoked. The waitress, seeing how much I had left, asked me if I wanted a doggie bag.

'No thank you,' I said through a thin smile, 'I don't believe I could find a dog that would eat it.'

On reflection, I can think of one eating experience even more dispiriting than dining at that café and that was the lunch-room at Callanan Junior High School in Des Moines. The lunch-room at Callanan was like something out of a prison movie. You would shuffle forward in a long, silent line and have lumpen, shapeless food dolloped on to your tray by lumpen, shapeless women – women who looked as if they were on day release from a mental institution, possibly for having poisoned food in public places. The food wasn't merely unappealing, it was unidentifiable. Adding to the displeasure was the presence of the deputy principal, Mr Snoyd, who was always stalking around behind you, ready to grab you by the neck and march you off to his office if you made gagging noises or were overheard inquiring of the person across from you, 'Say, what is this shit?' Eating at Callanan was like having your stomach pumped in reverse.

I went back to the motel feeling deeply hungry and unsatisfied. I watched some TV and read a book, and then slept that fitful sleep you get when all of your body is still and resting except your stomach, which is saying, 'WHERE THE FUCK IS MY DINNER? HEY, BILL, ARE YOU LISTENING TO ME? WHERE THE F-U-C-K IS MY EVENING SUSTENANCE?'

Chapter twenty-six

HERE, APROPOS OF nothing at all, is a true story. In 1958, my grandmother got cancer of the colon and came to our house to die. At this time my mother employed a cleaning lady named Mrs Goodman, who didn't have a whole lot upstairs but was possessed of a good Catholic heart. After my grandmother's arrival, Mrs Goodman grew uncharacteristically sullen. Then one afternoon at finishing time she told my mother that she would have to quit because she didn't want to catch cancer from my grandmother. My mother soothingly reassured Mrs Goodman that you cannot 'catch cancer', and gave her a small pay increase to compensate for the extra work occasioned by my grandmother's clammy and simpering presence. So with ill-disguised reluctance Mrs Goodman stayed on. And about three months later she caught cancer and with alarming swiftness died.

Well, as you can imagine, since it was my family that killed the poor woman, I've always wanted to commemorate her in some small way and I thought that here would be as good a place as any, especially as I had nothing of interest to tell you about the drive from Wells, Nevada, to Twin Falls, Idaho.

So, goodbye, Mrs Goodman, it was nice knowing you. And we're all very, very sorry.

Twin Falls was a nice enough place – Mrs Goodman, I've no doubt, would have liked it; but then when you think

340

about it a dead person would probably appreciate any change of scenery – and the landscape in southern Idaho was greener and more fertile than anything Nevada had to offer. Idaho is known for its potatoes, though in fact Maine, just a third of its size, produces more. Its real wealth comes from mining and timber, particularly in the higher reaches of the Rockies, up towards Canada, over 500 miles north of where I was now. I was headed for Sun Valley, the famous resort up in the Sawtooth Mountains, and the neighbouring town of Ketchum, where Ernest Hemingway spent the last year of his life and blew his brains out. This has always seemed to me (not that it's any of my business, mind you) a particularly thoughtless and selfish way to kill oneself. I mean to say, your family is going to be upset enough that you are dead without your having to spoil the furniture and gross everyone out on top of that.

In any case, Ketchum was touristy, though Sun Valley itself proved to be most agreeable. It was purpose-built as a ski resort in the 1930s by the Union Pacific Railroad as a way of enticing people to travel to the region during the winter. It certainly has a beautiful setting, in a bowl of jagged mountains, and is supposed to have some of the best skiing in the country. People like Clint Eastwood and Barbra Streisand have houses there. I looked in a window in a real estate office and didn't see anything for sale for less than $250,000.

The town part of Sun Valley – it's really just a little shopping centre – is built to look like a Bavarian village. I found it oddly charming. As so often with these things in America, it was superior to a real Bavarian village. There were two reasons for this: (1) it was better built and more

341

picturesque, and (2) the inhabitants of Sun Valley have never adopted Adolf Hitler as their leader or sent their neighbours off for gassing. Were I a skier and rich, I would on these grounds alone unhesitatingly choose it over Garmisch-Partenkirchen, say. In the meantime, being poor and skiless, there was nothing much for me to do but poke around in the shops. For the most part these sold swish skiing outfits and expensive gifts – things like large pewter elk for $200 and lead crystal paperweights at $150 – and the people who ran them were those snooty types who watch you as if they think you might do a poo in the corner given half a chance. Understandably, this soured me on the place and I declined to make any purchases. 'Your loss, not mine,' I murmured sniffily as I left.

Idaho is another big state – 550 miles from top to bottom, 300 miles across at the base – and it took me the rest of the day just to drive to Idaho Falls, near the border with Wyoming. *En route* I passed the little town of Arco, which on December 20, 1951, became the first town in the world to be lit with nuclear-powered electricity, supplied by the world's first peacetime nuclear reactor at a site ten miles south-west of town at the Idaho National Engineering Laboratory. The name is misleading because the so-called laboratory covers several hundred square miles of scrubby chaparral and is actually the biggest nuclear dump in the country. The highway between Arco and Idaho Falls runs for forty miles alongside the complex, but it is lined by high fences interspersed with military-style check-points. In the far distance stand large buildings where, presumably, workers in white space suits wander around in rooms that look like something out of a James Bond film.

I didn't realize it at the time, but the US government had recently admitted that plutonium had been found to be leaking from one of the storage facilities on the site and was working its way downward through the ground to a giant subterranean reservoir, which supplies the water for tens of thousands of people in southern Idaho. Plutonium is the most lethal substance known to man – a spoonful of it could wipe out a city. Once you make some plutonium, you have to keep it safe for 250,000 years. The United States government had managed to keep its plutonium safe for rather less than thirty-six years. This, it seems to me, is a convincing argument for not allowing your government to mess with plutonium.

And this was only one leak out of many. At a similar facility in the state of Washington, 500,000 gallons of highly radioactive substances drained away before anyone thought to put a dipstick in the tank and see how things were doing. How do you lose 500,000 gallons of anything? I don't know the answer to that question, but I do know that I would not like to be the real estate agent trying to sell houses in Pocatello or Idaho Falls five years from now when the ground starts to glow and women are giving birth to human flies.

For the time being, however, Idaho Falls remains an agreeable little city. The downtown was attractive and still evidently prospering. Trees and benches had been set out. A big banner was draped across one of the streets saying 'Idaho Falls says NO to drugs'. That's really going to keep the kids off the hard stuff, I thought. Small-town America is obsessed with drugs, yet I suspect that if you strip-searched every teenager in Idaho Falls you would come up with nothing more illicit than some dirty magazines, a packet of condoms and a half-empty bottle of Jack Daniels. Personally, I think the young people of Idaho Falls ought to be encouraged to take drugs. It will help them to cope when they find out there's plutonium in their drinking water.

I had an excellent dinner at Happy's Chinese Restaurant. The room was empty except for one other party consisting of a middle-aged couple, their teenaged daughter and a Swedish exchange student who was simply radiant – blonde, tanned, soft-spoken, hypnotically beautiful. I stared at her helplessly. I had never seen anyone so beautiful in a Chinese restaurant in Idaho before. After a while a man came in who was evidently a passing acquaintance of the family and stopped at their table to chat. He was introduced to the Swedish girl and asked her about her stay in Idaho Falls and if she had been to the local sights – the lava caves and hot springs. (She had. Zey were vairy nice.) Then he asked The Big Question. He said, 'Well, Greta, which do you like better, the United States or Sweden?'

The girl blushed. She obviously had not been in the country long enough to expect this question. Suddenly she looked more child than woman. With an embarrassed flutter of hands she said, 'Oh, I sink Sweden,' and a pall fell over the table. Everyone looked uncomfortable. 'Oh,' said the man in a flat, disappointed tone, and the conversation turned to potato prices.

People in middle America always ask that question. When you grow up in America you are inculcated from the earliest age with the belief – no, the *understanding* – that America is the richest and most powerful nation on earth because God likes us best. It has the most perfect form of government, the most exciting sporting events, the tastiest food and amplest portions, the largest cars, the cheapest gasoline, the most abundant natural resources, the most productive farms, the most devastating nuclear arsenal and the friendliest, most decent and most patriotic folks on Earth. Countries just don't come any better. So why anyone would want to live anywhere else is practically incomprehensible. In a foreigner it is puzzling; in a native it is seditious. I used to feel this way myself. In high school I shared a locker with a Dutch exchange student and I remember him asking me one day in a peevish tone why everybody, absolutely everybody, wanted him to like America better than The Netherlands. 'Holland is my home,' he said. 'Why can't people understand that it's where I want to live?'

I considered his point. 'Yes,' I said, 'but deep down, Anton, wouldn't you really rather live here?' And funnily enough, in the end, he decided he did. The last I heard he was a successful realtor in Florida, driving a Porsche, wearing wraparound sunglasses and saying, 'Hey, what's happening?' which of course is a considerable improvement on wearing wooden shoes, carrying pails of milk on a yoke over your shoulder and being invaded by Germany every couple of generations.

In the morning I drove to Wyoming, through scenery that looked like an illustration from some marvellous children's book of Western tales – snowy peaks, pine forests, snug farms, a twisting river, a mountain vale with a comely name: Swan Valley. That is the one thing that must be said for the men and women who carved out the West. They certainly knew how to name a place. Just on this corner of the map I could see Soda Springs, Massacre Rocks, Steamboat Mountain, Wind River, Flaming Gorge, Calamity Falls – places whose very names promised adventure and excitement, even if in reality all they contained were a DX gas station and a Tastee-Freez drive-in.

Most of the early settlers in America were oddly inept at devising place-names. They either chose unimaginative, semi-recycled names – New York, New Hampshire, New Jersey, New England – or toadying, kiss-ass names like Virginia, Georgia, Maryland and Jamestown in a generally pitiable attempt to secure favour with some monarch or powdered aristocrat back home. Or else they just accepted the names the Indians told them, not knowing whether Squashaninsect meant 'land of the twinkling lakes' or 'place where Big Chief Thunderclap paused to pass water'.

The Spanish were even worse because they gave everything religious names, so that every place in the south-west is called San this or Santa that. Driving across the south-west is like an 800-mile religious procession. The worst name on the whole continent is the Sangre de Cristo mountains in New Mexico, which means the 'Blood of Christ Mountains'. Have you ever heard of a more inane name for any geographical feature? It was only here in the real West, the land of beaver trappers and mountain men, that a dollop of romance and colour was brought to the business of giving names. And here I was about to enter one of the most beautiful and understatedly romantic of them all: Jackson Hole.

Jackson Hole isn't really a hole at all; it's just the name for a scenic valley that runs from north to south through the Grand Tetons, very probably the most majestic range in the Rockies. With their high white peaks and bluish-grey bases they look like some kind of exotic confection, like blueberry *frappés*. At the southern edge of Jackson Hole is the small town of Jackson, where I stopped now for lunch. It was a strange place, with an odd combination of bow-legged Yosemite Sams and upmarket stores like Benetton and Ralph Lauren, which are there for the benefit of the many well-heeled tenderfeet who come for the skiing in the winter and to dude ranches in the summer. Every place in town had a Wild West motif – the Antler Motel, the Silver Dollar Saloon, the Hitching Post Lodge. Even the Bank of Jackson, where I went to cash a traveller's cheque, had a stuffed buffalo head on the wall. Yet it all seemed quite natural. Wyoming is the most fiercely Western of all the Western states. It's still a land of cowboys and horses and wide open spaces, a place where a man's gotta do what a man's gotta do, which on the face of it primarily consists of driving around in a pickup truck and being kind of slow. I had never seen so many people in cowboy apparel, and almost everybody owns a gun. Only a couple of weeks before, the state legislature in Cheyenne had introduced a rule that all legislators would henceforth have to check their handguns at the front desk before being allowed into the Statehouse. That's the sort of state Wyoming is.

I drove on to Grand Teton National Park. And there's another arresting name for you. *'Tétons'* means 'tits' in French. That's an interesting fact – a topographical titbit, so to speak – that Miss Mucus, my junior high school geography teacher, failed to share with us in the eighth grade. Why do they always keep the most interesting stuff from you in school? If I'd known in high school that Thomas Jefferson kept a black slave to help him deal with sexual tension or that Ulysses S. Grant was a hopeless

347

drunk who couldn't button his own flies without falling over, I would have shown a livelier interest in my lessons, I can assure you.

At any rate, the first French explorers who passed through north-western Wyoming took one look at the mountains and said, '*Zut alors*! Hey, Jacques, clock those mountains. They look just like my wife's *tétons*.' Isn't it typical of the French to reduce everything to a level of sexual vulgarity? Thank goodness they didn't discover the Grand Canyon, that's all I can say. And the remarkable thing is that the Tetons look about as much like tits as . . . well, as a frying-pan or a pair of hiking boots. In a word, they don't look like tits at all, except perhaps to desperately lonely men who have been away from home for a very long time. They looked a little bit like tits to me.

Grand Teton National Park and Yellowstone National Park run together to form one enormous area of wilderness stretching over a hundred miles from north to south. The road connecting them, Route 191, had only just been reopened for the year, and the Teton visitors' centres were still closed. There were hardly any other people or cars around and for forty miles I drove in splendid isolation along the wild meadows of the Snake River, where herds of elk grazed against the backdrop of the tall and jagged Tetons. As I climbed into Yellowstone the clouds grew moody and looked heavy with snow. The road I was on is closed for six months of the year, which gives you some idea of the sort of winters they have there. Even now the snow along the roadside was five or six feet deep in places.

Yellowstone is the oldest national park in the world (it was created in 1872) and it is enormous, about the size of Connecticut. I drove for over an hour without seeing anyone, except for a park warden in a wooden hut who charged me $10 to get in. That must be an exciting job for a college graduate, to sit in a hut in the middle of nowhere and take $10 off a tourist every two or three hours. Eventually I came to a turn-off for Grant Village, and I followed it for a mile through the snowy woods. The village was good-sized, with a visitors' centre, motel, stores, post office and campgrounds, but everything was shut and every window was boarded. Snowdrifts rose almost to the rooftops of some of the buildings. I had now driven seventy miles without seeing an open place of business, and gave silent thanks that I had filled up with gasoline at Jackson.

Grant Village and the neighbouring village of West Thumb are on the banks of Yellowstone Lake, which the highway runs alongside. Steam was rising from fumaroles in the lake and bubbling up through the mud by the roadside. I was in the area of the park called the caldera. Once there was a great mountain here. But 600,000 years ago it blew up in a colossal volcanic eruption that sent 240 cubic miles of débris into the atmosphere. The geysers, fumaroles and steaming mudpots for which Yellowstone is famous are the spluttering relics of that cataclysm.

Just beyond West Thumb the highway split in two. One branch went to Old Faithful, the most famous of all the geysers, but a chain had been strung across the road with a red sign hanging from it saying 'Road Closed'. Old Faithful was seventeen miles away down the closed road, but eighty miles away down the alternative road. I drove on to Hayden Valley, where you can stop the car at frequent lay-bys and look out upon the plain of the Yellowstone River. This is where the grizzly bears roam and buffalo graze.

When you enter the park you are given a set of stern instructions telling you not to approach the animals as they are likely to kill or maim you, though I read later that more people have been killed in the park by other people than by animals. Even so, grizzlies are still a real threat to campers, one or two of whom get carried off every year. If you camp in the park you are instructed to change your clothes after eating or cooking and put them and all your food in a bag suspended from a branch ten feet above the ground, 100 yards from your tent. Stories abound of peckish campers who eat a bar of chocolate at bedtime and five minutes later a grizzly bear puts his head in the tent and says, 'Hey, have you guys got some chocolate in here?' According to the park literature, there is even evidence that sexual intercourse and menstruation attract grizzlies. This seemed a bit rough to me.

I peered through my dad's binoculars but I didn't see any bears, possibly because they were still hibernating, and possibly because there aren't very many left in the park. Most of them have been driven out by the crush of visitors in the summer, even though large tracts of Yellowstone have been closed to people to encourage the bears to stay. There were, however, herds of buffalo everywhere. They are quite an extraordinary animal, with such big heads and shoulders on tiny legs. It must have been something to see when herds numbering in the millions filled the plains.

I drove on to Geyser Basin. This is the most volatile and unstable landscape in the world. A few miles to the east the land is rising by almost an inch a year, suggesting that another big blow-out is on the way. Geyser Basin presented the most fantastic and eerie prospect, a lunar landscape of steam vents, hissing geysers and shallow pools of the deepest blue aquamarine. You can wander all over along wooden sidewalks built above the ground. If you were to step off them, according to the signs, you would sink in the crusty soil and be scalded to death by the water just below the surface. The whole place stank of sulphur.

I walked down to Steamboat Geyser, the biggest in the world. According to the sign, it shoots water up to 400 feet into the air, though only at widely-spaced intervals. The last big eruption was three and a half years earlier, on September 26, 1984. As I was watching it erupted – suddenly I understood the expression to jump out of one's skin. The steamy mudpack before me made a flapping sound like a colossal palpitating sphincter (my own sphincter, I can tell you, began to beat a modest counterpoint) and then with a whoosh like a whale coming up for air shot out a great, steaming plume of white water. It went up only about twenty or thirty feet, but it poured forth for many seconds. Then it died and came again, and it repeated this four times, filling the cool air with blankets of steam, before it went dormant. When it finished, I shut my mouth with my hand and walked back to the car, knowing that I had seen one of the more arresting sights of my life.

There was no need to drive on to Old Faithful, still forty miles down the road. I headed instead up the steep road over Roaring Mountain, past Nymph Lake, Grizzly Lake and Sheepeater Cliff – oh, how I love those names – and on down into Mammoth Hot Springs, home of the park headquarters. Here there was a visitors' centre open, so I had a look around, and a pee and a drink of water, before driving on. When I emerged from the park at its northern end, by the little town of Gardiner, I was in a new state, Montana. I drove the sixty miles or so to Livingston through a landscape that was less wild but more beautiful than anything Yellowstone had offered. Partly this was because the sun came out and filled the late afternoon with a sudden spring-like warmth. Long, flat shadows lay across the valley. There was no snow here, though the first infusion of green was just beginning to seep into the grassy and still yellow pastures along the highway. It was almost the first of May and winter was only just now withdrawing.

I got a room in the Del Mar Motel in Livingston, had some dinner and went for a walk out along the highway at the edge of town. With the sun sinking behind the nearby mountains, the evening quickly grew cold. A bleak wind came whipping down from the emptiness of Canada, 300 miles to the north, the kind of wind that slips up the back of your jacket and humiliates your hair. It resonated down the telephone lines, like a man whistling through his teeth, and made the tall grass seethe. Somewhere a gate creaked and banged, creaked and banged. The highway stretched out flat and straight ahead of me until it narrowed to a vanishing-point some miles away. Every so often a car would come at me down the highway from behind, sounding eerily like a jet taking off. As it came nearer and nearer I would half wonder for one moment if it was going to hit me – it sounded that close – and then it would flash past and I would watch its tail-lights disappear into the gathering gloom.

A freight train came along on some tracks that ran parallel to the highway. At first it was a distant light and short bursts of horn, and then it was rolling past me, slow and stately, on its nightly procession through Livingston. It was enormous – American trains are twice the size of European ones – and at least a mile long. I counted sixty freight cars on it before I lost track, all of them with names on them like Burlington & Northern, Rock Island, Santa Fe. It struck me as curious that train lines were so often named after towns that never amounted to much. I wondered how many people a century ago lost their shirts buying property in places like Atchison and Topeka on the assumption that one day they would be as big as Chicago and San Francisco. Towards the end of the train one car went by with its door open and I could see three shadowy figures inside: hoboes. I was amazed to find that such people still existed, that it was still possible to ride the rails. In the dusk it looked a very romantic way to spend your life. It was all I could do to keep from sprinting along and climbing aboard and just disappearing with them into the night. There is nothing like an evening train rolling past to make you take leave of your senses. But instead I just turned around and trudged back along the tracks into town, feeling oddly content.

Chapter twenty-seven

T HE NEXT DAY I was torn between driving back into Wyoming further east along Interstate 90 and going to the little town of Cody, or staying in Montana and visiting the Custer National Battlefield. Cody takes its name from Buffalo Bill Cody, who agreed to be buried there if they named the town after him. There were presumably two further stipulations: (1) that they waited until he was dead before they buried him, and (2) that they filled the town with as much tourist tat as they could possibly manage. Seeing the chance to collect a little lucre, the townspeople happily acceded and they have been cashing in on Cody's fame ever since. Today the town offers half a dozen cowboy museums and other diversions and of course many opportunities to purchase small crappy trinkets to take back home with you.

The people of Cody like you to think that Buffalo Bill was a native son. In fact, I'm awfully proud to tell you, he was an Iowa native, born in the little town of Le Claire in 1846. The people of Cody, in one of the more desperate commercial acts of this century, bought Buffalo Bill's birthplace and re-erected it in their town, but they are lying through their teeth when they hint that he was a local. And the thing is, they have a talented native son of their own. Jackson Pollock, the artist, was born in Cody. But they don't make anything of that because, I suppose,

Pollock was a complete wanker when it came to shooting buffalo.

So that was option one. Alternatively, as I say, I had the choice of driving on across Montana to Little Bighorn, where Custer came a cropper. To be perfectly frank, neither one of them seemed terribly exciting – I would have preferred something more in the way of a tall drink on a terrace over-looking the sea – but in Wyoming and Montana you don't get a lot to choose from. In the end, I opted for Custer's last stand. This rather surprised me because as a rule I don't like battlefields. I fail to see the appeal in them once they have carted off the bodies and swept up. My father used to love battlefields. He would go striding off with a guide-book and map, enthusiastically retracing the ebb and flow of the Battle of Lickspittle Ridge, or whatever.

Once I had the choice of going with my mother to a museum and looking at dresses of the Presidents' wives or staying with my dad, and I rashly chose the latter. I spent a long afternoon trailing behind him, certain that he had lost his mind. 'Now this must be the spot where General Goober accidentally shot himself in the armpit and had to be relieved of command by Lt-Col. Bowling-alley,' he would say as we hauled ourselves to the top of a steep summit. 'So that means Pillock's forces must have been regrouping over there at those trees' – and he would point to a grove of trees three hills away and stride off with his documents fluttering in the wind and I would think, 'Where's he going *now*?' Afterwards, to my great disgust, I discovered that the museum of First Ladies' dresses had only taken twenty minutes to see and my mother, brother and sister had spent the rest of the afternoon in a Howard Johnson's restaurant eating hot fudge sundaes.

So the Custer Battlefield National Monument came as a pleasant surprise. There's not much to it, but then there wasn't much to the battle. The visitors' centre contained a small but absorbing museum with relics from both the Indians and soldiers, and a topographical model of the battlefield, which employed tiny light bulbs to show you how the battle progressed. Mostly this consisted of a string of blue lights moving down the hill in a confident fashion and then scurrying back up the hill pursued by a much larger number of red lights. The blue lights formed into a cluster at the top of the hill where they blinked furiously for a while, but then one by one they winked out as the red lights swarmed over them. On the model the whole thing was over in a couple of minutes; in real life it didn't take much longer. Custer was an idiot and a brute and he deserved his fate. His plan was to slaughter the men, women and children of the Cheyenne and Sioux nations as they camped out beside the Little Bighorn River and it was just his bad luck that they were much more numerous and better armed than he had reckoned. Custer and his men fled back up the hill on which the visitors' centre now stands, but there was no place to hide and they were quickly overrun. I went outside and up a short slope to the spot where Custer made his last stand and had a look around.

It occupies a bleak and treeless hill, a place where the wind never stops blowing. From the hilltop I could see for perhaps fifty or sixty miles and there was not a tree in sight, just an unbroken sweep of yellowish grassland rolling away to a white horizon. It was a place so remote and lonely that I could see the wind coming before I felt it. The grass further down the hill would begin to ripple and a moment later a gust would swirl around me and be gone.

The site of Custer's last stand is enclosed by a black cast-iron fence. Inside this little compound, about fifty yards across, are scattered white stones to mark the spots where each soldier fell. Behind me, fifty yards or so down the far side of the hill, two white stones stood together where a pair of soldiers had obviously made a run for it and had been cut down. No-one knows where or how many Indians fell because they took their dead and injured away with them. In fact, nobody really knows what happened there that day in June 1876 because the Indians gave such conflicting accounts and none of the white participants lived to tell the tale. All that is known for sure is that Custer screwed up in a mighty big way and got himself and 260 other men killed.

Scattered as they are around such a desolate and windy bluff, the marker stones are surprisingly, almost disturbingly, poignant. It's impossible to look at them and not imagine what a strange and scary death it must have been for the soldiers who dropped there, and it left me yet again in a reflective frame of mind as I walked back down the hill to the car and returned to the endless American highway.

I drove to Buffalo, Wyoming, through a landscape of mossy brown hills. Montana is enormously vast and empty. It is even bigger and emptier than Nevada, largely because there are no population centres to speak of. Helena, the state capital, has a population of just 24,000. In the whole state there are fewer than 800,000 people – this in an area of 145,000 square miles. Yet it has a kind of haunting beauty with its endless empty plains and towering skies. Montana is called the Big Sky country and it really is true. I had always thought of the sky as something fixed and invariable, but here it seemed to have grown by a factor of at least ten. The Chevette was a tiny particle beneath a colossal white dome. Everything was dwarfed by the stupendous sky.

The highway led through a big Crow Indian reservation, but I saw no sign of Indians either on the road or off it. Beyond Lodge Grass and Wyola I passed back into Wyoming. The landscape stayed the same, though here there were more signs of ranching and the map once again filled up with diverting names: Spotted Horse, Recluse, Crazy Woman Creek, Thunder Basin.

I drove into Buffalo. In 1892 it was the scene of the famous Johnson County War, the incident that inspired the movie *Heaven's Gate*, though in fact the term 'war' is a gross over-exaggeration of events. All that happened was that the local ranchers, in the guise of the Wyoming Stock Growers' Association, hired a bunch of thugs to come to Johnson County and rough up some of the homesteaders who had recently, and quite legally, begun moving in. When the thugs killed a man, the homesteaders rose up and chased them to a ranch outside town, where they laid siege until the cavalry rode in and gave the humbled bullies safe passage out of town. And that was it: just one man killed and hardly any shots fired. That was the way the West really was, by and large. It was just farmers. That's all.

I reached Buffalo a little after four in the afternoon. The town has a museum dedicated to the Johnson County War, which I was hoping to see, but I discovered when I got there that it is only open from June to September. I drove around the business district, toying with the idea of stopping for the night, but it was such a dumpy little town that I decided to press on to Gillette, seventy miles down the road. Gillette was even worse. I drove around it for a few minutes, but I couldn't face the prospect of spending a Saturday night there, so I decided to press on once again.

Thus it was that I ended up in Sundance, thirty miles further down the road. Sundance is the town from which the Sundance Kid took his name, and from all appearances that was the only thing in town worth taking. He wasn't born in Sundance; he just spent some time in jail there. It was a small, charmless place, with just one road in and one road out. I got a room in the Bear Lodge Motel on Main Street and it was pleasant in a basic sort of way. The bed was soft, the television was hooked up to HBO, the cable movie network, and the toilet had a 'Sanitized For Your Protection' banner across the seat. On the far side of the street was a restaurant that looked acceptable. Clearly I was not about to have the Saturday night of a lifetime here, but things could have been worse. And indeed very soon they were.

I had a shower and afterwards as I dressed I switched on the television and watched the Reverend Jimmy Swaggart, a TV evangelist who had recently been caught dallying with a prostitute, the old rascal. Naturally this had put a certain strain on his credibility and he had taken to the airwaves, more or less continuously as far as I could tell, to beg for mercy. Here he was once again appealing for money and forgiveness, in that order. Tears rolled from his eyes and glistened on his cheeks. He told me he was a miserable sinner. 'No argument there, Jimbo,' I said, and switched off.

BILL BRYSON

I stepped out on to Main Street. It was ten of seven, as they say in this part of the world. The evening was warm and in the still air the aroma of charbroiled steaks floated over from the restaurant across the street and berthed in my nostrils. I hadn't eaten all day and the whiff of sirloin made me realize just how hungry I was. I smoothed down my wet hair, needlessly looked both ways before stepping off the sidewalk – there was nothing moving on the road for at least 100 miles in either direction – and went over. I opened the door and was taken aback to discover that the place was packed with Shriners.

The Shriners, if you are not familiar with them, are a social organization composed of middle-aged men of a certain disposition and mentality – the sort of men who like to engage in practical jokes and pinch the bottoms of passing waitresses. They get drunk a lot and drop water balloons out of hotel windows. Their idea of advanced wit is to stick a cupped hand under their armpit and make farting noises. You can always tell a Shriner because he's wearing a red fez and his socks don't match. Ostensibly, Shriners get together to raise money for charities. This is what they tell their wives. However, here's an interesting fact that may help you to put this claim into perspective. In 1984, according to *Harper's Magazine*, the amount of money raised by the Shriners was $17.5 million; of this sum, the amount they donated to charities was $182,000. In short, what Shriners do is get together and be assholes. So you can perhaps conceive of my disquiet at the prospect of eating dinner amid a group of fifty bald-headed men who are throwing pats of butter around the room and setting fire to one another's menus.

The hostess came over. She was chewing gum and didn't look overfriendly. 'Help you?' she said.

'I'd like a table for one, please.'

She clicked her chewing gum in an unattractive fashion. 'We're closed.'

I was taken aback once more. 'You look pretty open to me.'

'It's a private party. They've reserved the restaurant for the evening.'

I sighed. 'I'm a stranger in town. Can you tell me where else I can get something to eat?'

She grinned, clearly pleased to be able to give me some bad news. 'We're the only restaurant in Sundance,' she said. Some beaming Shriners at a nearby table watched my unfolding discomfort with simple-minded merriment. 'You might try the gas station down the street,' the lady added.

'The gas station serves food?' I responded in a tone of quiet amazement.

'No, but they've got potato chips and candy bars.'

'I don't believe this is happening,' I muttered.

'Or else you can go about a mile out of town on Highway 24 and you'll come to a Tastee-Freez drive-in.'

This was great. This was just too outstanding for words. The woman was telling me that on a Saturday night in Sundance, Wyoming, all I could have for dinner was potato chips and ice-cream.

'What about another town?' I asked.

'You can try Spearfish. That's thirty-one miles down Route 14 over the state line in South Dakota. But you won't find much there either.' She grinned again, and clicked her gum, as if proud to be living in such a turdy place.

'Well, thank you *so* much for your help,' I said with elaborate insincerity and departed.

And there you have the difference between the Midwest and the West, ladies and gentlemen. People in the Midwest are nice. In the Midwest the hostess would have felt bad about my going hungry. She would have found me a table at the back of the room or at least fixed me up with a couple of roast beef sandwiches and a slab of apple pie to take back to the motel. And the Shriners, sub-imbecile assholes that they may be, would have been happy to make room for me at one of their tables, and probably would even have given me some pats of butter to throw. People in the Midwest are good and they are kind to strangers. But here in Sundance the milk of human kindness was exceeded in tininess only by the size of the Shriners' brains.

I trudged up the road in the direction of the Tastee-Freez. I walked for some way, out past the last of the houses and on to an empty highway that appeared to stretch off into the distance for miles, but there was no sign of a Tastee-Freez, so I turned around and trudged back into town. I intended to get the car, but then I couldn't be bothered. There was something about the way they can't even spell 'freeze' right that's always put me off these places. How much faith can you place in a company that can't even spell a monosyllable? So instead I went to the gas station and bought about six dollar's worth of potato chips and candy bars, which I took back to my room and dumped on the bed. I lay there and pushed candy bars into my face, like logs into a sawmill, and watched some plotless piece of violent Hollywood excrescence on HBO, and then slept another fitful night, lying in the dark, full and yet unsatisfied, staring at the ceiling and listening to the Shriners across the street and to the ceaseless bleating of my stomach.

And so the night passed.

I woke early and peeked shivering through a gap in the curtains. It was a drizzly Sunday dawn. Not a soul was about. This would be an excellent time to firebomb the restaurant. I made a mental note to pack gelignite the next time I came to Wyoming. And sandwiches. Switching on the TV, I slipped back into bed and pulled the covers up to just below my eyeballs. Jimmy Swaggart was still appealing for forgiveness. Goodness me but that man can cry. He is a human waterfall. I watched for a while, but then got up and changed the channel. On all the other channels it was just more evangelists, usually with their dumpy wives sitting at their sides. You could see why they all went out for sex. Generally, the programme would also feature the evangelist's son-in-law, a graduate of the Pat Boone school of grooming, who would sing a song with a title like 'You've Got A Friend in Jesus And Please Send Us Lots of Money'. There can be few experiences more dispiriting than to lie alone in a darkened motel room in a place like Wyoming and watch TV early on a Sunday morning.

I can remember when we didn't even have TV on Sunday mornings; that's how old I am. You would turn on WOI and all you would get was a test pattern and you would sit there and watch that because there was nothing else. Then after a while they would take off the test pattern and show *Sky King*, which was an interesting and exciting programme, at least compared to a test pattern. Nowadays they don't show test patterns at all on American TV, which is a shame because given a choice between test patterns and TV evangelists, I would unhesitatingly choose the test patterns. They were soothing in an odd way and of course they didn't ask you for money or make you listen to their son-in-law sing.

It was just after eight when I left the motel. I drove through the drizzle to Devils Tower, about twenty-five miles away. Devils Tower was the mountain used by Steven Spielberg in *Close Encounters of the Third Kind*, the one on which the aliens landed. It is so singular and extraordinary that you cannot imagine what Spielberg would have used as an alternative if it hadn't been available. You can see it long before you get to it, but as you draw nearer the scale of it becomes really quite awesome. It is a flat-topped cone of rock 850 feet high, soaring out of an otherwise featureless plain. The scientific explanation is that it was a volcanic fluke – an outsized lump of warm rock that shot out of the earth and then cooled into its present arresting shape. In the moonlight it is said to glow, though even now on a wet Sunday morning with smoky clouds brushing across its summit it looked decidedly supernatural, as if it were placed there aeons ago for the eventual use of aliens. I only hope that when they do come they don't expect to eat out.

I stopped at a lay-by near the tower and got out to look at it, squinting through the drizzle. A wooden sign beside the road said that the tower was considered sacred by the Indians and that in 1906 it became the first designated national monument in America. I stared at the tower for a long time, hypnotized both by its majesty and by a dull need for coffee, and then realized that I was getting very wet, so I returned to the car and drove on. Having gone without dinner the night before, I intended to indulge myself in that greatest of all American gustatory pleasures – going out for Sunday breakfast.

Everybody in America goes out for Sunday breakfast. It is such a popular pastime that you generally have to queue for a table, but it's always worth the wait. Indeed, the inability to achieve instant oral gratification is such an unusual experience in America that queuing actually intensifies the pleasure. You wouldn't want to do it all the time, of course, you wouldn't want to get British about it or anything, but once a week for twenty minutes is kinda neat, as they say. One reason you have to queue is that it takes the waitress about thirty minutes just to take each order. First you have to tell her whether you want your eggs sunny side up, over easy, scrambled, poached, par-boiled or in an omelette, and if in an omelette whether you want it to be a plain, cheese, vegetable, hot 'n' spicy or chocolate nut 'n' fudge omelette, and then you have to decide whether you want your toast to be white, rye, whole wheat, sourdough, or pumpernickel bread and whether you want whipped butter, pat butter, or low-cholesterol butter substitute, and then there's a complicated period of negotiation in which you ask if you can have cornflakes instead of the cinnamon roll and link sausages instead of patties. So the waitress, who is only sixteen years old and not real smart, has to go off to the manager and ask him whether that's possible, and she comes back and tells you that you can't have cornflakes instead of the cinnamon roll, but you can have Idaho fries instead of the short stack of pancakes or you can have an English muffin and bacon instead of whole wheat toast, but only if you order a side of hashed browns and a large orange juice. This is unacceptable to you, and you decide that you will have waffles instead, so the waitress has to rub everything out with her nubby little eraser and start all over again. And across the room the queue on the other side of the 'Please Wait to Be Seated' board grows longer and longer, but the people don't mind because the food smells so good and anyway all this waiting is, as I say, kinda neat.

I drove along Highway 24 through a landscape of low hills, in a state of tingly anticipation. There were three little towns over the next twenty miles and I felt certain that one of them would have a roadside restaurant. I was nearly at the South Dakota state line. I was leaving the ranching country and entering more conventional farmland. Farmers cannot exist without a roadside restaurant every couple of miles, so I had no doubt that I would find one just around the next bend. One by one I passed through the little towns – Hulett, Alva, Aladdin – but there was nothing to them, just sleeping houses. No-one was awake. What kind of place was this? Even on Sundays farmers are up at dawn. Beyond Beulah I passed the larger community of Belle Fourche and then St Onge and Sturgis, but still there was nothing. I couldn't even get a cup of coffee.

At last I came to Deadwood, a town that, if nothing else, lived up to its first syllable. For a few years in the 1870s, after gold was discovered in the Black Hills, Deadwood was one of the liveliest and most famous towns in the West. It was the home of Calamity Jane. Wild Bill Hickock was shot dead while playing cards in a local saloon. Today the town makes a living by taking large sums of money off tourists and giving them in return some crappy little trinket to take home and put on their mantelpiece. Almost all the stores along the main street were souvenir emporia, and several of them were open even though it was a Sunday morning. There were even a couple of coffee shops, but they were closed.

I went into the Gold Nugget Trading Post and had a look around. It was a large room selling nothing but souvenirs – moccasins, beaded Indian bags, arrowheads, nuggets of fool's gold, Indian dolls. I was the only customer. I didn't see anything to buy, so I left and went into another store a couple of doors away, The World Famous Prospectors Gift Shop, and found exactly the same stuff at identical prices and again I was the only customer. At neither place did the people running things say hello or ask me how I was doing. They would have in the Midwest. I went back out into the miserable drizzle and walked around the town looking for a place to eat, but there was nothing. So I got back in the car and drove on to Mount Rushmore, forty miles down the road.

Mount Rushmore is just outside the little town of Keystone, which is even more touristy than Deadwood, but at least there were some restaurants open. I went in one and was seated immediately, which rather threw me. The waitress gave me a menu and went off. The menu had about forty breakfasts on it. I had only read to number 17 ('Pigs in a Blanket') when the waitress returned with a pencil ready, but I was so hungry that I just decided, more or less arbitrarily, that I would have breakfast number 3. 'But can I have link sausages instead of hashed browns?' I added. She tapped her pencil against a notice on the menu. It said NO SUBSTITUTIONS. What a drag. That was the most fun part. No wonder the place was half-empty. I started to make a protest, but I fancied I could see her forming a bolus of saliva at the back of her mouth and I broke off. I just smiled and said, 'OK, never mind, thank you!' in a bright tone. 'And please don't spit in my food!' I wanted to add as she went off, but somehow I felt this would only encourage her.

Afterwards I drove to Mount Rushmore, a couple of miles outside town up a steep road. I had always wanted to see Mount Rushmore, especially after watching Cary Grant clamber over Thomas Jefferson's nose in *North by Northwest* (a film that also left me with a strange urge to strafe someone in a cornfield from a low-flying aeroplane). I was delighted to discover that Mount Rushmore was free. There was a huge terraced parking lot, though hardly any cars in it. I parked and walked up to the visitors' centre. One whole wall was glass, so that you could gaze out at the monument, high up on the neighbouring mountainside. It was shrouded in fog. I couldn't believe my bad luck. It was like peering into a steam bath. I thought I could just make out Washington, but I wasn't sure. I waited for a long time, but nothing happened. And then, just as I was about to give up and depart, the fog mercifully drifted away and there they were – Washington, Jefferson, Lincoln and Teddy Roosevelt, staring glassily out over the Black Hills.

The monument looked smaller than I had expected. Everybody says that. It's just that, positioned as you are well below and looking at it from a distance of perhaps a quarter of a mile, it looks more modest than it is. In fact, Mount Rushmore is enormous. Washington's face is sixty feet high, his eyes eleven feet wide. If they had bodies, according to a sign on the wall, the Rushmore figures would be 465 feet tall.

In an adjoining room there was an excellent and more or less continuous movie presentation giving the history of Mount Rushmore, with lots of impressive statistics about the amount of rock that was shifted, and terrific silent film footage showing the work in progress. Mostly this consisted of smiling workmen packing dynamite into the rockface, followed by a big explosion and then the dust would clear and what had been rock before was now revealed to be Abraham Lincoln. It was remarkable. The whole thing is an extraordinary achievement, one of America's glories, and surely one of the great monuments of this century.

The project took from 1927 to 1941 to complete. Just before it was finished, Gutzon Borglum, the man behind it all, died. Isn't that tragic? He did all that work for all those years and then just when they were about to crack open the champagne and put out the little sausages on toothpicks, he keeled over and expired. On a bad luck scale of 0 to 10, I would call that an 11.

I drove east across South Dakota, past Rapid City. I had intended to stop off and see Badlands National Park, but the fog and drizzle were so dense that it seemed pointless. More than that, according to the radio I was just half a step ahead of another perilous frunnal system. Snow was expected on the higher reaches of the Black Hills. Already many roads in Colorado, Wyoming and Montana were shut by fresh snowfalls, including the highway between Jackson and Yellowstone. If I had gone to Yellowstone a day later, I would now be stranded, and if I didn't keep moving, I could well be stranded for a couple of days in South Dakota. On a bad luck scale of 0 to 10 I would call that a 12.

Fifty miles beyond Rapid City is the little town of Wall, home of the most famous drugstore in the West, Wall Drug. You know it's coming because every 100 yards or so along the whole of that fifty miles you pass a big billboard telling you so: STEAKS AND CAKES – WALL DRUG, 47 MILES, HOT BEEF SANDWICHES – WALL DRUG, 36 MILES, FIVE CENT COFFEE – WALL DRUG, 25 MILES, and so on. It is the advertising equivalent of the Chinese water torture. After a while the endless drip drip drip of billboards so unstabilizes your judgement that you have no choice but to leave the interstate and have a look at it.

It's an awful place, one of the world's biggest tourist traps, but I loved it and I won't have a word said against it. In 1931, a guy named Ted Hustead bought Wall Drug. Buying a drugstore in a town in South Dakota with a population of 300 people at the height of a great depression must be about as stupid a business decision as you can make. But Hustead realized that people driving across places like South Dakota were so delirious with boredom that they would stop and look at almost anything. So he put up a lot of gimmicks like a life-sized dinosaur, a 1908 Hupmobile, a stuffed buffalo, and a big pole with arrows giving the distances and directions from Wall Drug to places all over the world, like Paris and Hong Kong and Timbuctoo. Above all, he erected hundreds of billboards all along the highway between Sioux Falls and the Black Hills, and filled the store with the most exotic and comprehensive assortment of tourist crap human eyes have ever seen, and pretty soon people were pouring in. Now Wall Drug takes up most of the town and is surrounded by parking lots so enormous that you could land a jumbo jet on them. In the summer they get up to 20,000 visitors a day, though when I arrived things were decidedly more quiet and I was able to park right out front on Main Street.

I was hugely disappointed to discover that Wall Drug wasn't just an overgrown drugstore as I had always imagined. It was more a mini shopping mall, with about forty little stores selling all kinds of different things – postcards, film, Western wear, jewellery, cowboy boots, food, paintings and endless souvenirs. I bought a very nice kerosene lamp in the shape of Mount Rushmore. The wick and the glass jar that encloses it sprout directly out of George Washington's head. It was made in Japan and the four Presidents have a distinctly oriental slant to their eyes. There were many other gifts and keepsakes of this type, though none quite as beautiful or charming. Sadly, there were no baseball caps with plastic turds on the brim. Wall Drug is a family store, so that sort of thing is right out. It was a pity because this was the last souvenir place I was likely to encounter on the trip. Another dream would have to go unfulfilled.

Chapter twenty-eight

I DROVE ON and on across South Dakota. God, what a flat and empty state. You can't believe how remote and lonely it feels out in the endless fields of yellow grass. It is like the world's first drive-through sensory deprivation chamber. The car was still making ominous clonking noises, and the thought of breaking down out here filled me with disquiet. I was in a part of the world where you could drive hundreds of miles in any direction before you found civilization, or at least met another person who didn't like accordion music. In a forlorn attempt to pass the time, I thumbed through my Mobil guides, leaning them against the steering wheel while drifting just a trifle wildly in and out of my lane, and added up the populations and sizes of the four states of the high plains: North and South Dakota, Montana and Wyoming. Altogether they take up 385,000 square miles – an area about the size of France, Germany, Switzerland and the Low Countries combined – but they have a total population of just 2.6 million. There are almost four times as many people in Paris alone. Isn't that interesting? Here's another interesting fact for you. The population density of Wyoming is 1.9 people per square kilometre; in South Dakota it is a little over two people per square kilometre. In Britain, there are 236.2 people per square kilometre. The number of people airborne in the United States at any given time (136,000) is greater than the combined populations of the largest cities in each of these four states. And finally, here's a really interesting fact. According to a survey by *Current Health Magazine*, the percentage of salad bar customers in the United States seen 'touching or spilling food or otherwise being unsanitary' is sixty per cent. I am of course aware that this has nothing to do with the population of the northern plains states, but I thought a brief excursion into irrelevancy was a small price to pay for information that could change your life. It certainly has changed mine.

I stopped for the night in a nothing little town called Murdo, got a room in a Motel 6 overlooking Interstate 90 and went for dinner in a big truck stop across the highway. A highway patrol car was parked by the restaurant door. There is always a highway patrol car parked by the restaurant door. As you walk past it you can hear muffled squawking on the radio. 'Attention, attention! Zero Tango Charlie! A Boeing 747 has just crashed into the nuclear power plant on Highway 69. People are wandering around with their hair on fire. Do you read me?' Inside, oblivious of all this, are the two highway patrolmen, sitting at the counter eating apple pie with ice-cream and shooting the breeze with the waitress. Every once in a great while – perhaps twice in a day – the two patrolmen will get up from the counter and drive out to the highway to ticket some random motorists for trying to cross the state at seven miles an hour above the permitted limit. Then they will go and have some more pie. That is what it is to be a highway patrolman.

In the morning I continued on across South Dakota. It was like driving over an infinite sheet of sandpaper. The skies were low and dark. The radio said there was a tornado-watch in effect for the region. This always freaks out visitors from abroad – chambermaids in hotels in the Midwest are forever going into rooms and finding members of Japanese trade delegations cowering under the bed because they've heard a tornado siren – but locals pay no attention to these warnings because after years of living in the tornado belt you just take it as part of life. Besides, the chances of being hit by a tornado are about one in a million.

The only person I ever knew who came close was my grandfather. He and my grandmother (this is an absolutely true story, by the way) were sleeping one night when they were awakened by a roaring noise like the sound of a thousand chain-saws. The whole house shook. Pictures fell off the walls. A clock toppled off the mantelpiece in the living-room. My grandfather plodded over to the window and peered out, but he couldn't see a thing, just pitch blackness, so he climbed back into bed, remarking to my grandmother that it seemed a bit stormy out there, and went back to sleep. What he didn't realize was that a tornado, the most violent force in nature, had passed just beyond his nose. He could literally have reached out and touched it – though of course had he done so he would very probably have been sucked up and hurled into the next county.

In the morning, he and Grandma woke up to a fine clear day. They were surprised to see trees lying everywhere. They went outside and discovered, with little murmurings of astonishment, a swath of destruction stretching across the landscape in two directions and skirting the very edge of their house. Their garage was gone, but their old Chevy was standing on the concrete base without a scratch on it. They never saw a single splinter of the garage again, though later in the day a farmer brought them their mailbox, which he had found in a field two miles away. It just had a tiny dent in it. That's the sort of thing tornadoes do. All those stories you've ever read about tornadoes driving pieces of straw through telegraph poles or picking up cows and depositing them unharmed in a field four miles away are entirely true. In south-west Iowa there is a cow that has actually had this happen to it twice. People come from miles around to see it. This alone tells you a lot about the mysteries of tornadoes. It also tells you a little something about what there is to do for fun in south-west Iowa.

In mid afternoon, just beyond Sioux Falls, I at last left South Dakota and passed into Minnesota. This was the thirty-eighth state of my trip and the last new one I would visit, though really it hardly counted because I was just skimming along its southern edge for a while. Off to the right, only a couple of miles away over the fields, was Iowa. It was wonderful to be back in the Midwest, with its rolling fields and rich black earth. After weeks in the empty west, the sudden lushness of the countryside was almost giddying. Just beyond Worthington, Minnesota, I passed back into Iowa. As if on cue, the sun emerged from the clouds. A swift band of golden light swept over the fields and made everything instantly warm and spring-like. Every farm looked tidy and fruitful. Every little town looked clean and friendly. I drove on spellbound, unable to get over how striking the landscape was. There was nothing much to it, just rolling fields, but every colour was deep and vivid: the blue sky, the white clouds, the red barns, the

BILL BRYSON

chocolate soil. I felt as if I had never seen it before. I had no idea Iowa could be so beautiful.

I drove to Storm Lake. Somebody once told me that Storm Lake was a nice little town, so I decided to drive in and have a look. And by golly, it was wonderful. Built around the blue lake from which it takes its name, it is a college town of 8,000 people. Maybe it was the time of year, the mild spring air, the fresh breeze, I don't know, but it seemed just perfect. The little downtown was solid and unpretentious, full of old brick buildings and family-owned stores. Beyond it a whole series of broad, leafy streets, all of them lined with fine Victorian homes, ran down to the lakefront where a park stood along the water's edge. I stopped and parked and walked around. There were lots of churches. The whole town was spotless. Across the street, a boy on a bike slung newspapers on to front porches and I would almost swear that in the distance I saw two guys in 1940s suits cross the street without breaking stride. And somewhere at an open window, Deanna Durbin sang.

Suddenly I didn't want the trip to be over. I couldn't stand the thought that I would go to the car now and in an hour or two I would crest my last hill, drive around my last bend, and be finished with looking at America, possibly for ever. I pulled my wallet out and peered into it. I still had almost $75. It occurred to me to drive up to Minneapolis and take in a Minnesota Twins baseball game. Suddenly this seemed an excellent idea. If I drove just a little bit maniacally, I could be there in three hours – easily in time for a night game. I bought a copy of USA Today from a street-corner machine and went with it into a coffee shop. I slid into a booth and eagerly opened it to the sports pages to see if the Twins were at home. They were not. They were in Baltimore, a thousand miles away. I was desolate. I couldn't believe I had been in America all this time and it hadn't occurred to me before now, the last day of the trip, to go to a ball game. What an incredibly stupid oversight.

My father always took us to ball games. Every summer he and my brother and I would get in the car and drive to Chicago or Milwaukee or St Louis for three or four days and go to movies in the afternoon and to ball games in the evening. It was heaven. We would always go to the ballpark hours before the game started. Because dad was a sports writer of some standing – no, to hell with the modesty, my dad was one of the finest sports writers in the country and widely recognized as such – he could go into the press-box and on to the field before the game and to his eternal credit he always took us with him. We got to stand beside him at the batting cage while he interviewed people like Willie Mays and Stan Musial. If you're British this means nothing to you, I know, but believe me it was a real privilege. We got to sit in the dug-outs (they always smelled of tobacco juice and urine; I don't know what those guys got up to down there) and we got to go in the dressing-room and watch the players dress for the games. I've seen Ernie Banks naked. Not a lot of people can say that, even in Chicago.

The best feeling was to walk around the field knowing that kids in the stands were watching us enviously. Wearing my Little League baseball cap with its meticulously-creased brim and a pair of very sharp plastic sunglasses, I thought I was Mr Cool. And I was. I remember once at Commiskey Park in Chicago some kids calling to me from behind the first base dug-out, a few yards away. They were big city kids. They looked like they came from the Dead End Gang. I don't know where my brother was this trip, but he wasn't there. The kids said to me, 'Hey, buddy, how come you get to be down there?' and 'Hey, buddy, do me a favour, get me Nellie Fox's autograph, will ya?' But I paid no attention to them because I was . . . Too Cool.

So I was, as I say, desolate to discover that the Twins were a thousand miles away on the east coast and that I couldn't go to a game. My gaze drifted idly over the box scores from the previous day's games and I realized with a kind of dull shock that I didn't recognize a single name. It occurred to me that all these players were in junior high school when I left America. How could I go to a baseball game not knowing any of the players? The essence of baseball is knowing what's going on, knowing who's likely to do what in any given situation. Who did I think I was fooling? I was a foreigner now.

The waitress came over and put a paper mat and cutlery in front of me. 'Hi!' she said in a voice that was more shout than salutation. 'And how are you doin' today?' She sounded as if she really cared. I expect she did. Boy, are Midwestern people wonderful. She wore butterfly glasses and had a beehive hairdo.

'I'm very well, thank you,' I said. 'How are you?'

The waitress gave me a sideways look that was suspicious and yet friendly. 'Say, you don't come from around here, do ya?' she said.

I didn't know how to answer that. 'No, I'm afraid I don't,' I replied, just a trifle wistfully. 'But you know, it's so nice I sometimes kind of wish I did.'

*   *   *

Well, that was my trip, more or less. I visited all but ten of the lower forty-eight states and drove 13,978 miles. I saw pretty much everything I wanted to see and a good deal that I didn't. I had much to be grateful for. I didn't get shot or mugged. The car didn't break down. I wasn't once approached by a Jehovah's Witness. I still had $68 and a clean pair of underpants. Trips don't come much better than that.

I drove on into Des Moines and it looked very large and handsome in the afternoon sunshine. The golden dome of the state capitol building gleamed. Every yard was dark with trees. People were out cutting the grass or riding bikes. I could see why strangers came in off the interstate looking for hamburgers and gasoline and stayed for ever. There was just something about it that looked friendly and decent and nice. I could live here, I thought, and turned the car for home. It was the strangest thing, but for the first time in a long time I almost felt serene.

BILL BRYSON

Neither *here* Nor *there*

Bill Bryson's first travel book, *The Lost Continent*, was unanimously acclaimed as one of the funniest books in years. In *Neither Here nor There* he brings his unique brand of humour to bear on Europe as he shoulders his backback, keeps a tight hold on his wallet, and journeys from Hammerfest, the northernmost town on the continent, to Istanbul on the cusp of Asia. Fluent in, oh, at least one language, he retraces his travels as a student twenty years before.

Whether braving the homicidal motorists of Paris, being robbed by gypsies in Florence, attempting not to order tripe and eyeballs in a German restaurant, window–shopping in the sex shops of the Reeperbahn or disputing his hotel bill in Copenhagen, Bryson takes in the sights, dissects the culture and illuminates each place and person with his hilariously caustic observations. He even goes to Liechtenstein.

'This is the travel book that every inter-rail vagrant would love to write; the Animal House *of the genre*'
NEW STATESMAN

'Hugely funny (not snigger-snigger funny, but great-big-belly-laugh-till-you-cry funny)'
DAILY TELEGRAPH

BILL BRYSON

Down Under

It is the driest, flattest, hottest, most desiccated, infertile and climatically aggressive of all the inhabited continents and still Australia teems with life – a large portion of it quite deadly. In fact, Australia has more things that can kill you in a very nasty way than anywhere else.

Ignoring such dangers – and yet curiously obsessed by them – Bill Bryson journeyed to Australia and promptly fell in love with the country. And who can blame him? The people are cheerful, extrovert, quick-witted and unfailingly obliging: their cities are safe and clean and nearly always built on water; the food is excellent; the beer is cold and the sun nearly always shines. Life doesn't get much better than this…

'Bryson is the perfect travelling companion…when it comes to travel's peculiars the man still has no peers'
THE TIMES

'He arrives at his destination, finds a hotel, checks in, meanders around the neighbourhood, visits any museums or public monuments he happens to encounter, has a couple of drinks, eavesdrops on a conversation or two, then goes to bed. A year later, people on three continents are hospitalised as a result of ruptures caused by laughing so hard at his account of the experience'
THE AGE, MELBOURNE

BILL BRYSON

The Road to
Little Dribbling

Over twenty years ago, Bill Bryson went on a trip around
Britain to celebrate the green and kindly island that had
become his home. The hilarious book he wrote about that
journey, *Notes from a Small Island*, became one of the most
loved books of recent decades, and was voted in a BBC
poll as the book that best represents Britain.

Now, in this hotly anticipated new travel book, his first in
fifteen years and sure to be greeted as the funniest book of the
decade, Bryson sets out on a brand-new journey, on a route he
dubs the Bryson Line, from Bognor Regis on the south coast to
Cape Wrath on the northernmost tip of Scotland. Once again,
he will guide us through all that's best and worst about Britain
today – while doing that incredibly rare thing of making us
laugh out loud in public.

'The news that Bill Bryson is to
publish a follow-up to his 1995 travelogue around
the UK, Notes from a Small Island, *this
autumn, will bring cheer to readers
and booksellers alike.*'
GUARDIAN

The book every BODY should read

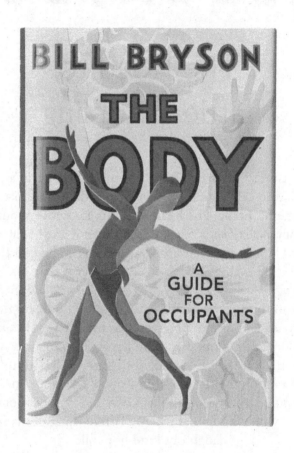

'We spend our whole lives in one body and yet most of us have practically no idea how it works and what goes on inside it. The idea of this book is simply to try to understand the extraordinary contraption that is us.'
Bill Bryson

October 2019